THE HILL OF THE M'

This popular but scholarly handbook to ⸺ of St. Albans Abbey covers the whole sweep of a⸺ ⸺ from the martyrdom of Alban to the modern shrine rest⸺ ⸺

Architectural books often describe a building in the form of a tour, leaving the mind in a muddled whirl of dates and with no clear picture of organic growth. This book is different. It is the biography of a building, a chronological narrative describing and explaining each feature – from the Saxon Benedictine monastery, *via* the great Romanesque church of the Normans, through mediaeval growth and change, then from near ruin to Victorian salvation and twentieth-century glory.

The building is related to its geographical setting, local building materials and to the lay of the land. The architects' point of view is stressed throughout, the problems they faced and how they solved them: Robert the Mason who re-cycled Roman bricks; Hawksmoor, Cottingham, Anderson and others, as the building was enlarged and adapted.

New light is cast on those 'hidden centuries' between the Dissolution and the restoration when, as a parish church, with box pews, galleries and three-decker pulpit re-ordered around the crossing, the abbey showed the influence of Wren and his City churches. On the nineteenth century restoration it puts the record straight. Scott consolidated the tower and pulled back the tottering wall of the nave; it was he who saved the abbey from collapse and ensured its present role as cathedral for Hertfordshire and Bedfordshire.

This absorbing book with its fund of facts contains both humour and suspense. Its one hundred specially prepared pictures, plans and diagrams give a rounded picture of the building; a bibliography with each chapter guides the interested reader to further exploration. In 1993, the twelfth centenary of the monastery's foundation was celebrated. This essential handbook, well indexed, pays tribute to centuries of living Christian witness.

Eileen Roberts has art history degrees from three countries, lectures widely on architectual subjects, advises on the care of churches and has lived in St. Albans for over thirty years.

PLAN OF THE NORMAN ABBEY

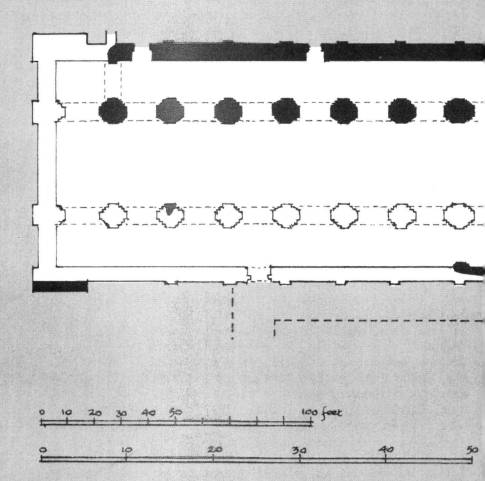

0 10 20 30 40 50   100 feet

0   10   20   30   40   50

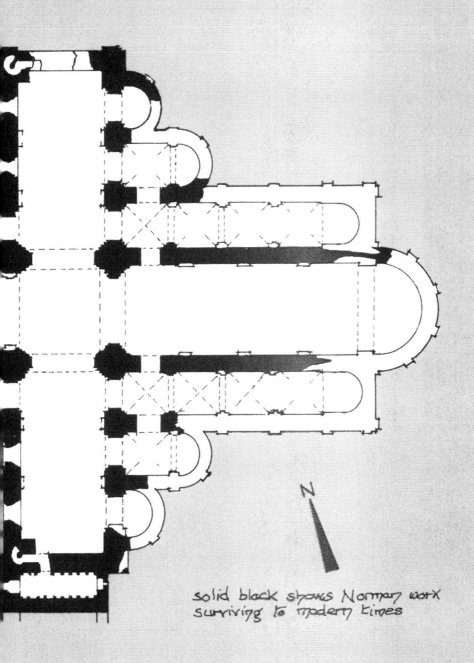

N

solid black shows Norman work
surviving to modern times

THE HILL OF THE MARTYR

an Architectural History of St. Albans Abbey

Eileen Roberts

First published May 1993
by The Book Castle
12 Church Street,
Dunstable,
Bedfordshire, LU4 5RU

Reprinted July 2008   November 2012

ISBN 978 1871199 26 0

Computer typeset by Keyword, Aldbury, Herts.

Printed in Great Britain by TJ International Ltd

Cover: Anonymous watercolour copy (first published by C.H.Ashdown, 1893) of a seventeenth century Dutch drawing in the British Library attributed to 'John Lievons' (see fig.71).

Non nobis, Domine, non nobis;
sed nomini tuo da gloriam.
Psalm 115:1

BY THE SAME AUTHOR

A guide to the medieval murals in St. Albans Abbey

The St. William of York mural and the Altar of the Relics in St. Albans Abbey

A school of masons in 15th century north Hertfordshire

St. Albans borough boundary and its significance in the Peasants' Revolt

CONTENTS

Foreword

by the Bishop of St. Albans

You often hear a casual enquirer asking of one of our ancient cathedrals, 'When was it built then?' as though they sprang up overnight! But even the least observant visitor to the Cathedral and Abbey Church of St. Alban is bound to realise that it bears the marks of different centuries. The contrasting columns in the nave and the vestigial outlines of the cloisters on the south wall speak of the complex history of form and function which makes the Abbey such a treasure trove for anyone who enjoys delving into the past. It also provides a wonderfully dramatic setting for teaching children about their social and Christian heritage. Such a work is carried out by the Cathedral's much praised education centre.

I am therefore very grateful indeed to Dr Eileen Roberts for producing an architectural history of the Abbey which brings each period of its development alive. It enables us to imagine the (usually) noble intentions of the major architects alongside the more humble aspirations of worshippers and pilgrims who have come to honour Alban and Amphibalus, to worship almighy God and to seek grace and healing for themselves and their loved ones.

On one level this is a record of the evolution of a great building. On another, it is the story of heroes and the occasional villain whose vision, or lack of it, still causes us to draw breath today. I was particularly interested to read of some of the failures and near disasters that have afflicted the Abbey. When one is staggered by how mediaeval man managed to construct buildings of such size and complexity, it is not surprising to hear tales of collapsing towers, crumbling masonry and cracks appearing in walls. The story of Gilbert Scott's work in rescuing the tower is a reminder that this is a history of saviours as well as creators. And to all of them we owe a debt of gratitude, not least because the history of the Abbey's architecture symbolises the reason for its very existence in bearing witness to God the creator and saviour of a world forever in need of restoration to a fuller glory.

So I congratulate Dr Roberts on her work. It is a book I have long wanted to read, combining as it does scholarship, readability and all the background history that anyone who lives in St. Albans and has a love for the Cathedral and Abbey Church would want to have at their fingertips. As the Abbey prepares to celebrate the 1200th anniversary of the Benedictine foundation on this site, this book has appeared at a timely moment and I am sure will be widely appreciated.

JOHN ST. ALBANS

Acknowledgements

Abbey interior views were photographed and reproduced by permission of the Dean and Cathedral Council. The list of officiating clergy on p. 263 has been reproduced from the one in the abbey, also with their permission.

The translations of the *Gesta Abbatum* by L F Salzman, in *Building in England* (1967), are quoted in chapters 7, 8 and 11 by permission of Oxford University Press.

R C Finucane in *History* is quoted in chapter 12 by permission of The Historical Association.

The account of the twentieth century restoration of St. Albans abbey is reprinted by permission of *Hertfordshire Countryside*.

Architectural drawings and maps are by Basil Miles Roberts, B. Arch., FRIBA.

Unless otherwise stated, photographs and drawings are by the author.

Introduction

This is the story of a building, from the martyrdom of Alban, a man of faith, through the founding of the monastery by the Christian king, Offa II, to the cathedral as it stands today. As we celebrate the twelfth centenary of the foundation, it forms a personal act of homage to a great and living church and to the faith which it inspires.

The building is seen as much as possible from the architect's point of view. Looking at it in terms of 'builds', it defines the problems faced by the architect and the means he employed to solve those problems. Bay elevations and the plans of the major developments recapture in part the designs laid out on his drawing board. Portraits of some architects, mediaeval and modern, are included.

The material is presented as a series of visual images, reflecting unashamedly its origins as a public lecture series. The illustrations, taken together, it is hoped, will provide a picture of the essential building; nor are furnishings and fittings overlooked. Some beautiful objects, like a fragment of a gilded screen or a cloister boss now lost, are included for the record.

This book is by no means the last word on the abbey, but may serve as an introduction to its architecture, giving the whole sweep of historical development from Roman times to the present. Presented as a chronological narrative, it ties the growth of the building to the practical circumstances and changing needs prompting the various changes. Key buildings and artefacts elsewhere in Europe are referred to throughout, so as to place the building in a wider cultural context than is often encountered, for example in church guides. A new and special feature, not found elsewhere, describes those 'lost centuries' between the dissolution of the monastery and the nineteenth century restoration.

The subject is the abbey church alone, although one or two conventual buildings are mentioned briefly in passing. Those few which still stand, and those revealed by excavation, form a specialist subject of their own which is outside the purview of this book.

Although it strives for accuracy, it does not claim to be a scholarly tome; it is an invitation to the general, non-specialist reader to understand the building better. A bibliography at the end of each chapter indicates the author's sources and presents the interested reader with signposts to wider knowledge.

A word is necessary on the designation of Lord Grimthorpe: what is confusing is that he thrice changed his name. Throughout the book generally he is referred to as 'Grimthorpe' but in chapters 17 and 18 he is called 'Denison' for activities between 1816 and 1874, 'Sir Edmund Beckett' between 1874 and 1886 and 'Lord Grimthorpe' between 1886 and his death in 1905.

Many people have contributed, directly and indirectly, to this book. Remembered with particular gratitude is the late distinguished churchwarden and cathedral archivist, Mr Rob Kell, for his kind encouragement over many years. Gareth Davies, former Director of the Verulamium Museum, generously sponsored and organised the original lecture series in the Town Hall, St. Albans in 1977. The courteous help is much appreciated of the staffs at the Bedford County Record Office, the British Library, the Central Library, St. Albans, Dowling de Lisle Ltd., the Hertfordshire College of Art and Design, the Hertford County Record Office, the St. Albans Museum, the National Monuments Record, the Society of Antiquaries of London, the Verulamium Museum and the Victoria and Albert Museum. Individuals who generously shared their time and expertise include the late Canon Murdoch Dahl, David Dean, Susan Evans, Veronica Gillmor, Carolyn Lewis-Barclay, Dr Rowland Mainstone, June Martin, Jean Peyton-Jones, Vivienne Prowse, Eric Rice, Philip Sturrock, the late Malcolm Tomkins, Marjorie Tomlinson, David Vesey, Joyce Wells and Dennis Yates. Mrs Jane Kelsall merits a special tribute. Her infectious enthusiasm encouraged me to seek publication in the first place and her loyal support over many weeks can be seen in the comprehensive index. Dr David Kelsall shared the work of the index and assisted with the illustrations, turning my coloured slides into black and white prints. My husband Basil helped most of all: without him, the book would never have been written. He drew up the glossary, did the architectural drawings and helped in a thousand other ways. To all these people, I tender warmest thanks.

Eileen Roberts.
St. Albans,
1992.

List of Illustrations

92. High-pitched roof with parapets constructed by Sir Edmund Beckett, from 1879. Re-leaded by J O Scott, 1909–1914.

93. West front as designed by Sir Edmund Beckett, 1880.

94. Reredos, 'The resurrection of Christ' by Alfred Gilbert, from 1890.

95. Rose window, north transept, designed by Lord Grimthorpe, 1888–89. Clear glazing now destroyed. Photomontage by, and published with permission of, Dr Rowland Mainstone.

96. Bishop's throne, designed by J Oldrid Scott, 1903.

97. George G Pace, 1916–1975.

98. Andrew Anderson, as portrayed in the corbel table of the restored nave.

99. South transept, south face, as rebuilt by Lord Grimthorpe after 1885. On the right, Chapter House, designed by William Whitfield, 1982.

100. Chapter house, longitudinal section looking north.

List of Abbreviations

FFSAA	Fraternity of the Friends of St. Albans Abbey
FRIBA	Fellow of the Royal Institute of British Architects
FSA	Fellow of the Society of Antiquaries
HMSO	Her Majesty's Stationery Office
n.d.	no date
PRO	Public Record Office
RIBA	Royal Institute of British Architects
Trans SAHAAS	Transactions of the St. Albans and Hertfordshire Architectural and Archaeological Society.

Part I

LET THESE STONES SPEAK

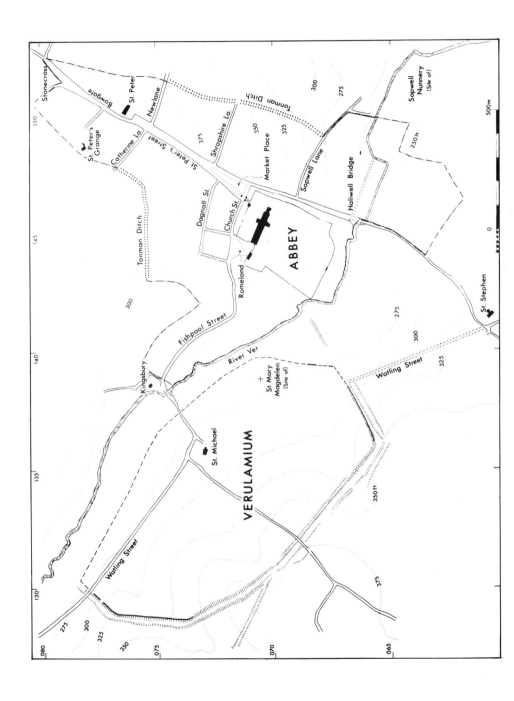

Chapter 1

THE ABBEY FABRIC

The twelfth centenary of the founding of St. Albans abbey church falls in the year 1993. Twelve centuries before, Offa II, King of Mercia travelled to a place already hallowed by pilgrimage, unearthed the bones of the martyr Alban and reverently placed them in a more worthy sanctuary which he had provided. A Benedictine community, newly formed, was entrusted with their care and the monastery endowed with ample lands in the south-west of what would one day be Hertfordshire. This royal act of vision and faith so long ago, in 793, set the scene for centuries of Christian prayer and service. The centenary has opened for us new perspectives and we now perceive this sacred place with a deeper sense of its significance.

Holmhurst, the hill where the abbey stands, may be one of the most important sites in Latin Europe, especially as a Roman city lies buried on the neighbouring hill across the river Ver. Man may have lived continuously in this spot from earliest times. Under green lawns lie hidden the monastic buildings numbered amongst the few very early foundations in England. Certainly the Norman church is one of the greatest surviving monuments of the generation following the Conquest. It was recognised as the premier abbey of England at the Council of Tours in 1163, made strong by its compact endowment of lands and its early control over its own diocese. It had many daughter houses and the superiority of its historical records gives it a special importance.

It was spared the fate of many monastic houses which fell into ruin or were destroyed at the Reformation, when taken over by the town to serve as a parish church. It was then adapted to Protestant worship, the small community struggling to maintain the extensive fabric. When raised to cathedral status in 1877, it became the focus of fierce arguments about how and how not mediaeval buildings should be restored. Lord Grimthorpe's name became a household word, still praised or denigrated vehemently even today.

The following pages attempt to assess the abbey's architectural history as a kind of summary in the twelfth centenary year. The architecture is examined in chronological sequence with attempts to place it in a wider context and to look at its associated arts insofar as they can be recovered.

Since architectural character is so closely interwoven with the structure of the land, we begin by considering the site and the building materials. The geological map of Britain shows Hertfordshire to be located in the south-east, lowland zone of Britain. It is shaped like two unequal squares ranged along the geological grain of the land. Most of Hertfordshire consists of a thick sheet of chalk tilted up at the north to form an escarpment overlooking the Aylesbury plain and sloping gently down towards London in the south. Hertfordshire is part of the London basin and forms one rim of it, most of its rivers eventually joining the Thames, either by way of the Colne or the Lea. Geography dictates that Hertfordshire in general and St. Albans in particular will look towards London and mirror what is happening there.

Looking at Hertfordshire specifically, a diagram of the geological zones shows the county to be divided into three main bands running south-west and north-east: in the north the chalk lies close to the surface forming the open downland of the Chiltern region. The middle band, where St. Albans lies, is covered with drift soils, sands and gravels, deeply cut by valleys to form an undulating landscape once densely forested. In the south, the London clay produces oak trees of gigantic size.

A descent into the famous Royston Cave emphasises the thickness and character of the chalk which makes up Hertfordshire. The county produces no top-quality building stone, yet it relied on local materials which influenced the style of building.

Flint is the only building stone abundant in Hertfordshire itself. It is found in the upper chalk in clearly defined stratae; in the Seine valley of France, especially at La Roche-Guyon, one sees the same geological formation. In a section of the chalk strata, huge flints can be seen in various horizontal beds. The quality of the flint varies according to its position, but the best comes from the floor bed. It is found in nodules, often egg-shaped, measuring from two inches to one foot in diameter. Outside is a thick crust called the cortex but inside it is like solid glass, translucent and pleasant to touch. It consists of almost pure silica, of the same

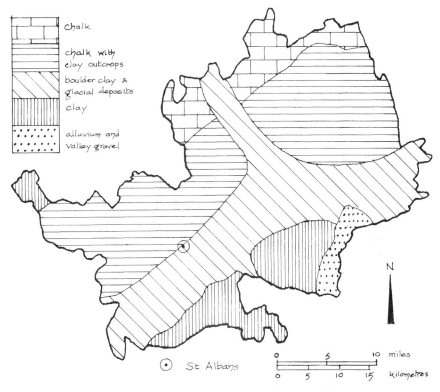

Chalk

chalk with
clay outcrops

boulder clay &
glacial deposits

clay

alluvium and
valley gravel

N

⊙ St Albans

0   5   10   miles

0   5   10   15   kilometres

Fig. 2   Diagram of the geology of Hertfordshire.

family as obsidian and quartz. Flint is completely non-absorbent and extremely durable but it cannot be worked. To knap flint, the surface is hit at right angles and it splits with one concave and one convex surface.

In a wall, flint needs an abundance of dryish lime mortar. The quoins are built up first, plumbed in and cords drawn to guide the line of the wall. It must be at least two feet thick. The flints are laid glassy side out with the rough pieces and lacing stones on the inside. No shuttering is used. The mortar can be left rough on the inside as a key to plaster. If the damp is kept out of the top and the mortar is good, it makes a very durable wall (see fig. 44).

The south clerestory wall of the abbey shows how flint was used by the Normans; with wide joints and liberal use of Roman bricks, it was intended to be plastered externally and whitewashed. As used by Lord Grimthorpe, for example on buttresses of the north transept, it was not plastered but presented its own handsome, glassy surface. Flints should be laid in

5

sweeping curves to give a pleasing overall texture if the Hertfordshire tradition is followed; it is considered to be of poor quality if it is coursed.

In Hertfordshire as a whole, bricks and tiles were the most important building materials. The local clays are excellent, for example, the superficial deposit of boulder clay at Hill End. The history of brick-making goes back to Roman times, when the thin, tile-like bricks were used at Verulamium. After the departure of the Romans, brick-making ceased but it was resumed in the fifteenth century during which the brickmakers developed great skill. In the late nineteenth century, Lord Grimthorpe manufactured imitation Roman bricks.

There is, of course, worked stone in St. Albans abbey. Some of it is Barnack stone, which has a shelly quality, with egg-like particles surrounded by layers of lime. It is white, pink or buff in colour and originates in the Stamford area of the Lincolnshire limestone belt where it was quarried from early times. The St. Albans' masons found their supply in Roman Verulamium and placed it in imposts, windowsills and wherever durability was required. In the external gallery of the central tower the Barnack stone was pieced together and extended with Roman brick making a decorative architectural feature (see fig. 20). It has stood up remarkably well to nine centuries of weathering.

Within the abbey, abundant use is made of freestone, but of another kind. This is Totternhoe stone, a compact, fine-grained stone, of which one sees an example in the Wallingford chantry (see fig. 67). It is often called clunch but clunch is, strictly speaking, a totally different stone, with a different weight, density and crushing resistance, which is found only in the chalk marl series of Cambridgeshire. Totternhoe stone is not native to Hertfordshire, but is quarried just over the border in Bedfordshire not far from Dunstable, where the edge of the escarpment drops down steeply to the Aylesbury plain. One well-known section forms part of the perimeter of Whipsnade zoo. A diagram of the escarpment shows the stratafied layers of limestone, the Upper Chalk where the flints are found, the Middle and the Lower Chalk. At Totternhoe in Bedfordshire, and nowhere else, a special bed occurs halfway down the lower chalk, fifteen to seventeen feet thick, resting upon an exceedingly sticky layer of chalk marl.

Chemically speaking, the stone is calcite, composed of little polygonal cylinders which are minute fragments of the shell *Inoceramus* which developed millions of years ago when Hertfordshire was covered by a clear and shallow lake. This shell gives Totternhoe stone its granular appearance and makes it hard and gritty. Iron pyrites give it its colour.

When the stone is first quarried it is full of water which is called 'quarry sap'. It requires about twelve months to 'settle', at which point hair-line cracks appear. The stone shrinks a little as it dries. In all, it must stand for two to three years in well ventilated conditions in the mason's yard until it is sufficiently dry for working. The masons say, 'If it looks right and if it feels right, it is right'.

Totternhoe stone is water holding and absorbs a great deal of moisture into its fine pores; for this reason, it weathers badly. The absorbed water expands and freezes, causing flakes of stone to fall off in scales, leaving hollows, called 'exfoliation'. Also, the iron pyrites form red patches which hasten decay. Used outside, Totternhoe stone requires a good damp proof course, lime wash as a protective covering and an overhanging roof. Lime wash, applied as a spray every five to six years, as often as the woodwork is painted, is the way good weathering qualities are given it, enabling it to endure for centuries in churches all over Hertfordshire.

Since it is a sedimentary rock, it is very important that the bedding planes lie horizontally in a building. The good mason personally selects the stone in the quarry and marks the bedding layers *in situ*, as they are not apparent later on. The bedding layers laid horizontally resist water penetration and improve the weathering quality.

The weathering qualities vary according to the strata in the quarry. The top stratum is softest but lower down, in a layer fifteen to twenty feet deep, it is very much harder. The best building stone comes from here. The 'blue layer' at the very bottom, immediately above the marl, is harder than the average Portland, almost approaching granite in density.

A demonstration of the weathering quality can be seen in the cloister arcades which survive on the south exterior wall of the abbey church (see fig. 55). These were never designed as external walls but were vaulted, roofed and protected by glazing. Lord Grimthorpe considered putting flying buttresses over them but, as the were 'getting worse yearly', built instead standard buttresses ruthlessly cutting through the designs. He thought they would soon be completely decayed away, when the walls could be refaced with flints and bricks. A century later, these traceries are still very much intact, which says a great deal for the skill of the masons who selected and laid the stone.

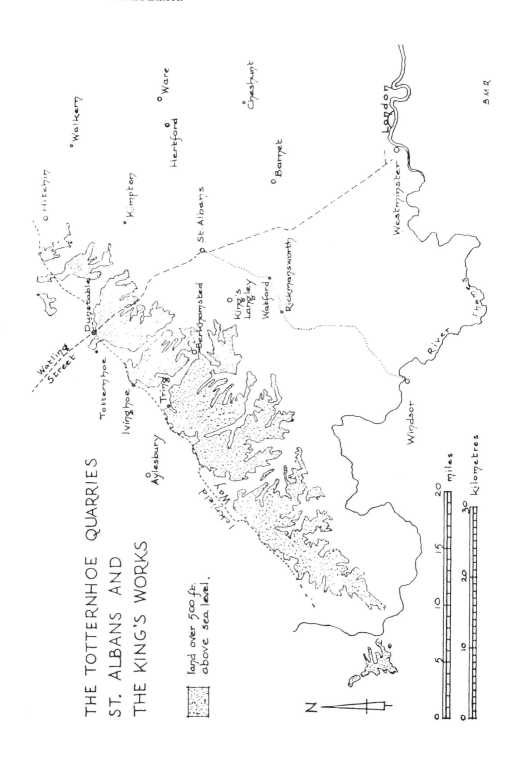

THE TOTTERNHOE QUARRIES
ST. ALBANS AND
THE KING'S WORKS

land over 500 ft.
above sea level.

N

20 miles

30 kilometres

The accompanying map shows the relation of the quarries to St. Albans. It also locates Windsor and Westminster, two places where this stone was used for important Kings' Works from the time of Henry II. Study of the terrain suggests that the stone-laden carts passed along Watling Street through St. Albans as the most convenient and economical route. In 1485, the road from St. Albans to Watford bore the name, 'Dunstableway'.

An aerial view of the quarry site was taken by Dr St. Joseph of Cambridge in 1971. At the top of the picture the motte-and-bailey castle built by the Normans is seen; one of its functions was the protection of the valuable quarries which take the form of horizontal passages entering the cliff face and tunnelling under the hill (see fig. 5). On the Totternhoe pre-enclosure map of 1829 the fields above are called 'Carthouse Furlongs' telling us something about the organisation of the quarrying industry.

In recent years, much of the upper chalk has been removed from the escarpment for cement manufacture. Consequently, subsidence began to occur over the tunnels making them unsafe for entry. They were sealed up in 1914. In 1972 stone began to be extracted by the open-cast method for the restoration of Woburn Abbey. Stones as large as twenty feet by nine feet by nine feet can be lifted out, weighing up to fifty-six and a half tonnes. The quarry contains sufficient stone for the restoration of Woburn Abbey in the forseeable future.

A detailed plan of the original quarry area however, shows a site resembling a giant handprint pressed into the soil. The fingers are the passages leading to the quarry entrances under the cliff edge of Hunger Hill.

A painting by G. Shepherd dated 1813 in the Bedfordshire Record Office shows the quarry as it must have looked for centuries. Near the quarry entrance stands one of the low carts used to bring the stone out of the quarry. Judging from the height of the men, the blocks of stone must have measured about five feet by three feet by three feet. The size was dictated by the width of the adits. The workshop on the left was probably the forge where the quarrying tools were sharpened, while the pond in the foreground, which assisted in quarry drainage, provided the water needed in the forging process as well as drinking water for the horses. The thatched lodge on the right of the picture allowed the masons to work the stone in the winter months in sheltered and heated conditions, cutting it to shape and squaring up the blocks. At the top of the cliff can be seen the horse-drawn sledges used to transport the stone southwards along Watling Street. The

*Fig. 4   'Entrance into the stone quarry at Totternhoe'.
Watercolour by G Shepherd, 1813.*

stone was drawn to the top of the escarpment by a gently circuitous route, with trace horses assisting the regular teams.

A painting of the interior, by the artist Nicholls in 1840, is no longer in this country; it is owned by Phyllis Jane Stanley of Bletchley, Bedfordshire and California. It shows how torches illuminated the inky blackness inside the mine, which was a labyrinth of passages going underground for half a mile.

A photograph inside an adit was taken in 1959 by the Manshead Archaeological Society of Dunstable who entered the quarry at that time. It shows the scale of the tunnels which honeycomb the cliff. The upright pillars of stone which were left to support the roof can be seen, as well as the recesses left to receive the backfill. On this visit, a block of stone on rollers was found, ready to be transported out. The adits were cut on a slope to facilitate rolling the stone.

At St. Albans abbey, Totternhoe stone was first used, apparently, in the time of Abbot John de Cella, 1195–1214, who was responsible for having the three west porches built (see fig. 35). The stone is not named in the chronicle, but its behaviour if badly chosen, badly laid and exposed to the weather, corresponds to Totternhoe stone. Certainly, those parts not renewed in the nineteenth century are Totternhoe stone. For decorative contrast in

Fig. 5   'View inside the Totternhoe quarry in 1959'
Archaeological Society of Dunstable.

the porches, some Purbeck marble was incorporated.

Quarries were actually purchased by Abbot Michael de Mentmore in 1336–1349, 'where, without cost or grudging, they could extract adequate supplies of stone ready for the various building works of the monastery, as often as necessary'. There are a number of documentary references to this stone being used for conventual buildings. In the fifteenth century, John of Wheathampstead purchased two additional quarries, one from William Hunt for twelve pounds, another from Thomas Jakes for eight pounds. This is the last mediaeval reference to the quarries.

Over the past century and a half, a variety of other limestones has been used. Gilbert Scott chose Chilmark stone from south Wiltshire, which had been employed so effectively in Salisbury cathedral. Buff to yellowish brown, it weathers to a greenish tint. It does not stand up well to atmospheric pollution, however, and in the abbey weathered badly in the form of scabbing and blisters. Lord Grimthorpe preferred Ancaster stone from Kesteven in the Lincolnshire limestone belt. This stone was used in St. Peter Mancroft, Norwich. A fine-grained, oolitic stone, it weathered somewhat better but also suffered from scabbing, exfoliation and pitting. In the twentieth century restoration, very hard York stone was used next to the tower, but elsewhere, especially in the parapets, Clipsham was chosen. Another oolitic stone from the Lincolnshire-Rutland border, it is creamy in colour and the hardest of the stones from the Lincolnshire limestone belt. For the carved corbel heads supporting the parapet, Ancaster hard white was used (see fig. 98).

References

CAMPBELL (E.M.J.) 'Hertfordshire'. The Domesday geography of south-east England. Eds. Darby and Campbell. Cambridge. 1971.

CATHEDRAL AND CITY: ST. ALBANS ANCIENT AND MODERN. Ed. by Robert Runcie. London. 1977.

ROBERTS (EILEEN). 'Totternhoe stone and flint in Hertfordshire churches'. *Medieval Archaeology*. XVIII. (1974) 66–89.

... 'The twentieth century restoration of St. Albans abbey'. *Hertfordshire Countryside*. XXXV. No. 253 (1980) 37–38.

SHERLOCK (R.L.) London and Thames Valley. British regional geology. Institute of Geological Sciences. London. 1960.

THOMSON (GLADYS SCOTT). Family background. London. 1949.

WARNES (ARTHUR R.). Building stones: their properties, decay and preservation. London. 1926.

Chapter 2

ST. ALBAN, PROTOMARTYR OF THE BRITISH

Christianity may have been brought to Britain by traders from the Mediterranean as early as the second century; certainly, Christians were meeting for worship together by the third century. Many religions were tolerated by the Romans alongside their State religion of Emperor worship. Because the Christians refused to participate in these official rites, they suffered on two separate occasions from severe persecution, under the Emperor Decius between January 250 and June 251 and under the Emperor Valerian between 257 and 259.

Persecution produces martyrs, and the first amongst the British martyrs was Alban who probably suffered about the middle of the third century A.D. The earlier date of A.D. 209 put forward by Dr John Morris, has unfortunately a number of cogent scholarly arguments to undermine it, explained by Charles Thomas in his book, *Christianity in Roman Britain to AD 500*. Constantius of Lyons, writing soon after 480, gives the earliest reference to St. Alban, followed by the later writers, Gildas and Venantius Fortunatus. By the early sixth century the first surviving full account of the martyrdom, the *Passio Albani*, had been set down in writing. Scholars who have studied the text, clearing away the later legends and correcting copyists' errors, note that the setting of the martyrdom, described so long ago, bears a striking resemblance to the site as it appears to this very day (see fig. 1).

The story of St. Alban is fully illustrated by Matthew Paris in his manuscript, *Lives of St. Alban and Amphibalus*, now in the library of Trinity College, Dublin (MS. 177). In a time of persecutions of Christians, Alban, a young Romano-British official of Verulamium gave shelter whilst still a pagan to a fugitive Christian priest. Dressing himself in the priest's vestments, Alban gave himself up to the authorities in his place. He refused all inducements to sacrifice to Jove and Apollo, the pagan gods, so

Fig. 6 *'The martyrdom of Alban'. Based upon* Lives of SS Alban and
Amphibalus, *Trinity College, Dublin.*

was beaten and cast into prison. Further questioning followed by
torture still failed to move him, so he was sentenced to die by the
sword. The place of execution lay outside the city so, crossing the
stream which divided the city wall from the arena, Alban was led
up a hill about five hundred paces away. This had 'nothing
difficult or steep about it . . in all directions smoothed by nature'
and here Alban was beheaded. Matthew Paris's drawing shows on
one side the armed guard and the executioner, with a crowd of
spectators on the other. Between them, the severed head of
St. Alban hangs with closed eyes from the branch of a tree where it
had been fixed. The corpse slumps to its knees, dropping the cross
which the priest had given him, which is retrieved by a
sympathiser. The soul of St. Alban ascends to heaven in the form
of a dove. The ruler, impressed by St. Alban's faith, orders the
persecution forthwith to cease.

It was customary to erect shrines over the graves of martyrs.
The shrine or *memoria* of St. Peter was discovered in 1946 below
the high altar of the present church of St. Peter in Rome. It was a
niche in a cemetery wall, following the pagan funerary custom of
the day. The upper portion of the shrine had not survived, so
archaeologists suggested a probable reconstruction of gabled
form. Gildas, the first British historian, who wrote the history of

the Celts in these islands from the time of the Romans to his own day, ca540, says there were a number of shrines about at that time. His reference to St. Alban of Verulamium is an important early confirmation of his authenticity.

Thus the site where St. Alban was buried became a holy place. What the shrine looked like we do not know, but the pagan practices of the time were no doubt modified for Christian use. Romano-Celtic sanctuaries have been discovered in excavations, a few with evidence of a shrine. A protected, ditched enclosure is an important feature within which privileged persons might be buried. Temples appear too, often stone built and square, while guest houses, baths, medicinal springs, healing centres and votive offerings are also indicated. Such a pagan sanctuary, reconstructed by the artist Alan Sorrell, shows some of these features (see Fox and Sorrell, *Roman Britain*, 1961, fig. 24).

The first burial place of the martyr continued to be treated with special respect. If a later church were built, dedicated to him, it would be so placed that the high altar stood over the spot where the bones were interred. On 2nd January 1257, when the great apse of the Norman abbey church was being demolished in preparation for the rebuilding and extension of the eastern arm, workmen discovered under the pavement a 'mausoleum' with a tomb of stone. It was thought to be the first resting place of St. Alban before the relics were translated to the shrine.

This process can be clearly seen in certain Early Christian sites in the Rhineland which came to light during the clearing, excavation and rebuilding following war damage. On the plan of Cologne showing the old Roman city, Colonia Agrippinensis, and the Roman roads radiating out from it, cemeteries can be seen alongside the roads. The earliest Christian sites were cemetery churches which grew up over the graves and shrines of saintly people. The plan of one of them, St. Severin, shows the earliest church from the end of the fourth century in a cemetery, originally pagan, with a cluster of Christian graves, strictly oriented, closely associated with it. The church was a very simple one, a rectangular box with an apsidal, western projection. From the excavation data, a reconstruction has been suggested. It was a small church of masonry with regular lacing courses of tile and a low-pitched roof (see fig. 7).

Alban, apparently, died in a cemetery outside Verulamium. Bede tells us that 'when the peace of Christian times was restored, a beautiful church worthy of his martydom was built, where sick folk are healed and frequent miracles take place to this day' (1.7).

The peace he referred to may have followed the Edict of Nantes of AD 313, when Constantine announced religious toleration and liberty of worship. Whether or not this church resembled the one of St. Severin, Cologne, would be very interesting to know.

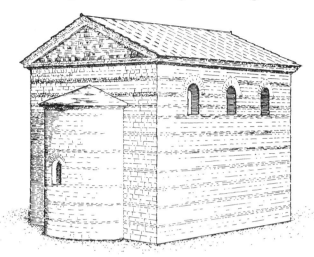

Fig. 7   Model of the cemetery chapel of St. Severin, Cologne, of the end of the fourth century.

Evidence of Early Christian worship in Britain is gradually coming to light. Some wealthy villa owners in prosperous areas had Christian house churches on their estates. An upper room in the Roman villa at Lullingstone in Kent was decorated with painted plaster featuring the *chi rho* symbol, the first two Greek letters of the word Christ, framed within a wreath and a portico. The *Alpha* and *Omega* symbols (the Beginning and the End) are also included. These murals were reconstructed by Crego Nicholson, FSA, grandson of Dr H J B Nicholson, an eminent rector of St. Albans abbey in the nineteenth century. A frieze on the west wall of the Lullingstone house church portrays members of the family with their arms outstretched in prayer.

A mosaic floor from the Roman villa at Hinton St. Mary in Dorset dating from the late fourth century shows the *chi rho* symbol again, behind which is probably the earliest representation of Christ in Britain and one of the very first in western Europe.

The collection of silver from Water Newton now in the British Museum is also identified as Christian by the presence of the *chi rho* symbol. It seems to be church plate of the third or fourth century, cups, bowls and flagons, which had been hidden during a period of religious persecution. Triangular plaques form votive offerings to hang in a sanctuary in fulfilment of vows, another borrowing from pagan practice.

In the late fourth and early fifth centuries, Verulamium was still a flourishing centre. Although Rome fell to the barbarians in AD 410, Roman culture survived in Britain for another generation. The heretical, humanistic teachings of Pelagius were very attractive to the British Christians but the Romans, overcome by cataclysmic events, adhered to the orthodox position. All had sinned, they preached; the sacraments of the church were necessary for salvation. With Papal approval, the bishops of Gaul sent to Britain one of their number, Germanus of Auxerre, to fight the Pelagian heresy. The debate which took place between Germanus and the Pelagians was illustrated centuries later in a drawing by Matthew Paris.

It is significant that Germanus visited the tomb of St. Alban and paid his respects there, proving that a cult was flourishing in AD 429 and that it was of national importance. Germanus' action at the shrine is very interesting: he had the tomb opened and deposited in it relics of all the apostles and of several martyrs. According to Bede, he 'took away with him a portion of earth from the place where the blessed martyr's blood had been shed. This earth appeared to have retained the martyr's blood and reddened the martyr's shrine.' (1.18). Bede describes in another place the enshrinement at Lichfield of Chad sometimes after 672: 'Chad's tomb is in the form of a little wooden house, covered, with an aperture in the side through which those who visit it out of devotion to him may insert their hand and take out some of the dust. They mix this in water, and give it to sick men or beasts to drink, by which means their ailment is quickly relieved and they are restored to health.' (IV.3). Not only did the actual bones of the saint have virtue, but all in physical contact with the saint, even the earth around. In County Kerry, in south-west Ireland, are a series of open air shrines made of stone slabs in the form of little tents set within rectangular yards. One has a circular hole six inches in diameter in the gable end, through which a hand could reach into the shallow grave inside. These stem from an ancient Mediterranean tradition carried to Early Christian Ireland. Bede believed that similar rites occurred at St. Alban's shrine.

In AD 731, when Bede was writing *A History of the English Church and People*, the cult of St. Alban still flourished with sick folk being healed and frequent miracles taking place. For this reason, reputable scholars like L F Rushbrooke Williams have rejected the claim by Matthew Paris that the church was destroyed by the Saxons and all memory of it lost between 586 and 793.

St. Alban's greatest patron was Offa II, king of Mercia from 757 to 796. This outstanding monarch, who treated on equal terms with Charlemagne, constructed Offa's Dyke, the major defensive earthwork in Europe at that time. His vigour and intensity is captured in portraits on silver coins in the British Museum; his reform of the coinage, making the penny standard, endured until the reign of King Henry III. Towards the end of Offa's life, in fulfilment of a vow, he was led in a dream to recover the bones of St. Alban and to found in 793 a monastery in his honour. As Offa was the first of our monarchs to strive to unify the English peoples into one nation, his choice of St. Alban, protomartyr of the British, was no doubt significant. Our account of the foundation comes from Matthew Paris, who mixes fact and fiction in a rather confusing way. Offa apparently established on the site regular clergy, men and women who followed the Benedictine rule at least for a time. He certainly endowed the community with lands, not a scattering of manors, but in a solid block in the Carolingian fashion. Offa's grant of lands to St. Alban's monastery helped to determine the county of Hertford boundary especially on the south-west (see fig. 2).

Although nothing is known of Offa's church, we can consider contemporary architecture on the continent and note its characteristic features. Centula (or St. Riquier) abbey church, near Abbeville in northern France, was an ambitious church built between 790 and 799 by the son-in-law of Charlemagne. It no longer survives today but is known to us through antiquarian drawings. There was an eastern apse separated from the nave by a pronounced chancel and two slender, circular staircase turrets. At each end of the nave was a transept and the main axis of the building was stressed by two crossing towers; they comprised tiered, open galleries in receding stages. The nave had aisles and a clerestory, with large round-

Fig. 8   Head of Offa II, King of Mercia, 757–796. From a coin in the British Museum.

Fig. 9   Sketch reconstruction of Centula abbey church, 790–799.

headed windows and some circular ones. The main entrance was at the west and was given special prominence by the *westwerk*, an entrance feature flanked by two more staircase turrets; they led into a raised gallery for a choir and an altar. A lively silhouette is given to the building by the combined effect of the crossing towers and the four tall turrets. This highly original church exerted much influence on contemporary northern architecture and Offa's church at St. Albans must be conceived in such a cultural context.

The remains in Britain from this period are modest compared to Centula. At Breamore parish church in Hampshire, one can see a survival of the Carolingian tradition: the crossing tower has a wooden structure above built like a pagoda in receding stages.

A Mercian church of the same general period as Offa's church which still stands about thirty miles north-west of St. Albans merits our close attention. Wing in Buckinghamshire was built between AD 600 and 800. At the eastern end is a seven-sided apse; outside embellishment includes strip decoration rising along the angles, with arches, blind recesses and triangles above. The chancel was apparently lit by three double-splayed, round-headed windows and there was a wide chancel arch. How to house relics and present them to pilgrims was a principal pre-occupation of church builders at this time. Under the chancel at Wing was a wide hall crypt lit by three windows. The reliquary chamber lay at the west and access was *via* two narrow passages from the nave; these are no longer viable. At a later date, a system of piers and arches was inserted into the crypt to strengthen it. A narrow door at the east end of the north aisle apparently gave access to an external ambulatory.

The nave of four bays opened to the aisles by means of three pairs of round-headed arches but the eastern bay retained its solid walls. A pair of doorways at the west end of the nave walls indicates the presence of a former western gallery. An internal offset on the nave wall twenty-six feet up possibly supported the floor of an upper room illuminated by the pair of windows over the chancel arch. Anyone interested in Offa's church at St. Albans should pay close attention to All Saints, Wing but the latter could have been the more ambitious of the two. The first wave of Viking invaders in the ninth century passed St. Albans by, suggesting that it was too obscure to tempt the raiders.

In the time of Abbot Wulnoth, ca.830–ca.840, there is an intriguing reference to the *major ecclesia*, the greater church, implying the existence also of a *minor ecclesia* or lesser church. Perhaps there were two churches at St. Albans, the early church mentioned by Bede and a later one built by Offa. If so, one would expect to find them in the axial alignment favoured by the Saxons. The Saxon churches at Jarrow, excavated by Professor Rosemary Cramp, were placed in this way and similar arrangements occur at Monkwearmouth and at the monastery of St. Augustine at Canterbury. There have long been two dedications on Holmhurst hill, one to St. Alban and the other to St. Andrew. The shield of arms of the city of St. Albans, which is very ancient, takes the form of St. Andrew's cross.

The artist's reconstruction of the Saxon monastery at Jarrow which is on display at the site, based upon the archaeological findings of 1975, help one to visualise the kind of monastery which flourished in this period.

References

BEDE. A history of the English church and people. Trans. by Leo Sherley-Price. The Penguin Classics. Harmondsworth. 1955.

CONANT (KENNETH JOHN). Carolingian and Romanesque architecture 800 to 1200. The Pelican History of Art. Harmondsworth. 1959.

GILDAS. The ruin of Britain and other documents. Ed. and trans. by Michael Winterbottom. History from the Sources. London and Chichester. 1978.

LA BAUME (PETER). Colonia Agrippinensis: a brief survey of Cologne in Roman times. Trans. Barry Jones. Cologne Archaeological Society No. 7, Cologne, 1967.

LEVISON (WILHELM). 'St. Alban and St. Albans'. *Antiquity*. XV (1941) 337–359.

LOWE (W R L), JACOB (E F) and JAMES (M R). Illustrations of the life of St. Alban. Oxford 1924.

MEYER (WILHELM). 'Die Legende des h. Albanus, des Protomartyr Angliae, in Texten vor Beda'. *Abhandlungen der Kgl. Gesellschaft der Wissenschaften zu Göttingen, Philol.–hist. Klasse.* Neue Folge (1904) VIII. 1–82.

MORRIS (JOHN). 'The date of St. Alban'. *Hertfordshire Archaeology*. I (1968) 1–8.

STENTON (FRANK M). 'The supremacy of the Mercian kings'. *English Historical Review*. XXXIII (1918) 433–452.

TATLOCK (J S P). 'St. Amphibalus'. *Essays and Studies*, University of California. 1934. 249–257.

TAYLOR (H M) and TAYLOR (JOAN). Anglo-Saxon architecture. Vol. II. Cambridge. 1965

THOMAS (CHARLES). Christianity in Roman Britain to AD 500. London 1981.

Chapter 3

THE LATER SAXON MONASTERY

We know almost nothing of the furnishings and fittings of the Saxon church at St. Albans. Survivals from any church of this period, like the Tassilo chalice, are generally very scarce, although the literary references are clearly to luxury goods of the highest order, vestments, shrines, golden candelabra and golden chalices blazing with gems. The Tassilo chalice, which dates from 777 now in Kremsmünster in Austria, is almost certainly by an English craftsman or one who trained in England. It is of gilt bronze with a carved chip decoration, interlaced ornament and portraits of the apostles and Christ. From this example, it is easy to understand why the skill of the Anglo-Saxon metalworker was prized throughout Europe.

Fig. 10   Tassilo chalice, Kremsmünster, Austria, 777–788.

When William the Conqueror returned to Normandy from a visit to England, his followers were astonished at the quality of the vestments he brought back with him. The Stole of St. Cuthbert, in the library at Durham cathedral, is a rare and precious relic of the embroidery of the period. It dates, apparently, between 909 and 916. It is embroidered in pinks, blues, greens and browns on a gold background and has the figures of the apostles within an acanthus border.

Fig. 11 Figure of Daniel on the stole of St. Cuthbert, 909–916. Durham cathedral library.

It is possible that St. Albans abbey was sacked in a Danish raid of the 890s which would account for the loss of early muniments and the subsequent forging of replacements. The dates for the Saxon abbots which Matthew Paris gives are very confused and unrelated to known historical facts. Pagan devastations virtually killed monasticism in England except at Canterbury and for a considerable time St. Albans was without an abbot. A great revival occurred under Dunstan and through his influence, the strict Benedictine Rule was re-introduced at St. Albans ca. 970. His reforms throughout England were accompanied by an architectural reawakening with many monastic houses built, rebuilt or remodelled to facilitate radical change.

St. Albans did not remain unaffected. A Saxon charter of the year 1005 seems to indicate that the site of Roman Verulamium was granted to the abbey in this year to be exploited for building materials (see fig. 1). For this reason the Roman wall of Verulamium as we see it today has been extensively robbed for tiles and flints. Thomas Wright, a fellow of the Society of Antiquaries, discussed this early excavation of the Roman city by the Saxon monks. He describes it as 'the earliest systematical excavations in England, of which we have a definite account.' Abbot Ealdred overthrew and filled up the subterranean crypts and winding, vaulted passages. He destroyed and filled up as much as possible of the fosses of the ancient city. He laid up the unbroken tiles or bricks and made great excavations in order to discover stone buildings, gathering together both stones, tiles and wood. His successor Eadmer uncovered the foundations of a vast palace, finding squared stones with bricks and columns which he reserved for the church he proposed to build. In the abbey church today, forming the bases of the central tower, are great squared oolitic blocks which

Fig. 12 The Roman god Mercury on a cameo of onyx, drawn by Matthew Paris in a catalogue of jewels of St. Albans abbey now in the British Library.

would fit the beds in the sleeper walls in the forum. The stone used in the Saxon baluster shafts corresponds to the stone used in the same building complex (see fig. 13). The Saxon abbots found statues, which they destroyed as being pagan gods, as well as altars overturned. Roman altars sometimes were decorated with chip carving, as one sees on an example found at Chester; it is interesting to note that a stone with a similar chip carving is built into the triforium of the present Norman nave. Whether or not it was rescued from the Roman city has never been established.

Glass funerary urns came to light as well as pots and amphorae. There is a special liturgy in the Anglo-Saxon prayer book for the hallowing of classical vases for use in churches: 'deign so to cleanse these vases, fabricated by the art of the Gentiles, that they may be used by the believers in peace and tranquillity'. Some fine Roman glass can be seen in the Verulamium Museum, and there is an internationally famous collection of such wares in Cologne.

Coins were also discovered and although there is no specific mention of it, they may have found in these or in other excavations the engraved gems which are detailed in later abbey inventories. A drawing of a river god is used by Matthew Paris to fill an empty space in a manuscript now in Trinity College, Cambridge, apparently copied from a cameo. Another cameo of onyx from a Matthew Paris inventory of jewels shows the god

Mercury; this was believed to be particularly helpful to women in childbirth and was lent out for this purpose. This gem was not found at Verulamium, but was given to the abbey by Ethelred the Unready, 978–1013. These cameos were collected for use on the shrine of St. Alban. Doubtless they were mounted in the same way as a cameo head of Augustus Caesar which adorns the Cross of Lothar ca. 990, now in the cathedral treasury at Aachen.

Re-building, then, was intended at St. Albans in the early eleventh century. Other monastic churches had similar hopes, Abingdon, St. Augustine at Canterbury, Bury St. Edmunds to name but a few. For some reason, their plans came to little, and why this should have been is very complicated: the renewed Viking attacks up until the accession of Cnut in 1016, the stultifying fear of attack, the money expended on repair after attack. Tribute money had to be paid to the Vikings; church treasure was broken up to raise funds and land was sold for cash. Skilled masons were in short supply. England suffered a recession in the early eleventh century and fell behind the continent, where Romanesque art was already developing with confidence.

Fig. 13 *Baluster shafts from the south transept triforium of St. Albans abbey. Saxon work of uncertain date.*

There remains to be considered the Saxon evidence within the abbey church beginning with the series of eight lathe-turned baluster shafts, six in the south transept, two in the north. They are fashioned from Bath stone, a medium to coarse grained oolite; the bedding layers are placed horizontally and watermarks are numerous. Some of the shafts are plain cylinders, some tapered shafts and others composite units of two or more parts. The splayed bases, Anglo-Saxon in style, are of a different stone. Baldwin Brown noted that some of the shafts are defective and have been made good with plaster in a makeshift manner, consonant with the re-use of materials from an older building store; they could be re-used Roman stone. Otherwise, the crisp condition of the detailing proves they were never used externally. They are decorated with moulded bands around the bases; the heads and the centres of the shafts and some of the intervals in between are thickened and bulbous. In 1911 the Royal Commission suggested that they could have been of the eighth century and hence survivals from Offa's church. Baldwin Brown, however, pointed out that they do not resemble the early lathe-turned shafts of Jarrow and Monkwearmouth; those are more stubby in proportion with rings shallower and more closely spaced. The shafts from Monkwearmouth retain traces of colour, and some believe they were part of a low chancel screen projecting into the nave of the church. They might have formed the posts between thin, flat panels, such as were used in the Early Christian chancel at Gerasa in Palestine. The St. Albans shafts are much closer to those at St. Mary-in-the-Castle at Dover which can be securely dated between 950 and 1000.

The St. Albans shafts strangely enough, have cushion capitals. The function of a capital is to effect the transition between the circular shaft and the square *abacus*. This type of plain cushion capital, a cube of stone with the lower corners rounded off, was found in England before the Conquest. The four plain faces would either have been painted or carved in low relief. This style of capital, which became one of the most popular forms in the Anglo-Norman style, is found above all in the great cathedrals and churches of the Rhineland, the homeland of this style, for it is very rare indeed in Normandy.

Another curious feature is the way some of the arches, supported by the baluster shafts, are turned. Since the plaster was stripped off here in the nineteenth century, the structure is exposed to view. The arches, the Bucklers noted in 1847, are 'built with little attention to exactness'. The voussoir joints do not all radiate from one centre. Instead, they are laid at an almost constant inclination, so that the lowest voussoirs on each side are titled sharply up from the faces of their imposts while, between the uppermost voussoirs, there is a large V-shaped gap. This is filled by a wedge-shaped stone or a large mass of mortar. Baldwin Brown first noted this system at Tredington, Warwickshire and applied the name 'Tredington-fashion'. Dr Harold Taylor calls it the 'non-radial setting of voussoirs'. It is interesting that this Anglo-Saxon method of construction was used in the Norman abbey church.

Documentary references cast some light on fittings in the later Saxon period. A noblewoman, Aethelgyfu, bequeathed to St. Albans abbey in her will of 980–90 her best wall hanging. Decorative textiles had long been important in a domestic setting and especially valuable ones were passed on to monasteries in the tenth and eleventh centuries. It was not until 1025, however, that the Council of Arras gave official approval to the use of figured hangings in churches as a means of instructing the illiterate.

In 1043, there is a reference to a 'great bell' given by Wynfled, wife of Egelwine. According to the *Regularis concordia* ca. 970 the ringing of bells at festivals was a 'custom of the people of this country'. Two bells hanging in a tiered belfry above a church are actually illustrated in *The Benedictional of St. Ethelwold* which dates between 971 and 984 (fol. 118b). Almost a third of surviving Anglo-Saxon churches in this country possessed towers and the presence of this bell at St. Albans points to the presence of one in the Anglo-Saxon church.

Little is known of books or learning at St. Albans before the Conquest. From this period, only three small booklets remain dating from ca. 1050–1075 and now in the Pierpont Morgan Library in New York (MS. 926). They were written, apparently, by local monks for their own personal use and decoration is not extensive. For example, a *Hymn to St. Alban* is

Fig. 14   The letter 'H' in the form of writhing dragons, from Hymn to St. Alban, second half of eleventh century. Pierpont Morgan Library, New York.

27

adorned with a fanciful letter 'H' composed of two writhing
dragons who grasp one another with fang and claw. The tail of
one creature has a second head which reaches, biting, into the text
itself; the tail of the other divides into three and sprouts leaves.
These muscular, winged creatures, executed in firm outline, are in
the Hiberno-Northumbrian tradition still in favour amongst the
Saxon monks at that time.

Under the Norman abbots, when building a library assumed
great importance, Saxon influence persisted. The only book
known to survive from Abbot Paul's time was certainly copied by
an English scribe (British Library, Harl. MS. 865). Its decorated
initials are slender, wiry creatures whose bodies twist into
interlace patterns terminating in foliage scrolls. Expert
Anglo-Saxons were obviously amongst those scribes drawn by
Abbot Paul into his new scriptorium.

*Fig. 15 'Faith battling against Idolatry'. Illumination made at St. Albans
ca. 1120 for the* Psychomachia *of Prudentius, now in the
British Library.*

Even after the death of Paul in 1093, a kind of bilingual art
remained, based broadly upon the Anglo-Saxon tradition but
gradually modified by Norman tastes. *The Psychomachia* by
Prudentius, for example, was illuminated at St. Albans in the early
years of the twelfth century. In this popular book, of which many
copies survive in England from the ninth and tenth centuries, the

ascetic life is described in terms of warfare. Vices and virtues are personified as women shown in deadly combat. The St. Albans example, now in the British Library (Cott. MS. Titus D. XVI) is the last in the series. It is clear that the artist worked from Anglo-Saxon models, as the little figures, intense, lively and passionate, are drawn in coloured lines on an empty background, without a frame and with only the slightest hint of a setting. They seem to dart about weightlessly and they wear jagged, linear draperies. A new trend toward monumentality is nevertheless present: in *The Psychomachia* we begin to witness the actual fusion of the Anglo-Saxon tradition with influences from abroad which would merge to create the Romanesque style.

References

GEM (RICHARD). 'A recession in English architecture during the early eleventh century, and its effect on the development of the Romanesque style.' *Journal of the British Archaeological Association*. Ser. 3. XXXVIII (1975) 28–49.

OMAN (CHARLES C). 'The Jewels of St. Albans Abbey'. *Burlington Magazine* LVII pt. 2. (1930) 81–2.

PAGE (WILLIAM). 'Houses of Benedictine monks: St. Albans abbey, before the Conquest'. *Victoria County History: Hertfordshire*. IV (1914) 367–372.

TAYLOR (H M) and TAYLOR (JOAN). Anglo-Saxon architecture. 3 vols. Cambridge. 1965–1978.

THOMSON (RODNEY M). Manuscripts from St. Albans Abbey, 1066–1235. 2 vols. University of Tasmania. 1982.

WRIGHT (THOMAS). 'On antiquarian excavations and researches in the middle ages.' *Archaeologia*. XXX (1844) 438–448.

Part II

THE NORMAN ABBEY

Chapter 4

ROBERT, MOST EXCELLENT MASON

Although Charlemagne who died in 814 had unified Europe, not many years passed before it broke up in chaos and anarchy. Invasion threatened, Huns from the east, Arabs from the south and Vikings from the north-west. In England, the Vikings were known as Danes, in France they were called Normans. Progress in architecture was non-existent and it was only with the emergence of the feudal system that order was gradually restored, monasticism established, art and learning took root and flourished once again.

The architecture which developed was the Romanesque, which lasted from the year 1000 until 1200, roughly speaking. It had many local schools, depending upon the materials at hand and on the models available for copying. We are concerned with only one of them, the Norman, evolved by the Vikings in north-western France. They settled in that area in 911 and after their conversion to Christianity began to create a state, using monasteries as their instruments. One of these was Jumièges, where they found a ruined Carolingian monastery which they set about restoring. What they built was the little church of S. Pierre, using cut stone, a remarkable achievement for so early a date, 934. As a sea-faring people, they had found superb stone at Caen, which they brought in by water transport and before long became consummate craftsmen in this medium. The building is still small in scale but the parts are clearly organised, unified by a strong rhythm, both in the repeated curves of the arches and circles and in the echoed pairs of motifs. These qualities point to the future.

In France of the year 1000, Normandy lay open to Burgundy *via* the great river system of the Seine. Cluny was the most vital monastic centre of the day and William of Dijon, an outstanding Burgundian churchman, was invited to Normandy to reform the monasteries there.

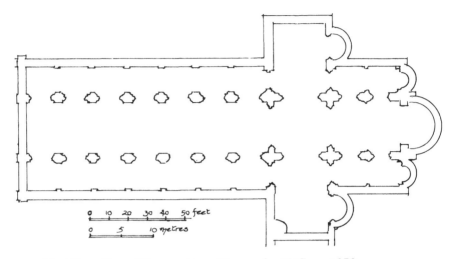

Fig. 16   Plan of Bernay abbey, Normandy, 1017–ca. 1050.

Bernay was the first Norman church to show the Cluny influence. Looking at its plan, which dates from 1017, one notices the sanctuary with an apse at the east, the nave for liturgical processions and corridors on either side to house the laity. Chapels east of the transepts accommodate extra altars, while nave and aisles hold a clear, mathematical relationship to one another. The main entrance is at the west, with neither porch nor narthex. Glancing inside the building today, one notes significant advances in less than half a century. Details are more elaborate, with oblong piers, rounded shafts and stepped mouldings. There is a hint of a triforium and string courses clearly define the space. In the clerestory, there is a single window per bay and the tower arch is daring for its time.

Only twenty years later, in 1037, the great church of Notre Dame, Jumièges, was built. Its scale is overpowering, built of superb quality ashlar, and with attached shafts rising from ground to vault. Round columns alternate in the nave arcade with rectangular ones. The Normans were clearly ambitious, capable and energetic men.

Soon after the Norman Conquest, the English church was re-organised at the Council of Windsor in 1070. Almost all the Saxon bishops were replaced by new men from Normandy who aimed to reform the lax English monasteries, and to conduct a vast programme of church rebuilding. They were experienced; they had resources. An architectural renaissance followed, one of the greatest in history. As William of Malmesbury wrote, 'You might see churches rising in every village, and monasteries in the towns and cities, built after a style unknown before.'

The new archbishop of Canterbury was Lanfranc, formerly abbot of St. Étienne monastery in Caen (see fig. 27). A lawyer from Pavia, he had founded a school at Bec, a leading intellectual centre of its day. He was a man of gigantic intellectual stature, lovable, but firm and energetic as well. When the abbacy of St. Albans became vacant in 1077, he appointed his kinsman, Paul, to the post. A monk under Lanfranc at Caen, Paul must have seen that great monastic church rise from the ground. It had been founded ca. 1063 by William the Conqueror himself and dedicated in the very year that St. Albans was begun. Many features from Caen reappeared in Paul's new church at St. Albans: the clear articulation of parts by means of flat pilaster buttresses splayed at the top and by horizontal string courses between the stages. The round headed arches have the same simple, stepped mouldings; the corbel table and the steep pitched roof appear in both churches (see fig. 23).

Paul was a proud and scornful man. He despised his Saxon predecessors, perhaps because their income was generous but their monastic buildings mean. He called them 'uneducated simpletons' and destroyed the tombs of those of their saints he considered unworthy of veneration. He did not even translate the bones of Offa. Paul's discipline was strict; he removed meat from the diet and placed the nuns in the almonry where they could specialise in nursing. Yet he did much good, establishing St. Albans as a centre of learning, founding a scriptorium and endowing three writers to copy books. Paul donated relics, vestments and ornaments. He was a notable musician and introduced the new liturgy and chant which had been developed on the continent. By his wise and strong rule, the monastery became a model to others; recruits flocked in and many benefactors made rich endowments.

We honour Paul as a patron of building, and he began at once to build a vast new church. His choice of architect was inspired: Robert the Mason, whose name and work both point to Norman roots. He was one of the first architects of England whose building still stands, of whom we know both name and some biographical details. His personality was outstanding, for he 'excelled all masons of his time' according to the chronicles. He had a house in St. Albans; exactly where it was we would like to know. A mason called Robert of St. Albans appears as a witness to a deed of land to Ramsey Abbey in 1122 and reappears in other documents until ca. 1135.

'Robert', John Harvey writes, 'reused Roman materials with beauty and ingenuity.' As a Norman mason, he would be accustomed to using the fine-grained freestone from Caen. From this he could have produced carved capitals and complex piers of moulded stone such as one sees at La Trinité, Caen. Now in England, he was faced with heaps of tatty Roman bricks and rough, hard flints collected by the Saxon abbots. He may have had some Norman assistants but his work force would be mainly Saxon, quite inexperienced in Norman methods.

Perhaps Robert wandered amongst the ruins of Verulamium as he pondered these problems. If so, what would he have seen? The Bucklers believed 'there still remained undisturbed very considerable portions of the walls and foundations of the city . . . very much more than now remains visible.' In the thirteenth century, a St. Albans author was moved to write 'O Verulamium, more of a ruin than a city. You are more blessed today, broken down that you are, in giving a message to all nations, than you were richly furnished in your former state. In pieces you teach more than you did whole'. (trans. Canon M E Dahl). Roger of Wendover, writing also in the thirteenth century, gives a description of Purgatory which is clearly based on the Roman theatre at Verulamium then standing with walls five feet high. We know that as late as 1700, much of the west gate was still to be seen. The antiquary, Stukeley, who drew a remarkably accurate plan of Verulamium, met in 1721 hundreds of cartloads of Roman bricks being taken away for road repairs. In the eleventh century, with very much more of the Roman city still standing, Robert the Mason may have found in Verulamium some guidelines on the use of his intractable materials.

He planned a much larger building than the Saxons had had in mind, so more materials would have had to be gathered. Apparently, as digging proceeded, he observed and learned. The Bucklers commented on the Roman methods of building which were copied in the abbey: foundations built with levelling courses of Roman bricks, nave pier bases copying hypocaust construction, and vaulted roofs based on Roman prototypes (see fig. 29). The austerity of this model has been maintained.

Siting the church involved important decisions. The Norman abbey was aligned with the existing roads at the north and east, very old routes, apparently part of the tenth century town plan.

This suggests that the Norman precinct followed the line of the Saxon one, at least on two sides. However, the church itself is not strictly oriented, as it is thirty degrees out of line and points south-east. This no doubt was due to the character of the available site. The Saxon monastery was already in existence, and had to remain in use during building operations. Sometimes a new and larger church was built around an existing earlier one; this was the case at St. Augustine, Canterbury. If this occurred at St. Albans, the holy place of St. Alban's burial might have remained at the heart of the Norman church.

The Bucklers observed with what care and forethought the site of the church had been chosen. The tower in particular, the heaviest part, had been placed on the best possible spot, where its foundations need descend only four feet to reach bedrock. The remainder of the hilltop site was terraced to support the building. This foresight of Robert the Mason ensured that much of the Norman building has survived the centuries.

Archbishop Lanfranc, seven years before, had begun rebuilding the metropolitan church at Canterbury. As former abbot of Caen, he copied the church of St. Étienne exactly, both in plan and in measurements (see fig. 17). It was a cruciform church, with a nave of nine bays, a crossing tower and an aisled chancel of two bays. The eastern arm has a total of five apses, all of them rounded. The church Paul built exceeded Canterbury in scale and elaboration: his chancel was elongated to four bays and his transepts project so far that seven apses, not five, were massed at the eastern end. The nave was not nine, but ten bays long. There is no question here of insubordination on Abbot Paul's part, because the archbishop supported his endeavour in every way. Perhaps it was to honour St. Alban, Protomartyr of the British, that the abbey church was made so grand. By elevating St. Alban, and appealing to common national pride, the country could be drawn together in greater unity under the Conqueror.

The Norman abbey church was very long, fifteen bays from end to end (see front plant). Projecting eastwards was a large, semi-circular apse and the shrine was placed on its chord. There was no crypt, although there was no danger of flooding on this hillside site; the body of St. Alban had, traditionally, been translated as long ago as the eighth century. The High Altar probably stood in front, in the chancel. Solid walls separated the chancel from the aisles. The chancel was apparently vaulted, to emphasise the sepulchral quality of the *martyrium* church.

If there had been only one altar, as in Early Christian times, the

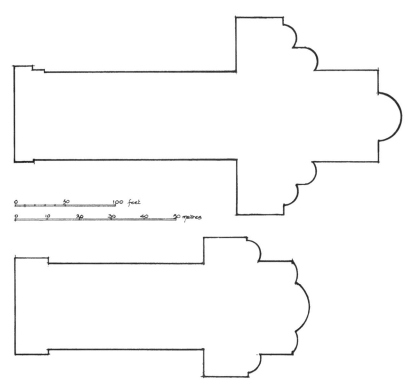

Fig. 17 Comparative plans to same scale of Canterbury cathedral (below) begun 1070/71, and St. Albans abbey (above) begun 1077.

design problem would have been simple. With the increased veneration of saints, many altars had to be provided. Whereas the solution in Carolingian times had been to subdivide the nave by means of screens into many chapels, here the solution is to group other chapels at the east in a stepped or *echelon* plan.

Next to the chancel, the aisles form long, high, narrow halls, very Anglo-Saxon in feeling, with altars at the east. These aisles have five divisions and were certainly vaulted, with access to the chancel in the western bay: these arches were used by officiating clergy and for processions. East of the transepts, four additional chapels project, first a pair with one vaulted bay and an apse and with access to the chancel aisle, then a pair with apses alone. The crossing tower is not square but narrower at north and south, because the nave is wider than the transepts. Their width and that of the nave is governed by the length of timbers available for the tie-beams of the roofs. The nave is aisled, and one nave bay equals two aisle bays in the orderly Norman fashion. The nave aisles were only partly vaulted. A door in the south aisle and another in the transept gave access to the cloister and were used for processions. The doors in the north nave aisle gave access to the parochial chapel. The whole plan is set out with remarkable regularity, especially in the nave; only the north transept is a little wider at the north.

This seven apse plan was copied at Binham, Norfolk, a daughter house of St. Albans, founded before 1093, although it has some variations in detail. The Norman nave of this priory still stands but the plan of the eastern arm was recovered by excavation.

Robert the Mason was scrupulous about foundations and both the Bucklers and Grimthorpe have remarked on their excellence. The Bucklers, who made excavations, are our chief authority on their construction. The ground had been terraced to different levels to get down to bedrock, only four feet under the tower, from six to twelve feet elsewhere. A continuous wall was built under the whole structure, openings as well as wall, tying the whole together and giving additional strength. Large blocks of stone were concentrated under the tower with some tiles added; the very tough mortar devised by Robert consisted of lime, gravel and pulverised brick.

In the other foundations, flints were laid in regular courses, proportionate in size to the superstructure they were to carry. The top of the foundations were levelled by tile courses which formed a flat, pavement-like surface to receive the upper walls.

The pier foundations, which Lord Grimthorpe found 'singularly large and strong' exceed the pier dimensions and are linked by connecting walls five feet six inches to seven feet six inches thick. The aisle foundations rise from a broad base and contract to meet the walls; there is extra footing inside but none outside. The pavement, according to the Bucklers, was covered in red tiles, six inches square and one inch thick, unpolished except from use. They had been purpose-made on the spot out of gravel, broken brick and lime.

We will now consider in detail the Presbytery, the space between the choir and the eastern wall of the church. The Bucklers were able to reconstruct the plan from their excavations before 1847 and found it to project farther than all the other members of the eastern arm. They discovered parts of the foundations of the great eastern apse: they were nine and a half feet thick and on either side, a three foot length survived which was clearly curved. Under the chord of the apse lay a cross wall which today forms

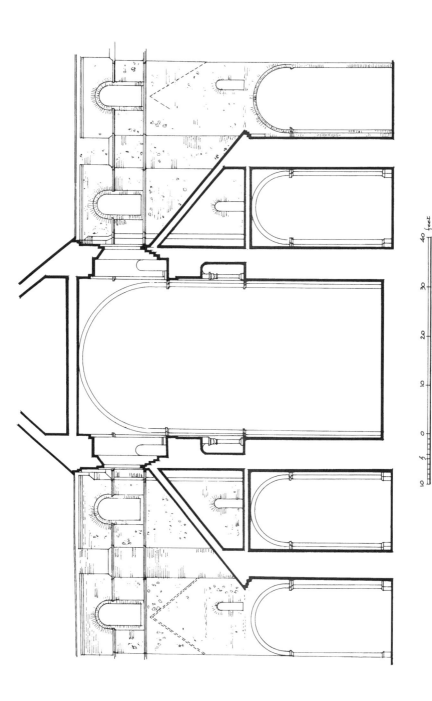

Fig. 18   Transverse section of Norman Presbytery, St. Albans, showing east elevation of transepts.

the foundation of the triple arches of the antechapel. The side walls of the Presbytery did not form an arcade but were solid; proof lies in the fact that the Presbytery bays, four in number, did not correspond to the five bays of the aisles. This indicates that the Presbytery was vaulted, as longer bays would be required to give a well-proportioned high vault. The side walls were originally seven feet three inches thick but were thinned down in the thirteenth century. Some of the pilaster buttresses still survive above the vault of the aisle.

The Bucklers made a drawing of the Norman Presbytery in section, of which the internal height can be calculated from the eastern side of the crossing tower. The walls were thick and solid in the lower stage as we have mentioned. Stage two had a triforium passage, for which the evidence again is found over the vault of the south aisle. The Bucklers also drew a plan and elevation of these details, showing a small, blocked Norman door which gave access to the triforium. A clerestory in stage three is inferred, simply because of the height of the structure; it, too, would have a passage in the wall. A clue to clerestory design may possibly survive in the south transept. Here, a solitary clerestory window is enriched by shafting which was henceforth discontinued, perhaps from lack of freestone or from financial constraints (see fig. 40).

Looking east from the crossing, we may picture an effect not unlike Lessay in Normandy, with two tiers of lights in its eastern apse. There, the clerestory is of large, single windows with similar windows, elaborated with shafting, in the triforium below. At Lessay, however, there is a Presbytery arcade, while St. Albans had solid walls pierced only by a pair of arches. The shrine would occupy the place of honour, on the chord of the apse to the north; this symbolised the right hand of God. The semi-dome hovered above, solemn and inspiring with the High Altar placed somewhat to the west of the apse. Paul de Caen gave a silver bowl to contain a light to hang before the High Altar and in the time of Abbot Geoffrey de Gorham, 1119–1146, a gold and silver altarpiece set with choice gems was made for it.

We know that Paul de Caen had decorated the recess behind the High Altar with a painting, which doubtless refers to the semi-dome. A contemporary mural from the priory of Berzé-la-Ville in Burgundy, dating from 1100–1140, helps us to picture the scheme. Christ, enthroned in an almond-shaped mandorla, raises his right hand in blessing and holds a book with his left. The cross inscribed in the halo indicates that he is divine.

Each Presbytery side aisle was like a hall, long, narrow and tall. Those which survive unaltered at La Trinité, Caen, are only three bays long, but at St. Albans each had four bays plus an apsidal eastern bay. These housed altars to English saints, to St. Oswin, King of Northumbria, d. 642 and to St. Wulstan, Bishop of Worcester, d.1095. These chapels were constructed entirely of masonry. In southern France and in Italy, where stone was abundant, vaults had developed early; they were mastered more slowly in the north, in Normandy and in England, which were peopled by a race of shipwrights and carpenters whose genius lay primarily in timberwork.

The groined cross vault with transverse ribs was the most popular form. First, the strong ribs were thrown across the space, as primary supports, then the gaps were filled in with two barrel vaults intersecting. When the centering was removed, the underside was plastered over and decorated with paint. At St. Albans, a masonry pattern was used. The vault rises naturally from the pavement level supported by its flat, pilaster buttresses and the simple, harmonious rhythms of springing curves are very satisfying.

We have already mentioned the Norman arches leading from the aisles into the Presbytery, the lines of which can still be detected from the aisles despite some later Gothic infill. A drawing by the Bucklers shows the original arches clearly as well as the construction of the wall above. Even the putlog holes of the Norman builders are visible.

Looking once more at the plan of the Norman abbey, one notes the free access from transept to chapel, aisle, Presbytery, aisle, chapel and transept. Next to each Presbytery aisle can be seen a chapel of a single vaulted bay plus an apse projecting eastwards. That on the north may have served as a sacristy or vestry, while the Norman Lady Chapel occupied the southern position. Similar chapels remain intact at La Trinité, Caen. Still in the south Presbytery aisle at St. Albans remains evidence of the large arched opening from the Lady Chapel to the aisle. There is a single window above it, and in the next bay east, a pair of round headed windows in the aisle wall; apparently they were just beyond the apse and illuminated the aisle. They provide important evidence of the appearance of the Norman aisle windows.

Each shallow outside chapel to the north-east and south-east consisted of an apse alone. A similar example can be seen at St. Aignan-sur-Cher in France. Chapels as small as this were often used as confessionals.

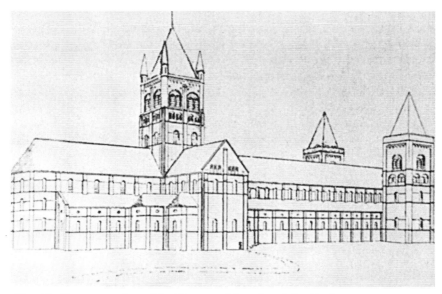

Fig. 19   Reconstruction of the Norman abbey church by Sir G G Scott, showing eastern apses and pyramidal spire. He mistakenly believed that a pair of western towers were built.

Sir George Gilbert Scott suggested a reconstruction of the eastern arm of the building. He conceived the great apse as having three tiers of windows and believed it was roofed in a single sweep, continuous with the Presbytery. The church of Lessay in Normandy, however, has only two tiers of lights in the main apse which is roofed separately from the Presbytery. The geometric forms of the great Norman churches have a monumental simplicity. The horizontal string courses, the pilaster buttresses and the corbel table under the eaves catch the light and break up otherwise monotonous surfaces. The side aisles at Lessay, as once at St. Albans, have square ends externally, a form which is easy to roof. The apsidal shape persisted within until, in time, this too fell out of fashion and was replaced by a rectangular form.

The priory church of St. Georges at St. Martin de Boscherville in Normandy is worth visiting to see how effective this Norman wall treatment can be in brilliant sunshine. In England, Romsey, Hampshire retains its eastern apses; its square-ended aisles are also round within.

The external eastern walls of the St. Albans transepts still retain in their fabric important evidence (see fig. 18). Although the

Norman apsidal chapels were removed in later centuries, one can see in certain lights, the lines of their high-pitched roofs. Below the roof level remain small Norman windows, blocked. This suggests a two-tier arrangement within the apses. In such cases, it was customary to hear confession in the floor below, while the altar was found in the high chapel above.

References

BOND (FRANCIS). Gothic architecture in England, an analysis of the origin and development of English church architecture from the Norman Conquest to the dissolution of the monasteries. London. 1905.

BUCKLER (J C) and BUCKLER (C A). A history of the architecture of the abbey church of St. Alban with special reference to the Norman structure. London. 1847.

CLAPHAM (SIR ALFRED). English Romanesque architecture. Vol. 2. After the Conquest. Oxford. 1934.

GRABAR (ANDRÉ). Martyrium. 2 vols. Paris. 1943–45.

HARVEY (JOHN). English mediaeval architects, a biographical dictionary down to 1550. Gloucester. 1984.

KIDSON (PETER), MURRAY (PETER) and THOMPSON (PAUL). A history of English architecture. Harmondsworth. 1965.

KNOWLES (DOM DAVID). Saints and scholars. Twenty-five medieval portraits. Cambridge. 1962.

. . . The monastic order in England. Cambridge. 1966.

PEVSNER (Sir NIKOLAUS). An outline of European architecture. Harmondsworth. 1943.

SAUNDERS (CHRISTOPHER). 'Unearthing secrets of city's past'. St. Albans Review and Express (6 May 1982) 2.

WEBB (GEOFFREY). Architecture in Britain in the middle ages. Harmondsworth. 1965.

Chapter 5

THE CROSSING TOWER AND THE TRANSEPTS

In Normandy one can scarcely find a cruciform church without a central tower; in England, it is the common form for all the greater churches. Erecting a tower is the logical way to put a roof over the crossing. Aesthetically, it serves two purposes: it gives the church a commanding outline, the strong vertical line balancing the four horizontals of nave, transepts and Presbytery. It also illuminates the most important part of the church. In many early cruciform churches the High Altar was placed in the crossing, where it was flooded by light in an otherwise gloomy interior.

The chief problem with crossing towers was how to achieve stability, in a day when methods were by rule of thumb, unaided by scientific disciplines. There were only four great legs to support an immense superstructure (see fig. 21). If they were too bulky, they obstructed movement and visibility; if too small, the tower came crashing down. Many are the tales of disaster: the towers at Winchester and Lincoln collapsed soon after completion; at Wells and York they tore away from the nave; at Chichester, the tower telescoped. Much additional underpinning was required at a later date at Hereford and Rochester. At Winchester, the tower was rebuilt, but the masons played for safety; a very short tower was built, rising only one stage above the ridge.

St. Albans is the only major church in England with a great crossing tower of the eleventh century still standing. What was Robert the Mason's secret? He built immensely thick walls; in all but the topmost stage he created a slightly pyramidal form and the materials he used proved extremely enduring, especially when held together by his own tough mortar. The scale of the mighty supports to the tower is disguised by the soaring verticals of the mouldings.

The external design of the tower is in four stages, with the walls slanting slightly inwards. Each face of each stage is divided into

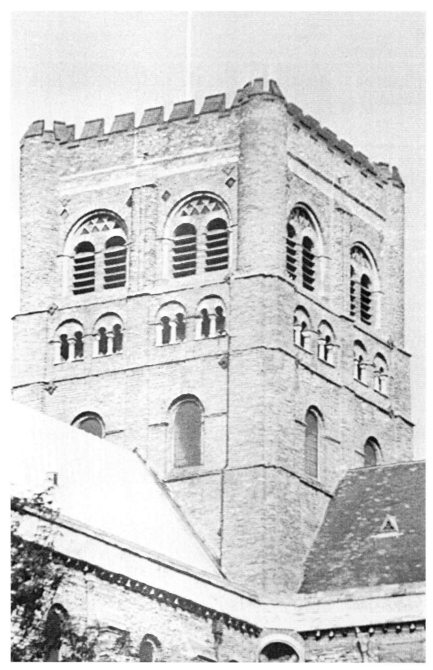

Fig. 20 The Norman crossing tower.

two bays by means of flat pilaster buttresses. The angles are supported by rectangular, clasping buttresses on the lower, pyramidal three stages. These are replaced by circular ones on the upper, vertical stage; each bore a circular turret capped by a small conical spire for access to the tower roof.

String courses have been used in a decorative way and the clasping buttresses have stepped profiles. The slight variations away from mathematical exactitude give a living and vibrant quality. The lowest stage is completely plain; an internal passage in the thickness of this wall gives access to the roof. Above is the lantern with a single, large, round-headed window in each bay adorned by a simple, stepped moulding and a string course at abacus level. In the next stage, the ringing chamber, is an external gallery with pairs of arched openings, each sub-divided; we will look at this in detail in a moment. The upper, belfry stage has a single arch in each bay, shafted and enriched by a roll moulding, the only place in the Norman abbey where this appears. This more elaborate form suggests that the building of the tower proceeded slowly and was completed last. Notice the buttresses between the bays on this level: they are made up of two half rounds and a triangle side by side. Each belfry window is divided by a brick shaft supporting the tympanum with its seven decorative triangles for ventilation and weight reduction. There is evidence of later flint patching and of iron tie rods inserted in recent times. The present battlements are not original.

From the external galleries, which are only twenty inches across, one obtains an extensive view of the countryside round about. Three of the galleries communicate by means of doors with the ringing chamber within. There are miniature groined cross vaults above the galleries, to which bits of wood from the original centering still adhere. The round shafts of Barnack stone have block capitals and chamfered bases, much weathered in nine hundred years. The wide mortar joints were meant to provide a key to the plaster which originally covered the entire building, so that it presented an exterior of gleaming white.

The plan of the tower at ringing chamber and gallery levels shows the two newel staircases and three intercommunicating doorways.

The roof treatment of Norman towers, we learn from manuscript evidence, was low and pyramidal (see fig. 19). A drawing of the Norman cathedral at Canterbury dating from the mid-twelfth century shows such a silhouette. Southwell Minster in Nottinghamshire is generally believed to have retained its original

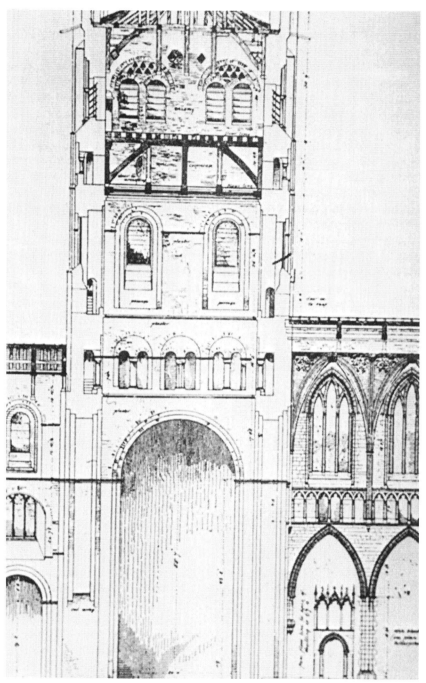

Fig. 21 Longtitudinal section of the crossing tower looking north by James Neale..

Norman tower roof shape, and to have been renewed to the old pattern. Lessay in Normandy also retains a pyramidal tower roof, and shows what St. Albans abbey must have looked like in its original state. Probably the pyramidal roof was shingled.

Having completed our survey of the tower exterior, we now turn to the section. The tower stands one hundred and forty-four feet tall and its five thousand ton weight is supported on four great piers canted slightly inwards. The four round tower arches are gently stilted and above them is an open arcade, screening a passage in the thickness of the wall. Each side has twin arches, sub-divided. Above is the lantern, eight large, round-headed windows with stepped mouldings and steeply sloping sills. In the tower wall, which is seven feet thick, is a newel staircase giving access to the upper parts. Above the lantern is located the ringing chamber and above that, the belfry, each with its own system of great roofing timbers. The sheer mechanical feat of raising these trusses into place testifies to Robert's skill.

We will now explain a few details of the tower, starting from the ground and moving upwards. The plan of the tower piers which the Bucklers drew shows the scale very clearly. The corners are chamfered in stepped order to improve circulation and visibility; their varied proportions are governed by the sizes of the Roman bricks available, mostly seventeen inches by twelve inches by one-and-a-half inches. The best quality bricks were selected for the pier angles. Considerable ingenuity has been used to effect the transition from the choir, aisles and crossing: each order supports an arched order above in the logical Norman manner, but extra ones at north and south form additional strengthening buttresses.

A general view of the crossing shows the relationships of the flat buttresses to the curved orders of the tower arches. The impost is marked by a simple moulding. In the time of Abbot Paul, a lighted lantern was carried round the choir at night to rouse the monks who had dozed off to sleep; there were fifty monks at St. Albans in 1190. The inner gallery of the tower can be seen above the arches.

The plan at gallery level shows newel staircases leading into the passage in two places with three exits into the roof space. The gallery shafts are varied in plan, with round ones at the east, but wide, thin rectangles elsewhere. Thus, most shafts are the widest where they are seen from below, but narrow where space is needed in the passage. All are pieced together from fragments of stone.

An elevation drawing of the gallery's north interior face shows

Fig. 22. View into lantern

the greater strength which has been given to the side supports as well as the variations which are beginning to break up the surfaces of the plain block capitals.

Looking up into the lantern from the pavement below reveals the brilliant light which pours down into the crossing. The wall passage, by contrast, remains in shadow and the stepped orders define the windows in light and shade. The architect J C Rogers made a careful study of the timber roof when he restored it in 1930. He found the tower ceiling to be supported on four enormous wall plates, each about thirty feet long, for the support of which the tower wall has been thickened out. These timbers form a great rectangular frame within which is a series of intermediate beams. The panels of the ceiling, three-quarters of an inch to one inch thick, are all of oak with lapped, tongued joints. Rogers made a careful drawing of this ceiling.

A sectional drawing of the tower roof trusses was also prepared by Rogers, a most careful craftsman in wood (see fig. 21). The floor of the ringing chamber consists of a double set of beams; within a space of ten feet are huge posts and curved braces framed together as trusses. These rise to support a second series of beams, the floor of the belfry and they also carry the bell frame. The timber trusses were obviously manoeuvred into place before the enclosing masonry walls were formed, which means that the timbers are at least as old as the masonry tower itself. Rogers described the roof as a 'veritable forest of timbers'. They were felled and squared no later than the eleventh century and mostly weigh a ton apiece. In some of the beams Rogers found mortices which suggested re-used timbers, perhaps from the Saxon church. Possibly we have here a key to the width of the Saxon nave; carbon dating tests would throw light on this problem.

Abbot Paul, we are told, put two bells in the tower and a drawing by Matthew Paris shows a bell-ringer at work. Another was given by a wealthy Englishman called Lyulf who sold his flocks to buy it and yet another was the gift of his wife. A fifth bell was donated by John, rector of Hoddesdon, and if the Saxon bell given by Wynfled still survived, the abbey bells would have reached a total of six.

The belfry is roofed by another set of great roof timbers (see fig. 21). In the Bucklers' drawing of the belfry interior, the twin apertures under relieving arches can be clearly seen, as well as the triangular openings in the tympana. The widely spaced Roman bricks are also shown. The cold and windy belfry, with its slatted shutters to keep out the rain, provides an excellent opportunity to

Fig. 23   Bay elevation of the Norman transept by John Carter.

study the quality of the Roman bricks. Some made with white earth can be seen up here. The texture of all of them is so close and fine, they are almost as durable as flint. The variations in shape are interesting too; some have been warped in the firing and others are vitrified.

Turning now to the transepts, we find that the bay elevation design repeats that of the crossing but on a smaller scale (compare fig. 21). A drawing by Carter shows the buttresses chamfered off before they meet the flat timber roof; this is typical of the Norman style and does not mean that the roof has been heightened. Originally, the buttresses sprang from pavement level; at a later date they were cut off in the lower stage to accommodate church furnishings. The principal transept arches are of matching height, whether they open on aisles or on chapels. String courses mark the division between triforium and clerestory. The effect is harmonious and well-proportioned, pleasing to modern taste in its simplicity and strength.

The design is close to its Norman roots. Mont St. Michel, completed in 1023, is clearly similar to St. Albans in bay design, although it is made of ashlar and has half-round shafts applied to the pilasters. At St. Albans, the transept walls are sixty-eight feet high and gradually reduce in thickness at each stage, especially so at clerestory level.

When the Saxon shafts used in the triforium ran out, the Normans used their own axe-hewn type, some octagonal, some with a raised fillet in front. They are monoliths of freshly quarried Barnack stone, a shelly oolite, set with the bedding planes vertical and coated in rendering. The Normans frequently used capitals of a stylised foliage design in two tiers, a simplification of the Corinthian style; examples of these can be seen at St. Étienne, Caen; at St. Albans, however, the cushion capitals from the Rhineland were used instead (see fig. 13). The Normans were not hostile to local achievement; once they adopted a feature, they carried on using it with enthusiasm.

At St. Albans we still see the flat timber roofs so typical of the great Anglo-Norman churches (see fig. 22).

The Saxon masons must have been amazed at the thick, sturdy walls of Master Robert, so different from the thin, plain walls they had used. The clerestory shows the typical construction method clearly (see fig. 18), with a wall on two planes, the window outside, the arch inside, and a long, continuous passage hollowed out between. The English took to this hollow wall technique eagerly, and experimented with it in many exciting ways. It persisted even in some Gothic buildings of the fourteenth century long after it had been dropped in France.

The imprint of the timber shuttering on the surface of the barrel vaults in the triforium passage still looks fresh and new.

Outside the north transept, looking east, we see the least altered part of the Norman exterior, 'elementary form, with the barest minimum of articulation' as Dr Peter Kidson puts it. Good, regular bricks were used on the exterior. The amount of projection of arches and buttresses depends directly on the size of bricks available. The angles are entirely of brick, but in between, brick is interspersed with rubble. The walls are coursed but variable mortar joints made the courses even. The roughness gave a key for plaster, which covered the whole exterior, but even after this fell off, damp did not penetrate because the mortar was so good. The cut stone found in Verulamium was rationed for use where it was needed most, in the window sills, *abaci* and cornices. As the Bucklers wrote, 'this re-markable simplicity of design with the largest scale of dimensions is without a counterpart in English architecture.' A fragment of the original external plaster which covered these walls still clings to the brickwork in the cock-loft over the north nave aisle.

Fig. 24 North elevation of the Norman north transept, as partially reconstructed by the Bucklers.

The evidence which the Bucklers and Neale found remaining in the transept ends permitted their design to be partly reconstructed. The face is divided into two by a central pilaster with broader, matching buttresses clasping the angles. Arcading stretched across the springing of the gable. Beneath it, at clerestory level, were two windows, with a second pair at a lower level. The design of the transept ends was therefore just like the tower with the belfry omitted. Happily, the lower stage of the north transept still retains the original scheme with its stepped windows, flat buttresses and small north door. The townsfolk had right of access to the north transept of the abbey church.

The angles of the gable were marked by small turrets topped by conical spires containing the newel staircases which gave access to the roof. An entry in the chronicles suggests that the church was complete or nearly so in 1089 when Anselm was enthroned as Archbishop of Canterbury. This may mean that the eastern arm was by then completed; Offa's church, if it had been in use up to now, could now be demolished and the new Norman east end brought into use. The dimensions of the pier pilasters in the upper orders east of the roodscreen are different in dimensions from the bays west of the roodscreen (see fig. 59). There is also a break in the aisle vaulting scheme as well as a (now blocked) processional door in the west wall of the south transept. This varied evidence confirms the theory of two building phases.

Abbot Paul rewarded Robert the Mason handsomely. He was given a house in St. Albans: it is interesting that the archaeological excavation of the Chequer Street site reported in 1982 the discovery of 'an elaborate Romanesque door jamb decorated at the top with a carving of a human head,' which suggested 'that an eleventh/twelfth century stone house may have stood in the vicinity of the new Riders and Saxby's shops' in the words of Christopher Saunders. Robert was also given manors at Sarratt with an income of sixty shillings per year. Moreover, Paul's successor gave him land at Sopwell with an income of eight shillings per year. Robert must have been a very prosperous man and the monks 'murmured against so princely a gift'. Robert gave ten shillings of his income annually to the abbey throughout his lifetime and on his deathbed returned the lands to the abbey, renouncing the claims of his heirs.

References

In addition to those listed on page 44

CARTER (JOHN). Some account of the abbey church of St. Alban. London. 1813.

NEALE (JAMES). The abbey church of St. Albans, Hertfordshire. London. 1877

ROGERS (JOHN C). 'The great tower of St. Albans abbey church, with a description of the repairs recently carried out among its ancient timbers'. *Trans. SAHAAS* (1930) 55-64.

Chapter 6

THE NAVE AND THE DECORATIVE ARTS

In the Norman nave is found a scheme of great simplicity and grandeur. A bay elevation closest to the original scheme is found behind the present organ; elsewhere, the middle stage was much altered in mediaeval times. In overall height, each bay is three times its width: the clerestory stage is one third the total height of the bay.

With the simple building materials used and with no carvings or moulded stones to relieve the austere simplicity, proportion is all important. Thus the three stages of each bay, the arcade, the gallery and the clerestory, are in the proportions of 4:2:3. Within these stages, arches rise, tier upon tier, each ascending arch contrasting in scale with those below.

The piers are almost square on plan, their vast bulk reduced by a series of recessions, each at right angles, each supporting a corresponding part of the arch above in the logical Norman fashion. (The three piers east of the roodscreen have a slightly different section, indicating a break in the building work at bay 4.) The arch openings between are only slightly wider than the piers themselves. In Pevsner's words, they are 'hardly piers at all, but chunks of solid wall masonry left standing.'

The middle stage is the narrowest of the three. Whereas the transepts have a triforium passage in the thickness of the wall, the nave being aisled can accommodate a gallery. This was not meant for worshippers, as access was only by newel stair; nor, so far as we know, did windows illuminate it from outside. Like St. Étienne at Caen, it opened on the nave with a single arch, but unlike Caen, which had a half-barrel masonry vault, St. Albans had a lean-to roof of timber. Some authorities suggest that the arched openings of this gallery had subdividing arches, but if so, no trace of them remains today.

The clerestory, as in the transepts, has single arched lights

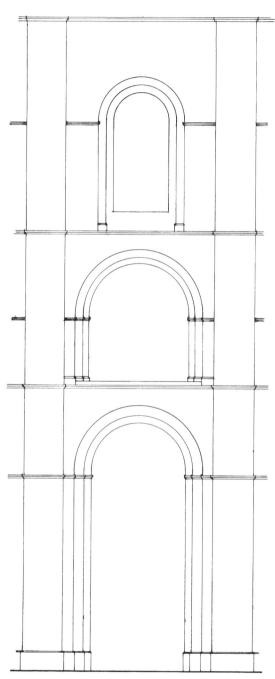

Fig. 25 *Norman nave bay elevation as it may have originally appeared.*

joined by a passage in the thickness of the wall.

The general effect today of the Norman bays is massive and fortress-like. The horizontal mouldings ran completely round the entire building giving it visual unity. This was enhanced by the flat timber roof in the *ecclesia* tradition (contrasting with the masonry vaults in the eastern arm in the *martyrium* tradition). Although these roofs are later, they have been constructed along the traditional lines. The nave aisle details suggest that these parts too were never vaulted but covered in timber roofs.

St. Albans is fortunate to retain its screens in the positions reflecting the monastic church. The choir therefore is still in the old position, west of the crossing. One can be thankful too that the internal plaster remains; St. Botolph, Colchester, also built from re-used ancient materials, is by contrast now a ruin, its plaster gone, its brick and mortar naked and unsightly.

The mouldings were built of Roman tiles and mortar to form the simplest profile. The plinths, with a single offset, stood over eleven inches above the pavement level; some are covered now, as the floor levels have been much altered in later centuries.

At one place, on the north side west of the crossing, a piece of sunk star decoration has been used in the gallery, but this is too slight to make any impact on the total effect of starkness.

A parochial chapel to St. Andrew located in the churchyard at the north-west of the abbey church was dedicated by Herbert de Losinga, Bishop of Norwich, between 1094 and 1119. The Norman doorway in the ninth bay west of the crossing gave access to this chapel. Otherwise little has been found of it, other than the fourth buttress from the west of the abbey which may incorporate part of its façade.

When the building was completed, architectural painting was applied to relieve the severity of the bare walls. Early in the twelfth century a yellow dado band was painted around the entire church interior about six feet from the pavement. Above this, in imitation of ashlar, a network of black lines was applied. On the soffits of the arches the favourite Norman patterns, chevron, lozenge and zigzag, were painted in solid blocks of colour from the simple palette of earth colours in red and yellow, black and white. The best idea of the original effect can be seen in

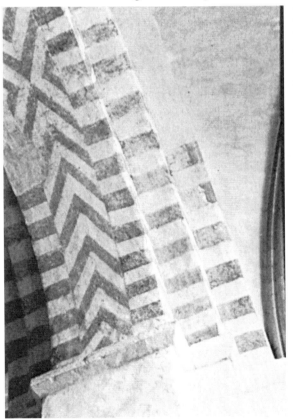

Fig. 26 Masonry pattern, south nave arcade.

the westernmost bay of the south Presbytery aisle.

Of the Norman exterior nave bay elevation, only the clerestory windows remain intact. Here also the Norman custom of topping the buttress with a splay, well below the corbel table, can be clearly seen. We can picture it in its extreme simplicity, not unlike the present appearance of Lessay in Normandy. St. Albans, plastered externally would, like Lessay, have been light in tone.

The appearance of the original west front remains a mystery, although there are two alternative viewpoints. The Bucklers examined the make-up of the foundations, flint with layered brick, which they claimed to have found throughout by excavation. They concluded that the Norman nave was thirteen bays long as it is today with a pair of western towers forty feet square outside the line of the aisles and a narthex-style porch between them and Scott accepted this view (see fig. 19). William Page, half a century later, disagreed with them. He found the south wall thickened along the third and fourth bays from the west, although nothing was found on the north where it had been much rebuilt on the site of St. Andrew's Chapel. The foundations suggested a front similar to that at St. Étienne, Caen. Page believed it was not especially remarkable in design, otherwise it would not have been rebuilt only eighty years later. The clinching argument was his observation of the mortar: the Normans used a white, gritty

Fig. 27 West front of St. Étienne, Caen.

mortar, but in the Early English period, the mortar contained bright yellow sand. The Royal Commission *Guide* of 1952 accepted Page's interpretation, that the Norman nave was ten bays long and had a plain façade without any western towers.

Abbot Paul did not live to see the great abbey consecrated. This event took place fully eighteen years after his death on Holy Innocents' Day in 1115. The new abbot was Richard d'Albini. The Archbishop of Rouen performed the ceremony in the presence of many nobles, as well as the bishops of Lincoln, Durham, Old Sarum and London. King Henry I and Queen Matilda were present and stayed for eleven days to be entertained by the abbot. Although the church designed by Robert the Mason was based on Norman models, it surpassed them all in scale and boldness; unlike them, however, it was devoid of architectural sculpture of any kind.

The starkness of the interior was relieved by woven woollen tapestries which at this date, like the Bayeux tapestry, were usually very long and rather narrow. One hanging, depicting the whole *Life of St. Alban*, was given to the abbey in the time of Abbot Richard d'Albini 1097–1119, a very early reference to a narrative based on Alban's sufferings. This gift is recorded in the cartulary of the ancient abbey of St. Vaast at Arras, the centre in the north-east of France long famous for its weaving supremacy. Later, in Abbot Geoffrey de Gorham's time, 1119–1146, three reredoses were ordered for the church, a great hanging on which the *Invention of St. Alban* was depicted on a gold ground, and two smaller pieces showing parables, the *Prodigal Son* on one, and on the other *The Man who fell among Thieves*. Survivals of such early tapestries are rare; one at Halberstadt abbey in East Germany not far from Goslar shows that manuscript illumination exerted a strong stylistic influence.

The oldest surviving picture of the martyrdom is found in the *St. Albans Psalter* which dates ca. 1119–1123. One would like to know how it relates to the lost tapestry. The judge, holding the staff of office, occupies the left with the executioner in the middle, sheathing his sword as his eyes fall out in punishment. On the right, the decapitated head of Alban falls to the ground, while his soul emerges from his mouth. A man behind holds the *signum*, symbol of Roman power while above, the saint's soul, in the form of a dove, is received into heaven.

The pages of the St. Albans Psalter help us to people the abbey with living figures. The original book is now in the library of St. Godehard, Hildesheim with one detached sheet in the Schnütgen Museum in Cologne. This Psalter was made in the scriptorium at

Fig. 28   'The martyrdom of St. Alban', from the St. Albans Psalter,
ca. 1119–1123, now at St. Godehard, Hildesheim.

St. Albans for Christina of Huntingdon before she became Prioress of the abbey cell at Markyate. An eminent embroidress, she was a friend both of Roger, the hermit of Markyate and of Abbot Geoffrey de Gorham. Fifty years after the Conquest, a great transformation has occurred in the style of painting. The picture of the *Garden of Eden*, for example, is now framed and the action within is organised by means of coloured shapes in the background of green, purple and blue. The setting, in this case a tree and two hillocks, is interposed like a backdrop. The figures of Adam and Eve, with the devil disgorging the serpent, are expressed in flat colour, rather like cloisonné enamels. Their proportions are long and narrow, their heads in profile and with hands and feet abnormally large in scale.

The Psalter, which contains forty-three pictures of the life of Christ, played an important role in reintroducing narrative back into English art. In the *Dream of the Magi*, we see the kings in a bed which fills the breadth of the page; they do not wear their crowns. An angel with outstretched wings hovers over them but the architectural background suggests an outside setting. The hands of three masters are discernible in this manuscript: the main artist is believed to have been the goldsmith, Antekil, with two assistants helping him.

In the *Descent from the Cross*, Joseph of Arimathea on a ladder supports the body of Christ and his is the only head not in profile. A boy with pincers removes the nails, while Mary and John embrace the hand of Christ. There are attendants on each side and ministering angels hovering above. As the style shows affinities with Ottonian, Italian and Byzantine art, the artist must have had an Italian training and brought sketchbooks back with him. He may have been one of those artists from many places whom Paul de Caen brought in to work in the scriptorium.

In the twelfth century during the reign of Henry I, 1100–1135, building in England continued as vigorously as before but a new element appeared: sculptural decoration began to be introduced into buildings. This movement was characteristic of Europe generally but in England at least, it is clear that it was not the Normans who executed the sculpture but rather the Anglo-Saxons. Geometric ornament was popular as seen in fragments found at various times on the monastic site and now in the Museum of St. Albans. Chevron ornament set at right angles to the wall was popular ca. 1150. Rolls edged in beading, bands of beaded fret and beaded chevron are believed to date ca. 1160, from Abbot Robert de Gorham's rule.

Fig. 29   The Slype, looking east, ca. 1877. Now destroyed.

One conventual building which survived internally almost intact until the late nineteenth century and whose remaining south wall was demolished in 1980 was the Slype. This was the passage between the south transept and the Chapter House which led from the cloister to the monks' cemetery. It may have been the Parlour which Abbot Robert built. The west door of the Slype was found in pieces about a century ago and re-erected in the south transept. The outer orders, which continue unbroken around the arch, are of the twelfth century but the inner order was added in the late nineteenth century. A principal motif of the original work consists of a double foliage scroll with beaded stems and curled tips held together by annulet bands; the Norman font at Aylesbury has similar motifs. Pattern books were circulated to assist the sculptors and similar decoration appears in manuscripts of the Winchester school from the mid twelfth century onwards.

Under the brick barrel vault inside the Slype, interlaced blank arcading decorated the walls on either side, a very English motif. It does not make sense from the structural point of view but creates a satisfactory pattern, emphasising the flat wall and giving a sense of enclosure. The arches were adorned with a bobbin motif which recalls the Saxon pilasters in the south transept. Pevsner likened them to bent spinal columns. The arcading from the north Slype interior was moved to the south wall of the south transept. This work is of the greatest interest, since it has much in common with sculptural fragments and carved work found *in situ* when the Chapter House was excavated as the scholar, Deborah Kahn, has pointed out. Robert de Gorham, who is associated with this work, is the abbot who obtained great privileges for the Abbey from Pope Adrian IV; because of his efforts, St. Albans was recognised as the premier abbey of England at the Council of Tours in 1163. This interlaced arcading gives us the best idea of this important abbot's building work.

The capitals are of particular interest. The interlaced zigzag pattern on the *abaci* link them with important work done at Reading Abbey ca. 1130 so influential for many years in the south Midlands. Perhaps the Reading masons moved on to St. Albans after completing the Reading cloister. One of the St. Albans capitals has decorative foliage with beading pattern in the scrolls. Another foliage design shows the influence of eastern textiles in the interlocking circles; it, too, has a decorated *abaci*. A third foliage design shows strong classical overtones in the acanthus leaf. Viking influence is apparent in another capital with intertwined dragons who turn to bite their own wings; work like this can be found on the famous crypt capitals at Canterbury. On another is a grotesque mask from the mouth of which issue living stems, a piece of pagan imagery showing the spirit of the tree, a legacy of ancient Druid rites. Finally, intricate lacy ornament, delicate and rich, with tiny cats' heads at each corner, adorns another capital.

Also from Robert de Gorham's period must come the two sculptured voussoir stones now in the Museum of St. Albans which were found at a site one and a quarter miles from the abbey. Apparently they enriched an arched doorway of considerable size, perhaps the lost processional door linking the south transept to the east walk of the cloister of which only the vestibule survives as a cupboard. The sturdy lion, which moves with energy and lightness, may represent the zodiac sign for the month of July.

An antiquarian drawing by Lee, dated 1849, shows a Norman door with elaborately coiled hinges which once stood in the abbey. The wood was very worn; it had been cut down to fit another

*Fig. 30 Sculptured voussoir stones of the Norman period
showing a lion in foliage scrolls. Museum of St. Albans.*

opening and some of the coils were missing. This magnificent
piece was thrown out in 1888 but was rescued and sent to the
Victoria and Albert Museum. There, the marks left on the wood
enabled the hinges to be reconstructed (see fig. 31). Most of the
ironwork on display at the Museum today is therefore new and is
mounted on a modern timber door. From three horizontal straps
spring pairs of tight coils from which in turn other coils emerge.
The straps are thickened at the junctions for strength and punched
with borders and chevron patterns. The ends become animal
heads, showing Viking influence. There are also leaf motifs,
rosettes and fleur-de-lys. The design is clearly related to some of
the Slype capitals. These Norman hinges are surely ancestors of
the famous examples of the Early English period to be seen at
Leighton Buzzard and Eaton Bray in Bedfordshire.

*Fig. 31   Coiled ironwork hinges, based upon an ancient
door from St. Albans abbey.*

References

BRANDT (MICHAEL). Der schatz von St. Godehard. Diözesan-museum. Hildesheim. 1988.

DODWELL (C R), PÄCHT (OTTO) and WORMALD(FRANCIS). The St. Albans Psalter. London. 1960.

HORLBECK (FRANK RALPH). 'Decorative painting in English medieval architecture'. PhD thesis. 1957. University of London.

KAHN (DEBORAH). 'Recent discoveries of Romanesque sculpture at St. Albans.' *Studies in Medieval Sculpture*. Ed. by F H Thompson. Society of Antiquaries. 1983. 71–89.

KNOWLES (DOM DAVID). The monastic order in England, 940–1216. Cambridge. 1966.

PAGE (WILLIAM). 'On some recent discoveries in the abbey church of St. Alban.' *Archaeologia*. LVI (1897) 1–6.

PEVSNER (Sir NIKOLAUS) and CHERRY (BRIDGET). Hertfordshire. The Buildings of England. Harmondsworth. 1977.

ROBERTS (EILEEN). 'A lion in foliage sculpture of the Romanesque period: its significance for the abbey of St. Alban.' *Hertfordshire Archaeology*. VIII (1980–82) 112–123.

. . . 'Two twelfth-century voussoir stones from Sopwell House, St. Albans.' *Studies in medieval sculpture*. Ed. by F H Thompson. Society of Antiquaries. 1983. 190–197.

ROYAL COMMISSION ON HISTORICAL MONUMENTS. St. Albans cathedral. HMSO. 1952.

THOMPSON (W G). A history of tapestry. Wakefield. 1973.

WIGRAM (SIR EDGAR). 'The ivory fragment from Orchard House'. *Trans. SAHAAS*. (1924) 29–34.

Part III

PREMIER ABBEY OF ENGLAND

Chapter 7

ABBOT JOHN DE CELLA AND THE
EARLY ENGLISH STYLE

The Gothic style was invented in 1140, when the new choir at the abbey of St. Denis near Paris was begun. The name of its brilliant architect is unknown, but he selected some features which had been well-known for many years, the pointed arch, the flying buttress and the rib vault, and combined them in a new way which had enormous potential: now energy seemed to be concentrated in a system of lines, there was a new stress upon the vertical and the whole building seemed poised with life and energy. Of equal if not more importance, the new system was more flexible to plan than the Romanesque style and much more efficient to build.

Gothic did not appear in England fully realised until 1175 at Canterbury. Here the monks were faced by a double problem: how to cope with the growing cult of St. Thomas Becket, recently murdered, and how to rebuild their choir, destroyed in a tragic fire. They chose a French architect, William of Sens, who was later succeeded by William the Englishman, whose work can be seen in the new choir. The tall pointed arches culminate in ribbed vaults above, the whole supported by flying buttresses outside the church. An innovation is the use of black Purbeck marble to contrast with the creamy Caen stone. The piers are built up of a number of units into complex shapes, the capitals are richly carved, the clustered colonettes give an impression of lightness and the jewel-like stained glass windows complete the effect. As the metropolitan cathedral, Canterbury exerted a strong influence and many churches followed her example, rebuilding their choirs in eastward extensions.

In the thirteenth century the great building patrons were the bishops, like Robert Grosseteste of Lincoln and Walter de Grey of

York. Their new buildings helped them reform the English church, so the landmarks of the new style will be found in the secular cathedrals such as Wells, Salisbury and Lincoln. A monastic church, like St. Albans, could not expect to be a pace-setter now; the monasteries had had their day in the Romanesque period. The Early English work at St. Albans, is nevertheless of considerable interest.

We shall begin with the late thirteenth century tomb recess in the south choir aisle where the hermits Sigar and Roger are buried. The 1428 *Inventory* tells us that they were buried 'nigh unto the door of the Church leading to the cloister, in an arch or recess of the wall'. Hermits filled a very important function in the twelfth century helping the English to adapt to the Norman Conquest. They acted as linkmen between the villagers and their

rulers in the outside world; living apart from both, they helped to resolve tensions in the advice they gave, and so prevented dangerous conflicts. Sigar was the hermit of Northaw Great Wood who walked nightly to the service in the abbey. Roger was a monk of St. Albans who became a hermit at Markyate; with a reputation for prophecy, he became the mentor of the anchoress of Markyate, Christina. Roger and Sigar both died in the early twelfth century so this recess must have been constructed long after their deaths, when their graves were attracting more and more pilgrims.

Fig. 32   Tomb recess of the hermits Roger of Markyate and Sigar of Northaw.

It is very different in style from the Romanesque period. The arch is lobed into seven leaf-shaped divisions, six rounded and one pointed. Its arch is moulded, no longer in the simple steps of the Romanesque style but in semi-sircular rounds and hollows, fine and delicate, which catch the light and give emphasis. The arch is supported, not on a massive chunk of wall but on clusters of slender colonnettes, large and small, which give an impression of fragility. The clumsy block capital has been replaced by an inverted bell, moulded in rolls and hollows; it was probably turned on a lathe. The base reflects the classical mouldings of ancient Greece, reminding us that the First Crusade took place in 1096, the Second in 1146; something of masonry techniques must have been absorbed by these experiences. Altogether the new style is one of elegance and grace. As an early example of a canopied tomb, this recess should received more attention than it does at present.

Few burials took place inside churches in the twelfth and thirteenth centuries except for founders and benefactors; abbots were buried in the Chapter House. Bodies were placed in coffins such as the one in the south Presbytery aisle, of hewn stone, with a flat lid over, engraved with some symbol of office such as a cross or a crosier. Later, effigies in low relief were represented on the coffin lids and from these beginnings, the three-dimensional effigy developed. When the coffins were buried outside, they were sunk to ground level but when inside, they stood upon the pavement. In time the coffin came to be encased in flat, decorated, rectangular slabs to form a tomb. The tomb of Roger the hermit once stood within the recess in the south choir aisle, according to the 1428 *Inventory*. No tomb chests with three-dimensional effigies survive in the abbey from the Middle Ages but we know they once existed; one example was the tomb of Geoffrey and Cristina Stukeley from the time of Edward III which stood in the west end of the south nave aisle. The canopied tombs which developed from low recesses were usually located near the Presbytery; Roger and Sigar's tomb is the only canopied tomb surviving in the abbey.

The thirteenth century is given special interest at St. Albans in that Matthew Paris, who was a monk here from 1217 until his death in 1259, has left us lively descriptions of contemporary building works. Drawings made by him in his *Vitae duorum Offarum* now in the British Library (MS Cotton Nero D. 1) show masons at work as well as the Master Mason and were probably inspired by actual building works taking place in those years. Whereas the work of Matthew Paris is of inestimable value, other aspects of the thirteenth century are disappointing. The brilliant work of the great goldsmith-sculptor, Walter of Colchester, has been almost completely wiped out. Three important building projects of the thirteenth century, the new west front, the broach spire and Trumpington's chapel at the south-east for the Altar of the Four Tapers, are for the most part destroyed. Considerable work does remain from the period, but the records which survive are confusing, plans were altered and the dates are far from clear. Despite these difficulties, we will attempt to discuss these works in the chronological order of their construction.

The major building project of the late twelfth and early thirteenth centuries was the great westward expansion of the abbey church. Why did St. Albans extend in that direction when so many other churches, like Rochester, Chichester and Lincoln, were extending eastwards? At St. Albans, of course, the eastern arm was already exceptionally large, and with its massing of seven great apses, there was little need for more embellishment. A longer nave, on the other hand, was a practical necessity. Under the brilliant but strict abbot, John de Cella, recruitment of monks markedly increased; from an average of fifty heretofore, numbers now had to be limited to one hundred. A much longer nave was required to accommodate the great processions so popular a liturgical practice in England at this time.

Equally important was the recently organised cult of St. Amphibalus and the need to make space in the nave for a cult centre with shrine and altar. The sixth and seventh bays west of the crossing were selected. Attention was newly focussed on St. Alban's anonymous mentor, the earliest-known Christian evangelist in Britain, when Geoffrey of Monmouth ca. 1139 assigned to him the proper name, Amphibalus. Under Abbot Simon, 1167–83, the life of St. Alban had been re-written to incorporate the legendary Anglo-Saxon passion of the fugitive priest. Bones believed to be his were exhumed on Redbourn heath and translated to the abbey. The physician abbot, Warin, 1183–1195, besides founding a new leper hospital at St. Mary de Pré, one of the new cult sites, gave a hundred marks to renew the front of the church.

The nave was extended three bays westward and rebuilding began at the west (see back plan). Since the view of the abbey from the important south-west approach was so very prominent, it required a commanding design. One can picture the original façade of Paul de Caen's time as plain and uncompromising, probably not unlike St. Étienne de Caen (see fig. 27). A severely military façade, however, would appear increasingly old-fashioned in the context of the new elegance achieved at Canterbury. Other places, such as Peterborough and Selby Abbey, were building new west fronts at this time.

An improved west front would provide a very difficult design problem. The body of the building was so long, and its tower so high; yet the important west entrance was on the narrow end. How could one make it impressive and still balance the length? One had also to give support, to withstand the thrust exerted by the line of the nave arcade. One solution was to go for width, setting a wide screen across the front, as at Wells; its front is covered in rows of arcading holding sculptures of scriptural subjects for the education of the laity. This had disadvantages: the sculpture is too high to be seen properly and the interior structure, instead of being reflected, is masked. In its overall surface pattern, however and in its grid of horizontals and verticals, it satisfies a deep aesthetic impulse of the English people.

Another solution was to go for height, a line chosen at Ripon. To compensate for the length of the building, a pair of western towers was built, which balance the long nave and buttress the thrust of the arcade. The advantage of this solution was stability, the disadvantage, cost, but the towers could be justified by providing them with bells.

At St. Albans we face great difficulties, not knowing for certain what was originally planned, if and how such plans were altered or even completed. The front, remodelled in the fifteenth century, deteriorated drastically between 1550 and 1850 and was almost entirely rebuilt after 1880. Four types of evidence relating to the thirteenth century façade survive. The first involves those portions which survive today, which include the triple western porches and the south-west tower arch. These we will examine shortly.

Secondly, we have the fragments which survived until destroyed in 1880. Behind the central porch and under Wheathampstead's window as a drawing by John Carter reveals, survived two small blind arches of the Early English period (see fig. 63), fragments, perhaps from a band of blind arcading which may have stretched across a screen-like front.

The third piece of evidence lies under the ground. J C and C A Buckler, as well as William Page, found outside the line of the aisles, foundations for a pair of western towers forty feet square. They were joined to the aisles by a pair of tower arches at south-west and north-west, one of which survives (see fig. 36). There seem to have been western doors to these towers, which

Fig. 33   King Offa II, founder of the monastery, holding a model church.
Sculpture detail from the base of St. Alban's shrine, 1308.

were never completed, although the northern one rose high enough to serve as a western entrance porch to St. Andrew's parochial chapel. If they had been completed, the west front would have been a hundred and forty-six feet in width, twenty feet wider than Wells. This is as near as we can come to what was planned.

The final piece of evidence may be found in the model church held by King Offa on the shrine base of 1308, put here after the completion of the Early English west front (assuming it was completed). It shows a cruciform church with a crossing tower and a spire correct for the period judging from the written description which we have. There is a façade with a tall lancet design and a foiled figure above, not unlike the west front of Ripon. There is a cross at the apex but no western towers. Possibly in this miniature, we have a replica of the lost Early English front of our abbey church as it was actually built.

Abbot John de Cella, 1195–1214, under whom the rebuilding work was commenced, ran into difficulties right from the start. The chronicle says (in the words of Salzman's translation) that he 'threw down to the ground the wall of the front of our church, built of ancient tiles and enduring mortar . . . the foundations were dug out, and in a very short time a hundred marks, and much more, not counting the daily allowances of food, were spent and yet the foundation wall had not risen to the level of the ground.' The tough, enduring mortar of the Norman walls may have made them excessively difficult to demolish. Untold problems may have arisen when the ground was opened up to dig the foundations if the remains of King Offa's monastery were uncovered. For some reason yet unknown, the cost of the rebuilding soared far beyond what had been anticipated.

The most spectacular survival of the lost west front is the group of three porches, apparently built with no expense spared in John de Cella's time. A plan by John Chapple shows how much of the original survived (see back plan). On plan, each porch is rectangular with chamfered corners. A double entrance leads into the nave, and single ones into each of the aisles. There are recesses to north and south, especially deep in the middle porch, forming niches with ample plinths. Separating the niches are slender, detached shafts and the setting is provided, here at the western entrance, for a programme of numerous sculptured figures, in the tradition developed in the Île de France and seen first at St. Denis in 1140. Such a scheme would be in keeping with what we know of John de Cella who was educated in Paris. The exterior of the porches has been completely rebuilt.

*Fig. 34   Interior view of south-west porch built in John de Cella's time,
1195–1214. Drawing by W S Weatherley.*

The architect, Hugh de Goldclif, whose work this seems to be, is described as 'a deceitful and unreliable man, but a craftsman of great reputation.' A drawing of the porch interior by W S Weatherley shows the beauty of the work, unequalled in England. The entrance arch is a simple two-centred one, with hood mould and end stops. Inside, a string course embraces two stiff-leaf brackets for images now lost. Over each bracket is an ingenious canopy, a twin-cusped arch with a central, still-leaf finial. At the side is a deep stone plinth with triple arches behind and a canopy over, supported by slender Purbeck shafts. The ribbed cross-vault springs from groups of triple shafts with crockets between. The severees are filled in the English manner, with the stones meeting the ridge-line at an angle.

The niches and brackets were certainly furnished with statues, for the chronicler refers to 'columns, bases and capitals' as well as to 'images and flowers', accurately describing the scheme. Tragically, the figures have been lost, but two sculptured heads from the same period, ca. 1200, survive in the easternmost corners of the Saint's Chapel, reset there from an earlier build. They are by two different hands. Once end stops, and thus horizontally laid, they have schematized curls, shallow eye sockets and (apart from the delicately carved eyelids), boldly carved facial features.

Vigorous carvings like these must have filled the west porch niches. St. Mary's abbey, York had such a western portal and ten of the life-sized sculptured figures dating from 1200–1210 can be seen in the Yorkshire Museum. They have the weighty bodies, the large heads and heavy draperies typical of this time.

The principal stone used in the porches is apparently from Totternhoe in Bedfordshire. It is not named in the documents, but the chalky quality, the finely detailed carving and the effect of weathering are typical of this stone. The *Gesta Abbatum* described how the stone reacted to the weather, due either to Hugh de Goldclif's carelessness or to his inexperience with this stone. 'And as the walls were left uncovered during the rainy season the stones, which were very soft, broke into little bits, and the wall, like the fallen and ruined stonework, with its columns, bases and capitals, slipped and fell by its own weight; so that the wreck of images and flowers was the cause of smiles and laughter to those that saw it.'

This light and porous stone is ideally adapted to the filling of vaulting cells and indeed it had been used at Windsor Castle for this purpose from the time of King Henry II, 1152–80 (see fig. 3). While the stone was still 'green', it was perfectly adapted to the undercut mouldings of rolls and hollows, and to the dog-tooth ornament popular at this time. The stiff-leaf capitals are particularly graceful, with their bending stems and windblown leaves. They compare quite well with capitals in the nave at Wells, 1192–1230, more or less contemporary to the St. Albans examples and considered to be the best in England.

A harmonious scheme was at first envisaged for the interior of the west end of the church, and indeed it was commenced. Deep niches, shafted and moulded, flank the four western doors. (The vault at present above them is not of

Fig. 35   *Stiff-leaf capital and dog- tooth ornament, in the north-west porch, 1195–1214. Unrestored.*

the thirteenth century.) At the west end of the south wall is the tall and slender tower arch, now blocked, with its complex mouldings and slender detached shafts with shaft rings; this feature was introduced to England by William de Sens at Canterbury sometime after 1174. The original scheme for the aisles apparently intended to line the walls with a double tier of blind arcading but this was soon abandoned. The capitals of the tower arch are moulded, not carved, suggesting at this point the change to a more modest plan, perhaps when Brother Gilbert de Eversolt was made warden of the work in 1198; Eversholt, incidentally, is under eight miles north of the Totternhoe quarries in Bedfordshire.

The Buckler brothers published a drawing of the parts of the unfinished tower which they excavated, showing the wide bench inside and the plan of the internal shafting.

Fig. 36 On the left, the blocked tower arch of the south-west external tower, planned but never completed, 1195–1214.

The respond detailing at the west end of the south aisle is another example of a handsome and elaborate scheme which had to be abandoned. The semi-octagonal shaft was supposed to be encircled by slender Purbeck shafts. Only two are in position, and whether the missing units were destroyed later or never inserted, we do not know. They were not customarily placed in position until sufficient time had elapsed for the building to settle; otherwise the stone would shatter. A similar scheme, completely realised, can be seen in the central pier in the Chapter House at Lincoln cathedral, 1220–35, which has all its surrounding shafts still in position.

A flight of five steps across the building leading from bay twelve down into bay thirteen shows how the changing levels of this hilltop site were accommodated in the pavement of the extended nave.

John de Cella was much criticised by his contemporaries for improvidence, and for 'attending but little to that admonition . . . in the Gospel . . . "This man began to build but was unable to finish it".' The nave extension dragged on interminably to the tedium and discomfort of those using the building. In fairness to John, one must consider his other problems. We have already mentioned the increased recruitment of monks; with numbers doubling between 1190 and 1210, more spacious accommodation was urgently required. Abbot John therefore had a refectory built, which in those days were lofty structures of masonry. He also commenced a larger dormitory. On top of these problems there was another. This was the period of King Richard I's capture and the ransom for his release was 150,000 marks. This would run into millions today, and most of it was paid from money raised in England, to which the monasteries contributed a goodly share.

Then, during the Interdict, 1208–1213, King John clashed with the abbot. John placed the monastery under the control of a secular custodian, Robert of London; to get rid of this man and his supporters, John de Cella first had to pay the king 500 marks, and then a further £600. There was clearly more to the problem than a simple improvidence; the wonder is that the nave extension got built at all.

Now, a brief sidelight. This clerk, Robert of London, had been sent earlier by the king as ambassador to the King of Morocco. While there, he had been given many rich presents and these he would bring out and display at the abbey with much pomp. Matthew Paris admired them, and Walter of Colchester became Robert's friend. What were these gifts and what influence if any had they upon the artistic life of the monastery? Martin Briggs noticed the strong eastern influence in an iron grille in the abbey, which is dated by most scholars to the thirteenth century, and is mounted at present next to the Gloucester Chantry (see fig. 77). This screen closely imitates the lattice screens of Moslem countries which, with their many fine openings, give a diffused light and afford a view of the street outside while acting as a screen to those within. The abbey screen is made of semi-circular iron bars, riveted together at the intersections with ornamental pins. Whether it was influenced by Robert of London or more generally by the Crusades when the skill of the Saracens in armour making and all metal work was greatly admired, it is impossible to say.

Turning now to the Early English bays at the west of the nave, we find four on the north and five on the south. The horizontal proportions of arcade, triforium and clerestory in this new work are rather conservative, 2:1:1, for the contiguous Norman work could not be ignored; the extension had to harmonise with it. As the Norman aisle walls were completely plain, blind arcading could not suitably be introduced. The piers at St. Albans are octagonal, with three-quarter round shafts applied to the cardinal points. All is in Totternhoe stone, to maintain harmony with the Norman work and to avoid the costly purchase and transport of

Fig. 37   Early English nave bay elevation, ca. 1214. Drawing by John Carter.

Purbeck marble. Moulded capitals, not stiff-leaf, are used here. As St. Albans was extending a thick Norman wall, the arcade mouldings are unusually rich and deep and the arches are quite sharply pointed. Horizontality is stressed, the vaulting shafts springing, not from the pavement, but from brackets in the spandrils of the main arcade. Again, this is a concession to existing Norman work, in which we have already noted the continuous, horizontal string course around the whole interior.

It is interesting to remember that John de Cella had studied at the University of Paris, specialising in grammar, poetry and medicine. He was there ca. 1170. Not long before this, in 1163, the choir at St. Germain des Prés had been consecrated. In the early Gothic style, it presents certain parallels to the St. Albans' scheme, such as twin lancets in the clerestory and twin arches, sub-divided, in the triforium. John must have seen this building while he was a student in Paris and marvelled over it, perhaps making sketches.

The new triforium at St. Albans, like the Norman design, has twin arches subdivided but the detailing is up-to-date in having arches which are sharply pointed and deeply moulded, with plenty of dog-tooth ornament in the strings and between the shafts. These shafts are in groups of four, the slender alternating with the sturdy. All capitals and bases are moulded. In each spandril is plate tracery, a quatrefoil motif with stiff-leaf sprigs. The hood is moulded but has no end stops. The passage floor is no longer sunk behind the shafts but level with their bases.

The Norman clerestory had a single, rounded window per bay with a passage through the wall (see fig. 25). In the new work, there are two pointed lancets per bay but they are still untraceried. The usual Early English clerestory has a set of triple lancets, two short and one tall but this has been rejected here, perhaps to harmonise with the Norman work, perhaps to admit more light into the dark western bays.

When the clerestory was begun, a vault was the intention. How it would have linked with the flat Norman roof is an interesting question. A sexpartite scheme was envisaged, which fits neatly in with a scheme of alternating bays. In this case, however, the alternate vaulting ribs rise, not above the columns, but above the apexes of the arches, an unusual solution, artistic but impractical. On the continent, a few scattered examples can be found, in the choir at Vézelay in 1185, at Avila in Spain before 1190 and at Coutances ca. 1218, but the potential weakness of the design must have led to its abandonment. If Hugh de Goldclif was responsible for this design, the vault proposal may be another example of his unreliability: admirable on design details, but weak on structures.

At St. Albans the vaulting scheme was not pursued. The faces prepared to receive the vaulting shafts, now bare and exposed, were decorated with parallel grooves to improve their appearance. As a result, St. Albans with its flat wooden ceiling retains the original atmosphere of the earlier church, of interest in itself. In the choir at Canterbury, 1175–1184, one can see an example of a sexpartite vault but all its ribs spring from the sturdy support of the piers.

The present aisle windows are of the late nineteenth century; there were no aisle windows in the new south bays due to contiguous conventual buildings beyond (see fig. 80). On the north, a deep vista opened up through the arcade of four arches into St. Andrew's Chapel, another source of light. Abbot John de Cella had assigned to the work in 1198 one sheaf of every acre sown during his abbacy and for ten years of the abbacy of his successor 'nor did the unlucky work ever show any visible advance' and the years passed 'uselessly so far as that work was concerned'. Then Brother Gilbert de Sisseverne was put in charge but in thirty years the work 'scarcely achieved two feet of increase altogether'. The *Victoria County History* authors believe, nevertheless, that much of the existing work was carried out before John de Cella's death in 1214.

References

HARVEY (JOHN). English mediaeval architects, a biographical dictionary down to 1550. Gloucester. 1984.

LLOYD (ROBERT RIDGWAY), ed. and trans. An account of the altars, monuments and tombs existing AD1428 in St. Alban's abbey. St. Albans. 1873.

MAYR-HARTING (H). 'Functions of a twelfth century recluse.' *History*. LX, no. 200 (October 1975) 337–352.

PAGE (WILLIAM). 'The parochial chapel of St. Andrew'. *Trans SAHAAS*. (1897–98) 82–104.

... 'On some recent discoveries in the abbey church of St. Alban.' *Archaeologia*. LVI (1897) 1–6.

PEVSNER (Sir NIKOLAUS). The Englishness of English art. New York. 1956.

ROBERTS (EILEEN). 'Amphibalus, the friend of Alban'. *Hertfordshire Countryside*. XXXVI. No. 262 (Feb. 1981) 14–15.

SALZMAN (L F). Building in England down to 1540: a documentary history. Oxford. 1952.

STONE (LAWRENCE). Sculpture in Britain: the middle ages. (The Pelican history of art.) Harmondsworth, 1955.

VAUGHAN (RICHARD), ed. and trans. Chronicles of Matthew Paris: monastic life in the thirteenth century. Gloucester and New York. 1984.

WILLIAM THE MONK. 'Other doings of Saints Alban and Amphibalus and their companions.' Trans. by Leslie Simpson. Introd. by Eileen Roberts. *Hertfordshire Archaeology*. VIII. 1980–82. 67–77.

Chapter 8

WILLIAM OF TRUMPINGTON AND WALTER OF COLCHESTER

The work was eventually brought to completion by Abbot William de Trumpington, 1214–1235. In what order did the building work proceed? William Page made a study of the masons' marks which abound in the western part of the church in an attempt to establish a sequence of building. The most frequent marks include a sharply pointed leaf, a banner on a staff, two segments of circle back to back and two triangles side by side. Usually, mediaeval builders erected one bay at a time, raising the work to the full height as they progressed; in this case, the programme seemed to have proceeded from west to east, with the lower stages completed before the higher ones began. The north side progressed more rapidly than the south and the fifth bay from the west on the south side was rebuilt as an afterthought.

Mouldings provide vital evidence for studying building work. The Early English piers show four different pier base designs, indicating that work progressed by fits and starts. One design has

a continuous plinth and water-holding mouldings, another example of eastern influence. A second design has mouldings in a single order; each shaft is treated individually and the half-round shafts are picked out with scalloped borders. Yet another design

Fig. 38   Early English nave pier base: one of four designs, ca. 1214.

has a continuous treatment.

The aisles were ceiled in wood; the existing vaulting dates from the nineteenth century. There were no windows in the new section of the south aisle at this stage, except for one opening into the abbot's chapel (see fig. 80). The cloister was apparently entered through a door towards the end of the south aisle, *via* a vaulted passage under the abbot's apartments.

There is a Norman pier in the north nave arcade not far from the roodscreen, the so-called Hollow Pillar, which presents an interesting problem. It is one of two, different from the other Norman piers in their rudely shaped capitals. This phenomenon, a rounded pillar, has been accounted for in various ways. Some explain it simply as accommodation for the newel staircase now blocked, which it contains; this is shown on the plans by Carter and Neale. Others suggest a break in the Norman work due to passage of time or a change of architect. Still others see it as an experiment with a scheme of alternate bays so often found in the Romanesque style. Some authorities even suggest that these two Norman piers were cut back and re-shaped to imitate the new Early English work, a scheme abandoned due to the sheer intractability of the Roman brick construction. We do not know how the Norman south arcade was treated; conceivably, it could have been cut back in the same way and suffered such disturbance in the process that it collapsed a century later.

Trumpington, we are told, in finishing the western extension, put on a wooden roof, covered it with lead and glazed the windows. The exterior of the clerestory wall shows a scheme with two lancet windows per bay, shafted and deeply moulded, alternating with blind arches of a similar design, which is most attractive (see fig. 80). It compares favourably with the exterior clerestory treatment at Lincoln which has the more usual triple light scheme.

The chronicle speaks of Trumpington's 'exquisite glass windows'. Perhaps the lancets in this rebuilding were glazed in the brilliant, jewel-like colours one sees in surviving windows at Canterbury dating from the late twelfth century. Beauty in the Middle Ages meant luminous, glittering, clear; Gothic architecture is but a frame for windows which admit the divine light of God, transforming and illuminating the world and people's lives.

One of Trumpington's achievements has almost disappeared, the remodelled chapel at the east end of the south Presbytery aisle where the walls, we are told, 'were awry and misshapen from their damaged and ruinous state.' The three eastern bays of this aisle were rebuilt between 1214 and 1235 under the direction of Matthew of Cambridge. A new altar was set up dedicated to Our Lady and St. Blaise, patron of diseased creatures, human and animal. The new altar was to be called the 'Altar of the Four Tapers', and here the important new Sung Mass was to be celebrated. This remodelling lasted only a generation, when more fundamental structural defects required demolition of the whole east end. Some details, nevertheless, have survived in the third bay east of the crossing, notably, a single bay of ribbed cross vaulting at a less steep pitch than the late thirteenth century work; the Early English boss has almost disintegrated. It is interesting to compare the three types of moulding which can be found hereabouts: Norman, early Early English and late Early English.

He set in 'two large glass windows, that . . . all might be illuminated with fitting light'. Only one survives, in bay three east of the crossing, and it is worth examining both inside and out. It consists of three simple, untraceried lancets under a two-centred arch as both Carter and Neale show, contrasting both in shape and proportions with the later window to the east. All external stonework details, including the tracery, are new. Inside, the original shafting survives, forming a contrast with the treatment of the later bay to the east.

Trumpington also did some work 'round the high altar', perhaps the two arches, of which only the heads survive, above the later Wallingford chantry. Perhaps they are part of sedilia, in which case the Norman High Altar must have occupied the same position as the present one. The doctrine of Transubstantiation had been confirmed at the Lateran Council of 1215. Once it had been accepted that the bread and wine of the Eucharist were converted into the actual body and blood of Christ, it followed that the setting for the Eucharist must be supremely beautiful, worthy of Christ himself.

Also in the time of William, 'the roofs of both aisles of the church were strengthened with oaken timber excellently tied and joined with rafters (see fig. 72); for previously they were so eaten up with rot and decay that they let in much rain.' The present roof to the north of the nave is a nineteenth century renewal of one of them. He also 'completed the stonework and glazing of very many (windows) in the north and south aisles of the church; so that the church, illuminated with the gift of fresh light, seemed almost like new'. The mouldings and shafting of the Trumpington windows are distinctive and similar examples are found in the south choir aisle. The series of stiff-leaf capitals which adorn many of

Trumpington's windows round the church are also worth noting (see fig. 40).

With the nave having been lengthened and the small Norman windows greatly enlarged to admit floods of light, the stage was set for a crucial change in the cult life of the church. Trumpington had purchased in London an important relic for the abbey, the cross of St. Amphibalus, supposedly the first Christian cross brought into England. He had given it to Alban before they parted, and both saints had held it during their respective martyrdoms. The cross, which had a round disc on top on which was an ancient form of crucifixion, had been purchased at great price from a London family who had handed it down for generations. This form of cross originated, apparently, in the new standard designed by the Emperor Constantine after his famous victory, which consisted of a cross surmounted by a laurel wreath symbolising victory. The cross with a great circular motif on top became a popular Early Christian symbol.

A suitable setting had to be found for this important relic. At the same time, the cult of St. Amphibalus was now separated from that of his pupil, St. Alban, and established in its own right. His shrine, hitherto in the great eastern apse, was now moved into the midst of the church. It probably stood at the sixth pier from the crossing, where a thirteen century mural depicts the parting of the two saints. Amphibalus wears the pilgrim's garb, with staff and scrip, Alban the robe he was soon to give to the fugitive. This mural apparently overlooked the shrine in the nave. This shrine we know stood upon marble pillars, and was probably the early, altar type of shrine base seen in contemporary miniatures by Matthew Paris (see fig. 46). An altar stood beside it, dedicated to the Holy Cross, Amphibalus and his friends. It had a *tabula* and super altar, beautifully painted and the whole was surrounded by an iron grille. John, Bishop of Ardfert consecrated the altar between 1218 and 1224. In this way the great abbey church, designed originally to house a single cult, was adapted to become a twin cult church, of SS. Alban and Amphibalus, his confessor.

Abbot Trumpington now turned his attention to the spire over the crossing which, as seen in the reconstruction drawn by Gilbert Scott, was still a low, pyramidal one (see fig. 19). By the thirteenth century it was 'threatening to fall' providing an opportunity to give the lengthened nave some higher element to balance it. Hence, the Chamberlain, Richard of Tyttenhanger, rebuilt 'the summit also of the tower, which stretches out like some huge scaffold . . . of the best timber well joined and raised much higher than the old . . .

and all these, at no small cost, were covered with lead . . Through the blending of the eight sides, it stretched out its smooth and graceful shape.' This description is entirely in line with the well-known developments in the thirteenth century of tower and spire design, for the earliest spires were simple elongations of the low cappings of the Norman towers. Nottingham St. Peter could be cited as having a spire of the type of the first build.

'But after the death of the same Richard of blessed memory', the *Gesta Abbatum* continues, 'the abbot himself caused the tower to be stripped, because it was improperly covered, and with the addition of no small quantity of lead, had it re-covered more properly and thoroughly, adding ornaments to the sides, namely, eight raised strips stretching from the cap to the parapet, so that the octangonal shape of the tower might show more clearly . . . And he changed the covering into that kind which has horizontal conical projections. And the above-mentioned strips, which are commonly called "herring-bones" both strengthened the tower wonderfully and when so strengthened adorned it and kept out the rain more completely.' A similar type of roof can still be seen today at St. Nicholas, Stevenage.

A (damaged) spire on the model church held by Offa on the shrine base of 1308 may represent the very spire Trumpington built (see fig. 33). It, too, is octagonal with little pyramids, known as broaches, filling in the canted sides to make a smooth transition to the square tower. Spires like this in stone were first developed in Northamptonshire in the second quarter of the thirteenth century but counties like Hertfordshire, lacking freestone, sometimes copied the broach form in timber and lead.

This same abbot, Trumpington, set up an altar to the Blessed Virgin Mary in the apsidal chapel at the north-east of the south transept. This served as a Lady Chapel until the present Lady Chapel at the east of the church was built.

Returning to the nave for a moment, there is one idiosyncrasy in the north nave arcade which deserves comment. This is the abrupt junction of the old Norman work with the new Early English style, found on the ninth pier from the crossing. The harshness of the transition seems naïve, although it does bring out the development in style occurring over one hundred years, in the contrasting height of arch, richness of moulding, design of profiles and the girth of the columns. Nevertheless, the incongruity is very striking. It had to do, supposedly, with the wall painting on the western face, the work it seems, of the famous artist, Walter of Colchester. This expedient was necessary to preserve the painting.

He had been, apparently, a monk at St. John's Priory in Colchester, but came to St. Albans ca. 1200 at the invitation of Brother Ralph Gubion, later the Prior of Tynemouth. In the England of his day, Walter was the outstanding worker in metals, as well as a sculptor and painter. He had as his assistants his brother Simon, his nephew Richard and a lay brother, Master Alan. Abbot John de Cella, a considerable patron of the arts, had given him great encouragement, making him Sacrist of the monastery in 1213 with responsibility for the service of the altar, the vestments and all the internal decoration and repairs of the church.

In the *Gesta Abbatum*, under a list of the works of John de Cella, are listed seven *tabulae* or altar tables which were painted by Walter, Simon and Richard. Some of the altars named were certainly in the nave in this period, although moved elsewhere later. Page and other authorities assume that the western facing murals on the Norman piers were painted by Walter of Colchester and his assistants at this time. These murals form the earliest surviving reredoses in England. The westernmost *Crucifixion* is a monumental, dignified work, showing Christ on the cross with the mourning figures of Mary and John. The style (at least in the underpainting which is all that remains) is one of firm outlines and stiff, angular drapery folds; this is particularly noticeable in the loincloth of Christ, suggesting its derivation from metalwork. Walter of Colchester was primarily a worker in metal.

On the figure of St. Benedict, the kneeling votive figure on the next Norman pier to the east, one fragment of brilliant pigment can be seen, reminding us of how much has been lost and that mainly underpainting survives. The well-meaning treatment they received in the nineteenth century proved to be disastrous. In the words of William Page, they 'were sized and varnished about the time of their discovery. The heat from the gas had dried the varnish, which was flaking off, carrying with it the colour from the pictures'. Page tried to glue the pigment back using more size, but obviously with little success.

Walter's most famous work was the shrine of St. Thomas of Canterbury which he was engaged to design, assisted by Elias of Derham, a canon of Salisbury. Doubtless Walter executed the shrine as well and it dated from ca. 1220. It survives only in a representation in stained glass at Canterbury Cathedral. Here it is represented as early in form, that is, a reliquary box resting on an altar-type base; it was not the later form which rested on a tomb-like base. In this context it is worth recalling the shrine of

*Fig. 39   Westernmost Crucifixion, ca. 1215, believed
to be by Walter of Colchester.*

St. Mary at Tournai in Belgium, by Nicholas of Verdun, Walter's great contemporary and rival. That shrine, which has a hipped roof, is adorned with arcades and roundels in which are figures, remarkably expressive and spiritual in quality. When the body of St. Thomas of Canterbury was translated on 7 July 1220 into Walter of Colchester's newly made shrine and moved from the crypt of the church at Canterbury into a splendid new chapel, Walter was himself present. That he was chosen by a rival monastery for this important work is a testimony to his skill. Matthew Paris, himself a goldsmith, described him as *praelectus pictor* and *sculptor et pictor incomparabilis*.

Back in St. Albans, where Walter served for almost fifty years, Abbot William de Trumpington, continued to give him warm support, 'desiring to use incessantly his labour and art while he enjoyed prosperity of life and age'. While Walter was Sacrist, he used sacristy funds to design, carve and paint a screen in the middle of the church with the statues of the great cross, Mary and John, as well as other carvings and adornments. Doubtless this stood on the site of the present roodscreen which replaced it, and to the east of the shrine of St. Amphibalus and its associated altar. An early thirteenth century roodscreen survives at Tynemouth Priory, Northumbria, a cell of St. Albans Abbey where Ralph of Gubion (who discovered Walter) became Prior. One wonders if possibly this contains some echoes of Walter's lost screen. The nave altar would have occupied the centre of the western face; flanking it were two doors through which the Sunday procession of monks passed in two files from the cloister before taking up their places in the choir stalls for High Mass.

Over the High Altar was placed an Altar Beam carved by Walter with scenes from the life of St. Alban. Such beams, of which few have survived, were either embedded in the lateral walls of the Presbytery or carried on brackets. They supported lamps or candles and on them reliquaries were often displayed. Walter's beam is tragically lost and one would like to know how, if at all, his cycle of pictures of St. Alban was reflected in later works. The fullest portrayal of the life of the saint now in existence is Matthew Paris' cycle in *Lives of SS Alban and Amphibalus* now in Trinity College, Dublin (see fig. 6).

Another of Walter's works was a 'most elegant Mariola', or image of the Virgin, dating ca. 1225. This statue is also lost, but it is worth examining the mural of a seated *Virgin and Child* on the fifth Norman pier from the west of the north nave arcade, which dates from roughly the same period. This is a monumental figure seated firmly in a frontal posture upon a broad, rectangular throne. She is swathed in ample draperies and supports the child in her left arm; there is a general feeling of solidity and calm. It may be that the mural of a flying angel which survives in the north-east corner of the south transept is a remnant of the painted setting for the statue by Walter.

Various steps were taken to enhance the statue's immediate environment: the Altar Beam made by Adam the Cellarer formerly over the High Altar was moved to this position. In order to hide the blackened beams of the roof above, panelling was placed above the statue, doubtless in the form of a *celure* or canopy. To illuminate it better, much enlarged windows of the Early English period replaced the small Norman windows opposite. With

pointed heads and moulded, they are deeply splayed to direct the light inwards. The slender shafts have moulded bases and stiff-leaf caps. Trumpington had no compunction about cutting into the old Norman triforium to achieve his ends, no doubt considering that style old-fashioned and of little account. *The Ordinal of the Minuti* (those blooded) was kept under these windows, which were later partially blocked when the cloister was rebuilt outside. Finally, the interior of the church was whitewashed.

Walter of Colchester died in 1248.

Fig. 40   Gothic windows inserted in the south transept by Abbot William de Trumpington to increase illumination, 1214–1235.

References

McCULLOCH (FLORENCE). 'Saints Alban and Amphibalus in the works of Matthew Paris: Dublin Trinity College MS 177.' *Speculum*. LVI, no. 4. 1981. 761–785.

PAGE (WILLIAM). 'The St. Albans school of painting, mural and miniature'. *Archaeologia*. LVIII (1902) 275–292.

ROBERTS (EILEEN). A guide to the abbey murals. FFSAA. 1971.

. . . 'The famous murals of St. Albans'. *This Hertfordshire*. I, no. 1 (1973) 38–41.

. . . 'Moulding analysis and architectural research: the late Middle Ages'. *Architectural History*. XX. 1977. 5–13.

SALZMAN (L F). Building in England down to 1540: a documentary history. Oxford. 1952.

TRISTRAM (E W). English medieval wall painting: the thirteenth century. 2 vols. Oxford. 1950.

Chapter 9

REBUILDING THE PRESBYTERY

In the year 1250, Matthew Paris recorded an earthquake. The tower was obviously unaffected, for it still stands, despite the heavy weight of the broach spire which it then carried. The old east end, however, may have been seriously weakened. By 1257, dangerous cracks had appeared and demolition became urgent. The three easternmost apses and the two easternmost bays of the two Norman aisles were taken down, but the thick walls of the Presbytery were retained to buttress the tower, a role they still perform. All this was in the time of Abbot John de Hertford, 1235–1263.

While building work proceeded, what served as a substitute Presbytery? It may be that the Chapter House filled in for the next thirty years, as Adrian Havercroft has suggested. Matthew Paris, before he died in 1257, wrote that the Norman graves in the Chapter House were then 'concealed by tiling' implying that it had been recently done in his lifetime. This improvement may have marked some temporary use. The relief tiles used in re-tiling the Chapter House have been thrice uncovered, in 1877, in 1937 and finally in 1978. They measure eight and a half inches square and one and a half inches thick and are highly glazed in a deep, rich, bottle green mottled with olive brown and Venetian red. They were set in groups of nine with bands of pattern framing them. This form of tile was invented in Alsace in the mid twelfth century and became very popular in the Rhineland and North Switzerland. They passed over to East Anglia in the thirteenth century and have been found subsequently over a wide area of England, suggesting the presence of itinerant craftsmen. They never took root here, as the raised designs wore badly and they were uncomfortable underfoot; the original purpose to which they were best suited was wall decoration.

It was at this time that the workmen uncovered the ancient

sarcophagus of Alban, buried under the chord of the great apse, the spot today under the steps giving access to the Saint's Chapel from the east (see fig. 42). Perhaps, before the translation of the relics, it had been buried under the High Altar as a relic.

The rebuilding scheme took place largely in the time of Abbot Roger de Norton, 1263–1290. Now that the abbey had reached the height of its power and influence, the opportunity was seized to give the shrine an even more impressive setting. The new Presbytery would be reliquary-shaped, five bays long, with the three eastern bays wider than the western ones (see back plan). It was raised like a platform above the surrounding area by means of steps on all sides. The platform itself increases in height from west to east by a series of steps. The shrine itself was to stand in the easternmost bay, with the High Altar in the next bay to the west, the whole surrounded by an open arcade except where the Norman walls had been retained. The High Altar screen was not interposed to divide the area until over two hundred years had passed. The ambulatory surrounding the shrine on three sides allowed pilgrims to circumambulate the relics, a custom deeply rooted in mankind's early history. The chantries and watching loft are also late additions, so a low wall probably marked the limit of the holy places. Both the aisles and the Presbytery itself are vaulted to stress their mausoleum function and we will consider a little later the elaborate star-like pattern of the ribs.

Comparing the internal elevation of the new Presbytery design with that of the Early English nave bays (see fig. 37), one notes a considerable alteration in proportions over the intervening half century. The triforium, conceived as a continuous band of blind arcading, is shrinking markedly, while the clerestory, with its shafted windows for the first time at St. Albans sub-divided into lights, is much more daring in the use of glass.

A view into the Presbytery from the west conveys the simplicity and elegance of the design (see fig. 74). The Norman wall, shaved back but retained to triforium level, has not been pierced by arches but instead had arches and pier mouldings applied to the surface, matching the new work farther east. The triforium passage is retained, long after it had been dropped in France; a passage persists at clerestory level as well. Between the clerestory windows, stone springers support the vaults.

It is instructive to look by comparison at Chartres, begun in 1194, fifty years earlier than the St. Albans scheme. Its vaulting ribs spring from the pavement with greater vertical thrust. Although the triforium passage is retained, there is none at

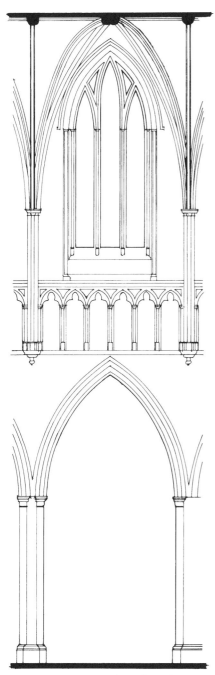

Fig. 41 *Bay elevation of Presbytery, before 1290.*

clerestory level, and in the windows, plate tracery has already appeared.

St. Albans seen in this context is conservative indeed. One must delete in the mind's eye not only the High Altar screen but also the chantries. A low screen only would have divided the Saint's Chapel from Presbytery proper so that the shrine, rising loftily above the High Altar, was for many years clearly visible from the choir.

The former Norman processional doors to the north and south of the bay next to the tower have been retained and adorned. That on the south is original work but the northern one is a modern copy. The big Norman opening has been filled in around a two-centred arch, shafted and with a hood. Above is an open arcade of triple arches under tabernacles with cusps, crockets and pinnacles. These may have been for the display of treasures, such as statues or reliquaries, during the Feast of the Relics. In design these doors are remarkably like the *sedilia* at Westminster Abbey, painted ca. 1308, about the same time as the Presbytery remodelling, which emphasises the close relationship between St. Albans and the Court School. Professor Tristram believed that Thomas of Durham, the artist who painted the figures on the Westminster

Fig. 42   Eastern wall of Presbytery with its triple arches as seen from the Lady Chapel.

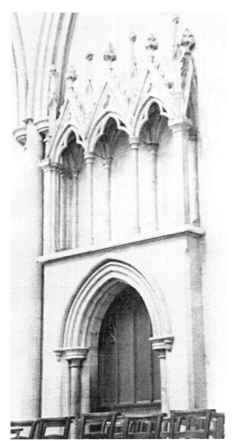

*Fig. 43   South processional door
in Presbytery.*

sedilia, lived at Bowgate, St. Albans, not far from St. Peter's church.

Standing in the Lady Chapel and looking west, one sees the eastern end wall of the Presbytery. One must picture its earliest state without the chantry chapel, the High Altar screen or the Watching Loft. The original low wall was probably built even lower, stretching continuously across the three arches, in order to control the flow of pilgrims. Three simple lancets form an elegant frame for the shrine, which we will discuss in due course. This wall, one notes, is ashlar below the hood mould but rubble above, proving that vaulting was intended for the antechapel; attached shafts to support the vaulting were probably envisaged between the lancets.

Looking north and south into the Presbytery aisles, one notes that aisle arcading has appeared at last, with two-centred arches, cusped, and foliage in the spandrils (see fig. 49, right). The slender shafts have moulded caps and bases. In the tracery of the windows above a new development has occurred: a quatrefoil has been added above the lancets (see fig. 79).

The architect James Neale has left us a pre-restoration view of the eastern exterior wall of the Presbytery, a drawing published in 1877. There is a group of three windows: a very slender lancet on either side and in the middle a large, traceried windows of four lights, the finest example of geometrical tracery in the abbey (see fig. 44). Comparing the window in its present form, the design after restoration remains much the same, with trefoils in the lower lights, and a great octofoiled circle in the head. In geometric tracery, all the forms can be drawn with compasses. It is sometimes called bar tracery, since the design is composed of short bars, carved in stone. This handsome window rises in culmination above the shrine and forms a splendid backdrop to it.

*Fig. 44   Group of windows with geometrical (bar) tracery
in east wall of Presbytery. Restored.*

Perhaps the Presbytery windows were glazed in grisaille glass which was popular between the years 1250 and 1270, with designs composed of circles and lozenges in double outline, filled with foliate patterns in white and greenish glass. A little colour was introduced into the borders. Fine examples remain in Lincoln and Salisbury cathedrals.

Bar tracery was invented at Rheims in France in 1211 but in England the earliest known example is at Binham Priory, Norfolk, a daughter house of St. Albans. The west front dates from before 1244 and although much mutilated, the magnificent window is very close to the St. Albans example.

The south elevation of the Presbytery shows its five bays, of which three and a half serve the Presbytery proper with one and a half devoted to the Saint's Chapel. The old Norman aisles are retained in bays one and two east of the crossing with taller, narrower Gothic aisles with their more pronounced buttresses farther east. The early thirteenth century Trumpington window with its differing proportions, occupies the middle bay. The tracery inserted in the clerestory windows during the late nineteenth century restoration has spoiled the effect as it is entirely wrong for this period.

Flying buttresses were intended to support this high vault: head stones have been built into the external face jutting out between the windows to receive their footings. This stone vault was never built, either for financial reasons or because the Norman walls would not have supported them. Roman brick has been used extensively for the last time at the abbey in the Presbytery walls.

A vault of wood was built instead. This was not common in the Middle Ages and it is sometimes criticised as insincere, copying a stone form in another medium, wood. Many masterpieces of

mediaeval woodwork, however, such as screens and traceried doors, imitate forms which were first evolved in stone. The big disadvantage of a wooden vault is its inflammability but it has many advantages. It is light and exerts little thrust on old, weak walls, it is easier to construct than a stone vault, and is therefore less expensive, it lends itself to light and airy designs and is easily decorated with paintings. Other examples of wooden vaults exist at Warmington, Northamptonshire and in the cloister at Lincoln, but St. Albans' vault, which dates after 1280, is the earliest major example

Fig. 45   Detail of the timber vault over the Presbytery.

in England.

A very careful craftsman in wood, the architect J C Rogers, studied the structure of the vault while he was repairing it and published his findings in the *Transactions of the St. Albans and Hertfordshire Architectural and Archaeological Society* in 1931. He includes a diagram, seen from below, of the vaults, resting on the caps of the applied wall shafts. These springers, carved in stone, rise and spread like funnels up to the points where the shields of arms are seen today. The stones are deeply bonded into the wall and end in flat platforms five feet square. These provide the support for the timber vault. The main ridge rib, eighty-five feet long (although not all in one piece) marks the highest point of the vault. The ribs, each in one piece, curve up to meet it. The transverse ridge ribs are eighteen feet long, the diagonal ribs twenty feet long.

Another diagram shows the truss construction which rests on the stone corbels. The curved ribs meet the ridge rib at the apex. The ribs are supported by horizontal struts tenoned in two places. A sturdy post rests against the wall within each pocket of the vault and the feet of the principal rafters are tied to it with one great tenon. Mortise and tenon joints are used and bosses conceal the junctions of the ribs.

The bosses which are on display in the south transept are not from the Presbytery but probably from the former Lady Chapel vault. It is interesting to observe how they are made: the largest are two feet in diameter and are like large bowls hollowed to prevent the splitting of the wood.

In 1256, King Henry III gave a gift of timbers to the abbey, probably used in the construction of the vault. When the timber was first examined, it seemed at first to include both oak and chestnut, but laboratory tests proved it to be entirely oak. Green timber was used, chosen from trees of moderate size which had been hewn and riven. Every tool mark is visible but the irregularities are very few.

Cecil A Hewett made a three-dimensional diagram of the vault timbers. The moulding section of the great ribs, with its rolls and hollows, must have required endless labour to complete. Horizontal struts fan out like a road sign from the tall post, joining the top surface of the diagonal and transverse ribs at two different levels. Rogers found these useful for climbing on during his inspection. The space above the vault is now lit by an eastern window placed in the gable end in the late nineteenth century.

A fine set of carpenter marks is found on the timbers, varying in every pocket, each member of a set bearing the same mark. They are composed of segments of circles combined in different ways to form five complicated shapes and there are in addition incised lines which are neither letters nor numerals. The whole vault was assembled at ground level where it was adjusted and marked, then taken apart and put together again on top of the walls.

Looking up at the vault from below one sees how spaces were provided for the clerestory windows; the window splays had crescents and roses painted on them at one time but only traces of this decoration are left. The vaulting cells have been filled with boards of riven oak, three-quarters of an inch thick and seven to eight inches wide, jointed horizontally. The nail heads appear as black spots; they fix the boards to small ribs hidden above, which hold and stiffen the boards. They are tongued and grooved together with joints which are so deep, narrow and regular, that a special grooving plane must have been used; no tool exists today which could do a similar job. The ribs are richly moulded, are about twelve inches square in section and thicker at the bottom for stability.

Near the window some tiercerons are found which are curved in an awkward way. These surface ribs, serving no structural purpose and fixed to the stone corbels by means of iron straps, were a later alteration when the vault was redecorated. The line of the original tiercerons can still be seen but these had to be moved to accommodate the later roundel pattern.

Originally, the vaulting pattern must have looked quite different from what we see today. The earliest painted decoration, which still survives under the fifteenth century repainting, was first detected by Professor Tristram during restoration work in the 1930s. He was able, under very strong light, to reconstruct the design. The carved bosses were gilded, with red in the hollows, the ribbed mouldings picked out in blue, red, grey, yellow and white. Some are marbled and some have counterchanged chevrons and indented patterns. The cells had scroll ornament in gold and bright colours outlined in black which sprouted foliage, fruit and flowers as it sprang from the bosses. The ground within the scrolls was coloured but the rest of the vault was white with masonry pattern in red.

The vault and the wall decoration were conceived as a unified whole but only fragments of wall painting survive: there was a dado band of scrolls between borders of yellow and grey indents. The window mouldings were picked out in red, yellow and grey while an indented border picked out the mouldings on the walls.

The fragmentary mural of an archbishop in the south-east corner of the Saint's Chapel is a precious survival of this earliest decorative programme.

The scheme culminated in the painting of *Christ in Majesty*, another of Professor Tristram's exciting discoveries. Christ is seated on a double rainbow against a ground of diaper pattern, within a great lobed mandorla. His crossed halo shows he is divine. He raises his right hand in blessing and holds the chalice in the left. On either side, in pinnacled tabernacles, stand two apostles, Peter with the key on the right and (doubtless) Paul with the sword on the left. There is scroll work around the western arch and on the wall, masonry pattern with crescents and roses. This great vision of the end of time, the Church Triumphant, fittingly looks down upon the altar and the shrine.

High in the lantern of the crossing tower are the earliest examples of heraldry found in the abbey (see fig. 22). These large, heater-shaped shields are shown hanging on straps; the shield of Kind Edward I is on the eastern wall, of his wife Eleanor of Castile on the west, the Prince of Wales, Edward of Caernarvon on the south, and Edmund, Earl of Cornwall, founder of Ashridge College on the north. The shields may commemorate the resting of Queen Eleanor's body before the High Altar on its passage from Lincolnshire to London in 1290. Alternatively, they may mark the completion of the new work in the Presbytery. In 1290, the first burial took place before the High Altar, that of Abbot Roger de Norton, which is taken to mean that building work was completed by that date.

About this time, the oldest surviving bell in the abbey was cast, the so-called 'Sanctus' bell, now mounted above the porch at the west end of the nave. It is similar in proportions to a bell at Aldbourne in Sussex by Adam le Potter.

After 1290, the apsidal chapels stretching east from the south transept were demolished and remodelled. New, squarish chapels replaced them, with stone screens partly filling in the arched openings at the west. These screens in turn were pierced by pointed arches under hood moulds. A new window was inserted near the western end of the south Presbytery aisle. The earlier Norman arch giving access to the apse from the north was blocked. The sculptured capitals which adorn the screens have developed far beyond the stylised, stiff-leaf capitals seen in the western porches: the basic form is still an inverted bell, now covered with wreaths of maple leaves, deeply undercut. The familiar plants of the English countryside are carefully observed and lovingly reproduced. This change of attitude reflects the influence of St. France of Assissi, d. 1226; he wrote:

'Be Thou praised, O Lord, for our Sister, Mother Earth,
Who doth nourish us and ruleth over us,
And bringeth forth divers fruit and bright flower and herbs.'

The beauty of creation is no longer regarded as a snare and delusion, but something in which to rejoice. With this fundamental change of attitude, we can fittingly leave the Early English period at St. Albans.

References

HEWETT (CECIL). English cathedral carpentry. London. 1974.

PERRYCOSTE (W B C). 'The Sanctus Bell'. *The Abbey Magazine*. IX, no. 1. (January 1969) 8–10.

PEVSNER (Sir NIKOLAUS). The leaves of Southwell. Harmondsworth. 1945.

ROGERS (JOHN C). 'St. Albans abbey church: the painted wooden vault over the presbytery and the saint's chapel. A description of its history, structure and recent repair.' *Trans. SAHAAS* (1931) 121–137.

ROGERS (JOHN C) and TRISTRAM (E W). 'Saint Alban's Abbey: the restoration of the presbytery roof.' *Country Life* (28 March 1931). 390–392.

ROBERTS (EILEEN). 'The coronation chair'. *Hertfordshire Countryside*. XXIII, no. 117. January (1969) 42–43.

ROBSON (FRANCES). 'Abbey artists had to use binoculars: Heraldry of the cathedral and abbey church of St. Alban/' *St. Albans Review and Express*. 12 May 1977.

ROUSE (E CLIVE). 'Paintings on the walls and timber ceilings of the central tower of St. Albans cathedral.' *Trans. SAHAAS* (1953) 98–102.

Part IV

INDIAN SUMMER OF THE ABBEY

Fig. 46   *The shrine of St. Alban as it appeared in
the lifetine of Matthew Paris, before 1259.*

Chapter 10

THE SHRINE OF ST. ALBAN AND THE LADY CHAPEL

In Matthew Paris' time, Alban's tomb was placed on a flat slab upheld by pillars, a kind of altar, within the great apse. This early type of shrine base is perfectly illustrated in a manuscript he wrote, *The Lives of SS Alban and Amphibalus,* which is now in Trinity College Dublin (MS 177, fol. 61a). King Henry III visited the shrine in 1259. He was a deeply religious man who gave great impetus to the cult of saints by the work at Westminster for his patron saint, St. Edward the Confessor, and by his many visits and gifts to shrines throughout his realm.

The height of shrines was an indication of their status. They rose up behind High Altars and were clearly seen from farther down the churches. At Ste. Chappelle, in Paris, for example, which dates from 1250, the important relics of the Passion were raised aloft on a platform under a canopy above the altar, accessible to devotees by means of two winding stairs. Another example, although of the eighteenth century, reconstructs the mediaeval layout at Pontigny in Burgundy, where the relics of an Englishman, St. Edmund de Rich, d. 1240, are raised high for all to see.

In England, all of the shrine bases which survived the Reformation date between 1270 and 1350, and of the eight major ones surviving from the hundreds destroyed, St. Albans possesses two.

The new Presbytery at St. Albans, one recalls, had been built between 1257 and 1290. Abbot John de Maryns (1302–1309), we read in the *Gesta Abbatum,* 'caused the *tumba* and *Feretrum* of St. Alban to be moved, whilst decorating it nobly, and expended on it, not to reckon too closely, more than a hundred and sixty marks in counted money'. The plan of the new arrangement shows the

Fig. 47   The shrine of St. Alban, 1302–1309, as reassembled in 1872.

Saint's Chapel to occupy one and a half bays to the east of the High Altar. (The High Altar screen, one must remember, was not introduced until two centuries later.) In 1290, the shrine was situated farther west than at present, closer to the High Altar itself. A low fence of iron probably surrounded it. A lofty, open arcade of nine masonry arches, probably with low walls within, allowed views of the shrine from north, east and south (see rear plan).

The description of the shrine base which follows is based on the 1872 reconstruction; in that year, a plan of the structure at niche level was published in *The Builder* for 4th May. It is rectangular in shape, three feet two inches by eight feet seven inches and rests on two steps. On the lower step are six sockets for hexagonal bases holding twisted columns for the six tapers which Trumpington had directed should burn on feast days. On the next step are the fourteen buttress bases. The slab of the basement is subdivided by panels to form the bases of ten niches; there are four square shaped niches in the middle, two triangular shaped niches at the ends, and four trapezium shaped niches in between. The two end niches are both subdivided by means of central shafts.

A 'marble tomb of splendid workmanship' is how the 1428 *Inventory* describes the shrine. It stands eight feet three inches tall, carved from Purbeck marble except for the vaults within the niches which are of clunch. It rises in three stages, tomb, niches and cornice and is divided into bays, four on each side and two at each end. The plinth, consisting of two steps, very worn, seems older than the rest; it supports the twisted columns and the buttresses. Above the plinth comes the 'tomb' (it contained no body) adorned with quatrefoil shapes in raised mouldings; the ones at the ends are split quatrefoils, a motif which is found in France at Ste. Urbaine de Troyes. Some of the quatrefoils are pierced with diamond shaped openings. A cavetto moulding with foliage decoration gives a suitable finish to the top of the tomb. This tomb form of shrine base replaced the earlier altar type after the murder of Thomas Becket at Canterbury in 1170; the tomb in which his body rested became the focus of an immensely popular cult.

In the next stage of the shrine, the open arcades form niches for gifts or relics, although some suggest they were 'squeezing places' for the sick to crouch in. Blue and red colouring survives on the panelling which had gold decoration: three lions for England, the *fleur de lys* of France as well as dots and stars. The blind, reticulated tracery is the earliest known example of this pattern and we will see it again in the Lady Chapel (see fig. 50 left).

There are a number of details which are worthy of close attention: the twisted columns on their hexagonal bases are notable, as are the diamond shaped apertures designed to receive models of diseased limbs or the clothes that wrapped them. Mediaeval illustrations survive showing pilgrims making votive offerings of model limbs to St. William's shrine in York Minster. Pilgrims creeping into apertures in the tomb of St. Edward the Confessor in Westminster to spend the night there are shown in the manuscript *La Estoire de Saint Aedward le Rei. (Cambridge University Library MS. Ee. III. 59.)*

The individual niches should be closely examined. Each one has an arch, continuously moulded, cusped and recusped and a pointed gable over with crockets and finials (see fig. 33). In the spandrels are sprays of foliage, including the oak with acorns. Between the gables are seated figures on pedestals: on the south, King Offa with his model church, on the north clerics, perhaps Oswin and Wulsin. There are angels at each end.

The type of gable decoration used on the shrine was the hallmark of the Court School of Westminster, where a series of tombs, like that of Aveline of Lancaster, dating 1296, and especially the Eleanor Crosses, helped to spread the fashion through the provinces. On the Eleanor Cross at Northampton one sees the same crocketed gable over a niche; the crest used there by the mason John of Battle is often compared with the cornice of the St. Alban shrine base.

The sculpture on the shrine is significant also. *The Scourging of Alban* fills the spandrel at the east end, with censing angels on either side, a motif popular on French tombs. The seated figure on the spandril below may represent King Offa. At the west end, the *Martyrdom of Alban* is represented. He is dressed in loose, classical drapery; modern representations often show him erroneously as a Roman soldier, whereas St. Alban was, of course, a Romano-British citizen.

The cornice of the shrine base is six inches high, heavy and overhanging, carved with maple and whitethorn leaves. Laid on top is a final slab, five inches deep, with formalized leaf border in a twelfth century style, re-used in this position from some earlier monument. Rising to the cornice are the tall, free-standing buttresses, joined to the pinnacles between the niches by little bridge-like members. The entire monument would have been thinly covered with gesso, painted and gilded.

The reliquary which rested on this Purbeck marble base was made by Master John the goldsmith in gold and silver (compare fig. 46). It had scenes in relief on the sides showing the life of Alban; there was the crucifixion at the eastern end, the Virgin and Child to the west and scenes from the martyrdom on the roof. When taken in procession around the monastery or the town boundary, four men were required to carry it. Shrines were usually kept locked under wooden covers which were raised by means of a pulley arrangement, to be revealed to pilgrims and visitors. These were apparently composed of niche-work like the elaborate mediaeval font covers which survive in some places. St. Albans had an especially extravagant cover, not of wood, but of silver and gilt, the work of John the Goldsmith. No wonder a constant watch had to be kept upon the shrine.

Leaving the Saint's Chapel, we will pause now to consider the rebuilding works so far. A view of the building from the Vintry Garden on the north-east shows how the eastern arm has been transformed and how very different it is from Paul de Caen's time. It descends in a series of diminishing boxes from the High Tower, down to the Presbytery with its aisles and ambulatory, to the Lady Chapel beyond. This square-ended plan has Cistercian roots but it developed in a purely English way and is characteristic of the south and west of England. Salisbury cathedral is similar in many ways, with its high Presbytery, double-aisle ambulatory and its low, two-bayed Lady Chapel. Inside, if vaulted with piers and

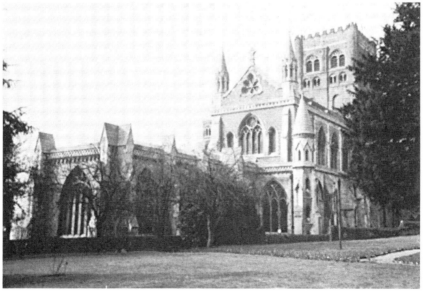

Fig. 48. North-east perspective of St. Albans abbey as seen from the Vintry Garden.

arches, mysterious and shadowy vistas are created, such as one sees at Southwark and at Winchester. The St. Albans plan east of the Presbytery has three eastern arches, an antechapel of three aisles flanked by two additional aisles and a Lady Chapel three bays long (see end plan).

The nine bays of the antechapel were meant to be vaulted in stone for which three forms of evidence survive: there are sleepers still existing under the floor to support the four missing piers, there is visible evidence for vaulting on the western wall with its triple arches (see fig. 42) and unfinished work can be observed in the arcades at north and south. The antechapel was destined as the cult centre of St. Amphibalus and his shrine, aligned with the High Altar and St. Alban's shrine, would shortly take up a central place here. Pre-restoration drawings shown how rich was the detailing. One view looks south-east across the antechapel toward the clustered responds with their shaft rings: an altar to St. Peter stood in this position. A little door opened onto a passage, allowing the clergy, officiating in the Lady Chapel, to bypass the crowds gathered round Amphibalus' shrine. Slender, gabled niches can also be seen. A view by the artist Shepherd dated 1804 shows the exterior aspect with its angle buttresses and geometric tracery.

Before turning our attention to the Lady Chapel, a few observations on the cult of the Virgin would be appropriate. Mary the mother of Jesus rarely appears in the gospels and when she does, she says little. However, great curiosity existed about her and in time, apocryphal tales developed to fill the void. The cult of the Virgin began in the twelfth century and developed rapidly in the thirteenth. The mendicant orders and St. Bernard of Clairvaux were strong promoters of the cult, in which the rich imagery of the *Song of Songs* was applied to Mary. Her office was recited daily and important chapels dedicated to her on the main axis of churches, near the High Altar. There is ample evidence of the cult of the Virgin at St. Albans: the *Assumption of the Virgin* was painted on the flat ceiling of the Antechapel and a mural in the nave shows her coronation in heaven by her son. The oak and acorn motif, popular in this century, is found on this mural.

The chapel of Our Lady was at the east, long and rectangular like the chancel of a parish church. Its altar was for the people, so big ambulatories were needed to give them access. The secular cathedrals adopted Lady Chapels in the twelfth century, hence the eastward growth of most of them. Monastic churches resisted for a long time, fearing to distract from their existing Saint's Chapels but they capitulated to the fashion by the thirteenth century.

The plan of the St. Alban's Lady Chapel is standard, a simple rectangle, long and wide, measuring internally twenty-five feet by fifty-eight feet (see end plan). Three steps at the east form a platform for the altar. There are three bays, and large windows with five lights at the east and four lights north and south, occupy the area between the deeply projecting buttresses. The chapel was vaulted in wood. This unaisled, rectangular plan had an interesting later history; it grew wider in the fourteenth century, supporting a higher structure and was finally adopted in the fifteenth century for the Royal Chapels at Windsor and at Westminster.

Special attention was concentrated on these chapels to make them little gems, separate entities from the rest of the church. The Lady Chapel at Chester cathedral, 1260–80, is like St. Albans', a low, broad, rectangular hall of three bays with a raised altar and tierceron vaulting. The window tracery and sedilia are in the Early English style.

Photographs taken after the restrained Scott restorations are valuable records of its unaltered state. William Boyden is said to have been the original architect; the official in charge was Reginald of St. Albans. The latter was often absent on legal

Fig. 49 View north-east into Lady Chapel after Scott's sensitive restoration. The original timber vault is still in situ and the shrine of St. Amphibalus is in its mediaeval position (left).

business and the work languished but the two hundred marks left in his will helped to bring it to completion under Abbot Hugh de Eversden, 1309–1327. The Bucklers observed the frame and cornice of an oaken screen across the chapel which were still in position in the 1840s. Scott re-erected the shrine of St. Amphibalus in its later mediaeval position in the midst of the antechapel. The 'choice timber vaulting' over the Lady Chapel was of a lower pitch than the present stone vault and gave a sense of sheltered breadth.

The interior today has altered proportions, although the present vault copies the tracery of the original one. The ridge rib and the tiercerons with elaborate bosses at the intersections form a rich, overall surface pattern. Both the Bucklers and Ashdown noted traces of wall arcading surviving on the lowest stage which were used as models in the restoration of the arcading.

A drawing by Frederick Kitton made before 1871 shows the interior bay elevation with its large traceried window. The deeply splayed jambs characteristic of this period are enriched with ballflower ornament and saints in niches. There are nine of these to each window, three on each side and three on each central mullion. Between the windows were shallow niches from whose canopies the vaulting ribs sprang.

The massing of figures of saints on the window jambs and mullions protected the openings against the entry of an evil, an idea which had its roots in the Coptic church. Above the little figures are nodding ogee canopies with pinnacles and finials. Ogee arches are said to have first appeared on the Eleanor Crosses. Shafting is no longer used to enrich the windows; ballflower ornament has replaced it, the components linked by trailing vines on an inner and an outer order. This motif was much used in the reign of King Edward II, 1307–27.

In the south-east corner of the Lady Chapel canopy work is found over the sedilia. There are eight different niches in three different sizes of varying depths, some with projecting canopies with double gables and stubby little spires behind, crowded with crockets. Many heads, both human and grotesque, all smiling, are incorporated in the design.

An exterior view of the chapel after 1874 but before the Grimthorpe restoration, shows the broad and low proportions. The hipped roof is low-pitched, which was fashionable in the Decorated period, and which lead to the use of parapets. These are often richly decorated; the Bucklers noted ballflower here in the 1840s. Buttresses are deep with gabled offsets rising to eaves level and angle buttresses are found at the corners. There are flint-faced walls, a string-course below the window sills and a deeply-moulded base course.

Window tracery is the chief glory of the Lady Chapel, as in all Decorated work. A sectional drawing by the architect James Neale shows how the Gothic ideal of a stone framework supporting walls of glass has been fully realised. The windows are of four lights under two-centred arches. The crisp and regular geometric patterns of an earlier period now begin to break up; one could still draw the forms with compasses, but they are pulled out and elongated, and the use of the ogee prepares the way for the future flowing tracery. Large windows are sometimes organised as two smaller ones, both under a containing arch. Neale's drawing shows fragments of wall arcading on the right and the left.

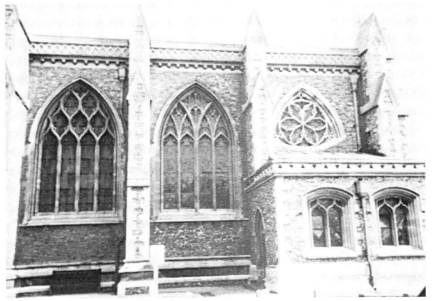

Fig. 50 Lady Chapel, south elevation, restored, showing window tracery.

The window tracery can best be appreciated outside the building. The glass in its moulded frames is recessed some inches from the surface of the wall, gaining interest through the play of light and shade. One window has reticulated tracery, a number of quatrefoils each the same width as the lights below, but each tier having a diminishing number of units, three, two and one.

The eastern window elaborates the theme of the Presbytery, its five ascending lancets having three petals above (see fig. 49). The *Gesta Abbatum* describes them as 'most beautiful stained glass windows, a magnificent sight'.

The original glass from the Lady Chapel windows is lost but glass in the church of Deerhurst, Gloucestershire, shows the most popular style of glass for the period, figure and canopy panels set in a ground of quarries with foliage.

Above the sedilia of the Lady Chapel there was insufficient room for a full-sized window so a triangular one with curved sides was inserted instead. These 'spherical triangles' were a popular way to fill in odd corners. There is a famous series of them in the Westminster Abbey triforium: the tracery consists of a large central circle subdivided into petals. Another example is found in the parish church of Abbot's Langley, St. Lawrence, four miles to the south-west of St. Albans; spherical triangles illuminate the south chancel, another Decorated monument in the St. Albans Liberty. This chapel has the broad windows and deep buttresses typical of the period.

One window of the St. Albans Lady Chapel stands apart from the rest in its tracery design: it might be called Transitional. Although there is fluid trefoil ornament below, a new motif, vertical panelling, is found in the head. This motif appeared after 1330 when the Perpendicular style was invented.

Before leaving the Lady Chapel, one should consider a particular red velvet cope sumptuously decorated with a network of niches containing saints. A St. Albans inventory of the early fifteenth century describes in detail a cope which corresponds exactly with the Butler-Bowden cope in the Victoria and Albert Museum. Either that vestment, or its double, was owned by St. Albans abbey. The architectural details on the orphrey, with their cusped and panelled niches, correspond with work in the Lady Chapel. The cope has been dated on stylistic grounds between 1330 and 1350. The luxurious quality, with gold and silver threads, coloured silks, some details covered densely with seed pearls, others picked out in green glass beads, is typical of the period. Angels seated on faldstools decorate the spandrils. The three main panels on the back depict scenes from the life of the Virgin; obviously the cult of the Virgin was at its height when the vestment was designed. Oak leaves and acorns are also found on the cope. This piece of *opus anglicanum* may give some idea of the kind of rich appointments which once furnished the abbey.

References

COLDSTREAM (NICOLA). 'English Decorated shrine bases'. *Journal of the British Archaeological Association.* CXXIX (1976) 15–34.

. . . 'The shrine of St. Alban'. *The Alban Link.* XXVI. Winter, 1987. 3.

LLOYD (ROBERT RIDGWAY). Altars, monuments and tombs existing AD 1428 in St. Albans abbey, translated from the original Latin with notes. St. Albans. 1873.

HASTINGS (MAURICE). St. Stephen's Chapel and its place in the development of Perpendicular style in England. Cambridge. 1955.

MICKLETHWAITE (J T). 'The shrine of St. Alban'. *Archaeological Journal.* XXIX (1872).

OMAN (CHARLES C). 'The shrine of St. Alban: two illustrations'. *The Burlington Magazine. LXIII (May 1933) 237–241.*

ROBERTS (EILEEN). 'The St. William of York mural in St. Albans Abbey and *opus anglicanum.' The Burlington Magazine.* CX, no. 782 (1968) 236–241.

Chapter 11

THE DAMAGED NAVE AND ITS REBUILDING

When King Edward of Caernarvon, 1307–27, making a journey through St. Albans, examined the old choir at night in the presence of the convent, the abbot mentioned that it had been his father's wish to make a new choir. The king at once said that he would like to fulfil his father's promise, so he gave one hundred marks as well as much timber from Temple Dinsley, a house of the Knights Templars near Hitchin, Hertfordshire. In 1904, the foundations of these stalls were found, stretching from the east side of the crossing as far as the roodscreen. To construct the choir stalls, the abbot hired various workmen highly skilled in carpentry, cutting and carving and put them under the supervision of one Master Geoffrey, a cunning man. He worked for many years, receiving four shillings weekly for himself and his assistants, as well as a robe of the abbot's esquires and other benefits. His assistant received the robe of a palfreyman.

These choir stalls exist no more but those still to be seen at Winchester cathedral are nearly contemporary. They are amongst the earliest to have survived complete with two stalls to each canopy. The back stall is panelled with geometric tracery and the front rises to a very steep gable with pinnacles, crockets and finials. The foliage is less naturalistic than heretofore, and rather more knobbly.

A great candlestick, we learn from the 1428 *Inventory*, stood in the midst of the Presbytery. St. Bernard of Clairvaux had vividly described the great candelabra of his day, 'standing like trees of massive bronze fashioned with marvellous subtlety of art, and glistening no less brightly with gems than with the lights they carry.' Artists have drawn reconstructions of one which survives only in part at St. Remi, Rheims; it stood four times the height of a man when it was intact.

A dreadful calamity occurred on 10th October, 1323. 'For when there was a great crowd of men and women in the church to pray or to hear mass, suddenly two great columns of the south side of the church, giving way first from the foundation, fell successively to the ground with a terrible noise and crash. So, laity and brethren running together from all sides, stupefied with terror, to gaze upon this fearful sight, scarcely an hour had passed when, behold! the whole wooden roof, which was built upon the said columns, with beams, rafters and ties, and the aisle on the south side of the church, and almost all that side of the cloister followed in the same way'. (The chronicler goes on to describe the damage done by the falling of the 'wooden props which were placed for the support of the ruins spoken of'; it is not quite clear whether or not this part of the arcade had already shown structural deficiencies.) Indeed, although only two piers fell, five bays had to be replaced, numbers four to eight from the tower.

The mason chosen to repair the damage was Henry Wy and a male head wearing a mason's cap, forming an end stop above a south nave pier, is believed to be his portrait. It is a strong, decisive, idealistic yet extroverted face. Placed in the company of the King, the Queen and the abbot, it is clear that architects enjoyed high status in the early fourteenth century.

The rebuilt bays have been consciously designed to harmonise with the Early English bays to the west, with a triforium wider and a clerestory narrower than had become the custom and with proportions that are more old-fashioned even than the Presbytery (compare with fig. 41). With a similar pier section, then twin arches sub-divided in the stage above, and twin lancets in stage three, we have a definite example of revival architecture. Nave vaulting was still aspired to, which would have sprung from the clerestory string-course, but it was never achieved and the strongly

Fig. 51 Portrait of Henry Wy, Master Mason, fl. ca. 1324–26, from carved head on nave spandril.

123

Fig. 52 Decorated nave bay elevation, 1324–26. Drawn by James Neale.

horizontal scheme established elsewhere in the nave has been maintained.

The mouldings, however, both of the nave arcades and of the bases, are very different from the Early English work. The bases, for example, are in two moulded orders rather than in one. The detailing is quite up to date with keeled shafts, ogee arches and heavy hood moulds with portrait end stops. There is abundant use of ballflower ornament and of fleuron bands with grotesque heads and shields of arms as further enrichment. The foliage capitals still refer to nature but have grown more stylised with undulating surfaces. The pure and aspiring ideal of the thirteenth century has given way to one more sensuous, extravagant and luxurious, reflecting the period when the merchant classes were growing in wealth.

Fig. 53   Detail of Decorated nave triforium, 1324–26.

The aisles are vaulted and a horizontal string course is cut by keeled wall shafts in clusters of five. The aisle windows are still adorned with shafting but the lower half has been blocked to accommodate the cloister beyond.

A print of 1832 shows the original tracery (see fig. 84), which combines two trefoiled motifs with one quatrefoil, ogee curves appearing throughout. This tracery, unfortunately, was lost in the restoration, although it harmonised perfectly with the cloister below.

*Fig. 54   Shrine of St. Amphibalus, second quarter of the fourteenth century.
Engraving by F G Kitton.*

New work carried out in the nave of Exeter cathedral in 1328 forms an interesting contrast: with its expanse of window glass and luxurious tracery, it helps put the St. Albans work into context. Antiquarianism was practised at St. Albans, with the clerestory modelled fairly closely on the Early English work. Blind arcading between the lancets has been abandoned but the shafting of the windows and their hood moulds have been retained.

There was no necessity to harmonise the aisle bays with those of the cloister immediately outside (see fig. 80).

The shrine of St. Amphibalus which had stood in the midst of the nave for over a hundred years, was also damaged in the fall of masonry. The sacrist, Ralph de Whitechurche, gave a new shrine base of Totternhoe stone which now took its place in the antechapel (see fig. 49). Some of the original colouring and gilding still remained on it when the fragments were recovered by Sir G G Scott. It had the usual plinth, basement, nichwork and cornice. The basement surface was decorated in low relief by a fretwork pattern (*opus interrsile*) with decorative motifs (the initial RW, a lion and a *fleur de lys*) superimposed. On the gable bulbous leaves are carved, in a form popular just before the Black Death in 1349; the tomb of the Percys at Beverly Minster in Yorkshire is adorned with leaves in this style. The large brackets on Amphibalus' shrine base probably supported tapers.

Fig. 55   Detail of cloister tracery, 1327–36.

Abbot Richard de Wallingford laid the foundation stone of the cloisters between 1327 and 1336 and paid the band of craftsmen working on it thirty shillings per week. There were thirty-six bays to the cloister, each one sixteen feet square, larger than the average living room today. It was thus a project of considerable scale. The cloister tracery, consisting of pointed trefoil figures using ogee curves, forms an ample, sensuous design. The central light measures ten feet high and over three feet wide (see fig. 55).

The internal vaulting must have presented a rich effect; one would like to know the details of the vaulting scheme. A fragment survives immediately outside the abbot's door in the north-east re-entrant angle of the cloister; it is tierceron vaulting with dense, foliage bosses, exceeding in complexity the Lady Chapel vaults.

A carved boss from the cloister still survived ca. 1800, known to us from antiquarian drawings. H G Oldfield recorded it, as did one 'TF' whose pencil study, dated 1806, states it was then 'preserved in a house in the town near the abbey.' In elegant carving, St. Amphibalus is depicted at his martyrdom, standing serene although bound, stabbed and disembowelled, with two attendant knights clad in armour of the fourteenth century.

Fig. 56 Carved boss from the cloisters, now lost, showing Martyrdom of St. Amphibalus, *based on drawing by T.F., 1806.*

Because of the sloping hilltop site, the cloister pavement was much lower than the abbey aisles; one descended a flight of twelve steps from the abbot's door to reach it. A few fragments of patterned tiles can still be seen on the site of the cloister and many similar pieces have been relaid in the north transept. The patterns, yellow on red, are mostly stamped and the fuzzy edges of this process are still detectable. The patterned tiles were used in combination with plain ones. They were quite economical at the time, costing four to eight shillings per thousand, although as many as four thousand might be needed for one project. They must have been soothing underfoot as the monks processed barefoot around the cloisters on Wednesdays and Saturdays.

The London Museum has a considerable collection of tiles showing designs found at St. Albans; masks, animals, leaves and petals are all popular motifs (see fig. 57). Some quadrant tiles in the collection are amongst the earliest printed tiles in the country. Others are from the famous kiln at Penn in Buckinghamshire which operated during the 1330s.

Later in the century, Abbot de la Mare (1349–1396) installed monks' carrels with their wooden seats and shelves for books. At Gloucester cathedral, twenty stone carrels still survive in the cloister but they have lost their desks and other wooden fittings. De la Mare also glazed two of the cloister walks at a cost of ten marks. Four royal shields now in the south-east window of the north transept are suggested survivals of this glazing project. These shields, of Edward III and three of his sons, the Black Prince, Lionel Duke of Clarence and John of Gaunt, must date between 1362 and 1368. In the history of stained glass world wide, they are important examples of a fashion new amongst sovereigns and great lords in fourteenth century England, to display their heraldic devices in the crisp outlines and glowing colours of the glass painter's art.

Another casualty of the 1323 disaster was the 'whole wooden roof, which was built upon the same columns, with beams, rafters and ties'. Sometime after 1323 the damaged ceiling must have been repaired. Neale tells us that it was not completely flat, but one foot higher in the centre, to prevent the optical illusion that it was sagging.

One wonders if the Monks' Choir ceiling was involved in this repair. It is composed of flat wooden panels painted with the sacred monogram alternating with angels holding shields bearing quotations from *Te Deum* and the responses at Mattins and Lauds. At the centre of the ceiling a pair of panels shows the *Coronation of the Virgin*. Stylistic features which could be closely dated are elusive: tall crowns, vanishing point perspective and weighty figures are of the fourteenth and fifteenth centuries rather than before. A complete set of high quality photographs would enable a detailed study to be made. The style of lettering might also be considered, but 'black letter' was used for a long time. On heraldic grounds, it could not date after 1405 as studies made by Mrs Fay Robson have shown; she demonstrated the many puzzles involved in the series of shields. Perhaps some panels at the west have been lost which would complete the series. Obviously this problem needs further study.

Fig. 57   Stamped tiles of types found at St. Albans, in the London Museum.

Richard de Wallingford (1327–1336), son of a blacksmith and brilliant Oxford graduate specialising in astronomy, designed and constructed during his term as abbot, a remarkable, weight-driven, astronomical clock. His detailed notebooks in the Bodleian Library have been translated by Dr J D North and replicas of the clock constructed. A full-scale, working model of the diurnal part of this famous clock made by local people was placed in the north transept of the abbey in 1988 and it is hoped to add the astronomical section at a future date.

References

GARROD (H W). 'Richard of Wallingford's connection with Merton College, Oxford'. *Trans SAHAAS*. (1926) 230–231.

GUNTHER (ROBERT T). 'Wallingford's scientific instruments'. *Trans SAHAAS*. (1926) 235–239.

HARVEY (JOHN). English mediaeval architects, a biographical dictionary down to 1550. Gloucester. 1984.

HENWOOD (GEORGE A). Abbot Richard of Wallingford, a fourteenth century scholar, astronomer and instrument maker. Wallingford. 1988.

HOWGRAVE-GRAHAM (R P). 'Early clocks and horloges. Richard of Wallingford's clock'. *Trans. SAHAAS*. (1926) 231–235.

LLOYD (ROBERT RIDGWAY). An architectural and historical account of the shrines of Saint Alban and Saint Amphibalus in Saint Alban's Abbey. St. Albans. 1873.

NORTH (J D). Richard of Wallingford. Oxford. 1976.

TURNER (H H). 'Richard of Wallingford'. *Trans. SAHAAS*. (1926) 233–25.

WALLER (J G). A critical examination of the armorial bearings and decorations on the ceiling of the monks' choir in the abbey church of St. Alban. Westminster. 1889.

WALLINGFORD (RICHARD DE). 'Tractatus horologii astronomici'. ca. 1327.

WARD PERKINS (JOHN B). London Museum medieval catalogue. London. HMSO. 1940.

WIGRAM (W A). 'Richard of Wallingford, the abbot'. *Trans. SAHAAS*. (1926) 225–229.

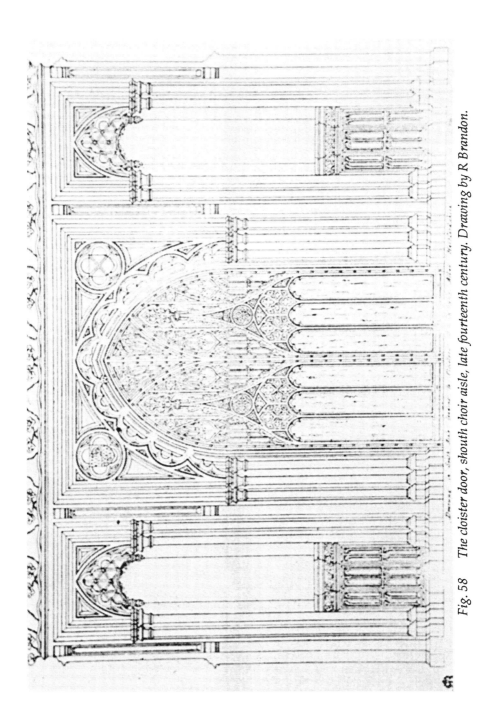

Fig. 58   The cloister door, shouth choir aisle, late fourteenth century. Drawing by R Brandon.

Chapter 12

THE PERPENDICULAR PERIOD

The Decorated period was a short-lived one in English art, lasting only a few decades; the exuberance and indulgence was too extreme for the English temperament and a reaction set in: the sober, disciplined Perpendicular style which replaced it was so natural and acceptable that it lasted for two hundred years.

A good example of the style is the fine doorway in the south choir aisle which gave access by a flight of twelve steps down to the north cloister walk. It is of special interest in that the door is dated: it was constructed while John de la Moote was Prior, that is, before 1396. It also bears the arms of King Richard II, d. 1399, in its eastern spandril. In the western spandril, incidentally, is the earliest known shield of St. Alban, *azure a saltire or*, which was later adopted as the shield of St. Albans city.

The architect Brandon made a handsome drawing of the door. The stone surround provides a clear example of the Perpendicular style: all is organised within a rectangular frame with horizontals and verticals predominating. Supports are long and slender; the capitals and bases are polygonal on plan. Blind panelling is a popular decorative motif and foliage tends towards rectangular shapes. In the heads of the flanking niches is lierne vaulting, a network of matchstick patterns with tiny bosses. These side niches are very like the ones at the west door of Westminster Abbey designed by the King's Mason, Henry Yeveley, who was called in by Abbot de la Mare on two occasions to advise about repairs to the monastery walls. Possible Henry Yeveley designed this door.

Turning to the wooden door within this framework, the outside face is on the church side, while the inside faced the cloister. It is a large door hung in two leaves with a little wicket door cleverly accommodated in the design to retain the symmetry. By this time it was the joiner rather than the smith who enriched doors and the marks of his tools can still be seen here. He has imitated window tracery in carved wood and applied it to the boards in sweeping ogees and blind panelling, with other three dimensional carvings added. This door is one of the finest mediaeval pieces in the abbey.

On the inside, a framework of diagonal battens has been dovetailed into place and much care given to mouldings, cusping and carvings. Although this door was designed to be kept under cover, it was buffeted by wind and rain for centuries after the destruction of the cloister. The special hinge design for this particular door should also be noted.

Fig. 59   The roodscreen, second half of the fourteenth century.

Walter of Colchester's roodscreen may have been destroyed in 1323, for it was replaced by one dated on stylistic grounds to the second half of the fourteenth century. Only a few roodscreens survive, at Ewenny, Boxgrove, Crowland, Davington and Tynemouth. These screens separated the laity's church from the monks' church, so the doors in the screen were usually kept locked, and entry into the side aisles must have been blocked off in some way. At St. Albans the Jesus altar stood in the centre and there were two side altars, one to St. Thomas of Canterbury on the north and one to St. Benedict on the south. At first glance the roodscreen appears to be assymmetrical; the design has to fit into a low Norman arch on the north and a higher, Decorated arch on the south. Otherwise, it is quite balanced. The Perpendicular design is highly developed, the whole surface presenting a grid of niches and panels. At Durham, the roodscreen showed scenes from the life of Christ and of the twelve apostles; here, the thirteen niches with their elaborate canopies were long ago robbed of their statues.

On Sundays the Great Procession moved around the cloister, up the nave and into the choir through the doors on either side of the Jesus altar, after asperging all the altars in the church and making the stations of the cross. A print of 1819 shows the parallel lines on the pavement surface which guided the procession (see fig. 78). Archdeacon Stubbs repaved the nave in the early eighteenth century but he apparently retained this feature of the old design.

Particular parts of the screen repay detailed examination. There is, for example, openwork cresting at the top of the screen and the nichework comprises lacy gables with three faces and a slender spire with delicate crockets above. The doors have square labels with crenellation and pinnacles, as well as carved spandrils and fleurons in the jambs. There is fine detailing around the central

reredos. At the northern end, the reredos of St. Thomas' altar has vaulted canopies and niches below. In the centre one would find a sacred group, such as the *Virgin and Child* or *Christ in Majesty*, while saints and martyrs would fill the niches on either side. St. Thomas would occupy the northernmost niche. The wooden doors in the roodscreen which are original and of high quality, are divided by transoms, crenellated, with three tiers of tracery and a continuous border all around. The door furniture is interesting too; on the choir side is an exquisite door ring with alternate, punched designs and a pair of salamanders twisting round the ring.

Fig. 60   Fragment of wooden screen, formerly in east tower arch.

A fragment of a lost wooden screen is displayed in the

Exhibition Gallery. The nineteenth century rector, Dr H J B Nicholson, records that it was removed from the eastern tower (where the stump still remains). It was part of a light wooden screen, richly coloured and gilded as were all mediaeval furnishings. St. David's cathedral in Wales still retains an open mediaeval screen in this position.

Between 1400 and 1420, the *Book of Benefactors* tells us, Robert of Malton gave twenty shillings for the *'nova Camera feretarii juxta maius altare'*. This refers to the watching loft which bears the white hart badge of King Richard II, 1377–99; the work must have commenced before this king's death. Besides one at Christ Church, Oxford, this is the only watching loft to have survived from the Middle Ages in England.

A complete little building in itself, it fills an arch in the north of the Saint's Chapel. It is framed in the mode of the carpenters' craft, with massive oak beams mortised and tenoned together. The plinth on the north side is two feet deeper than on the south. First of all, a double sill was laid, supporting uprights which carry in turn the hidden, first floor beams. Across these, transverse joists were laid projecting north and south to form the floor of the first floor watching chamber. From these, further uprights bear the cornice, seventeen feet above chapel pavement level.

The two façades, north and south, are individually treated. On the south, a series of traceried openings are grouped in pairs, separated by slender buttresses. These openings were never glazed but the grooves for the shutters remain, as well as peg-holes for propping the shutters open. Below are three pairs of cupboard doors behind which, presumably, relics were stored. Between these doors, clusters of ribs fan out from moulded capitals, adding support to the chamber above. At the east is the door projection; the steps within consist of massive, triangular baulks of wood nailed to sloping supports.

The northern façade, serving no special function, is differently treated, although similar sets of ribs fan out from moulded capitals. Here the panelling features ogee arches with crocket and finial adornment. On the horizontal fascias to north and south are carved a remarkable series of figural scenes. Besides the decollation of Alban with angel witnesses, are vignettes of the peasant life which teemed in town and manor beyond the abbey. Rural pursuits like the piping shepherd, the sheep scratching its ear, the milkmaid, the dog leading a boar by the ear are shown while the recreations of bear-baiting on the north-west corner and the hunting scene on the north-east are especially detailed and

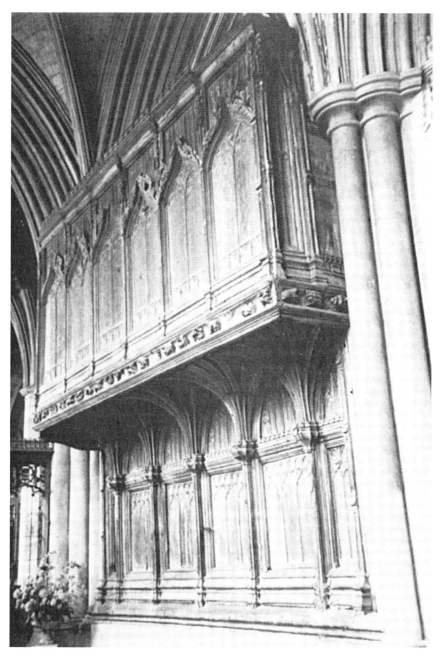

Fig. 61   Watching loft, 1400–1420.

well preserved. Incidentally, the Watchers occupying this chamber were not the monks themselves but the abbey tenants who served this function as part of their feudal service. An entry for 1431 in *The Court Book of Park* in the British Library makes this clear.

All the oak in the watching chamber is quarter cut, most carefully chosen for beauty of grain. The tracery is not applied, but fashioned throughout by woodcarvers' tools to a high degree of excellence. The entire structure is a prodigy of sculpture in oak. The pinkish-grey bloom on the wood is doubtless the ghost of the gesso grounding laid to receive vivid colour and gilding overall. No trace of pigment, however, has as yet been found.

Pilgrims, sick and sound, filled the Saint's Chapel by day and by night. As R C Finucane so vividly wrote, 'wretched cripples writhing on the floor, . . . the screams of fettered madmen straining at their bonds, the stench of poverty and disease. The pious are noisily praying in the semi-darkness, or offering their desperate pennies and home- made candles; a pilgrim is explaining his miraculous cure to a monk sitting at the tomb, while in a far corner someone is being sick . . . The nobility are here, and a clutch of clerics, but they disdain the humble common folk, remaining aloof until the moment comes for them to present their precious stones, their silver or wax images.' The pilgrims, before they left, could purchase as a souvenir a leaden badge showing the martyrdom of St. Alban.

Fig. 62   *Leaden pilgrim badge show-*
ing martyrdom of St. Alban.
Fourteenth century.

Abbot Wheathampstead's great west window was the most ambitious alteration of the early fifteenth century, but it survives today only in drawings and photographs; some bits of moulded stonework were found in the 1980 restoration. The *Book of Benefactors* describes a window with a stone framework from the northern parts, implying stone from the Lincolnshire limestone belt cut to the mason's specification at the quarry and perhaps even glass from the famous York School. The nine lights of this window entirely filled the central bay of the west front and its deep head was covered in tracery. Strong mullions divided it into groups of three lights with subsidiary arches at the sides.

Fig. 63   The west front, showing Wheathampstead's great west window. Drawing by John Carter.

The architect responsible for the design of this window is not recorded, but we do know that Thomas Wolvey, the former King's Mason, lived at the abbey manor of Childwick two miles north-west of St. Albans. In 1398, Wolvey had constructed as a sub-contractor under Yeveley, the great north window of Westminster Great Hall, similar in some ways to the St. Albans western window. Perhaps he was granted residence on the abbey manor in part remuneration for services as Master Mason. He died at Childwick and was buried in St. Michael's churchyard. On the other hand, we do know that money was being spent here for glazing as late as 1447 when a bequest was left for that purpose by one Robert Bellamy.

The fifteenth century saw other alterations, affecting the exterior aspect of the church; Nicholas Hawksmoor's drawing of 1721 gives a good idea of the effect of these changes (see fig. 79). The broach spire on the crossing tower was replaced by a small leaded spirelet, the well-known 'Hertfordshire spike'. The pitch of the roofs was lowered and battlements applied to the aisles, tower and Presbytery. This had the effect of making the Norman triforium into a second clerestory (see fig. 78). The tracery here was three cinquefoiled lights, flanked by two extra blank panels which are not clear on the Hawksmoor drawing but can still be clearly seen inside the cock-loft. The apsidal chapels on the east of the north transept were demolished, the arches filled in and provided with lights. A small chamber was hollowed out of the thickness of the wall in the south transept near the south choir aisle; this was illuminated by two cinquefoiled lights. The twenty angel busts adorning the brackets of the nave ceiling also date from this time. There are twenty of them, half with clasped or crossed hands, half holding shields.

Fig. 64   Traceried window placed in south transept by Abbot William Wallingford, 1476–1492.

The transept fronts were given great traceried windows by Abbot William Wallingford, 1476–92, which cost fifty pounds each. These consisted of seven lights under four-centred arches, with sub arches over the end lights. Daggers and short transoms were included in the tracery. The abbey was now filled with light.

A pair of traceried oaken doors from the main west entrance also date from this century. The two mediaeval layers of wood are fixed together by square nailheads with diamond patterns, arranged in a decorative way. Tracery, in a pattern of blind panelling, has been applied to the surface. Not only is a dense overall pattern formed

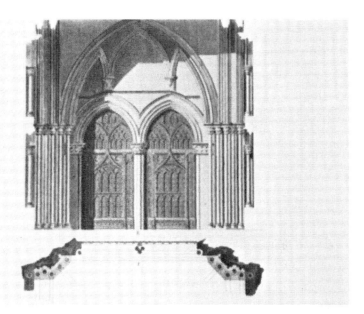

Fig. 65   *Old west doors in their original position.*
Drawing by John Carter, 1813. Now in the Slype.

from the cusping and rosettes; the tracery is cleverly laid over the joints to make the door waterproof. A wicket door has been ingeniously fitted in. The design has been built up in sections pegged together, and relief carving has been applied. These doors, which have suffered damage through the centuries and could do with some sympathetic repairs, are now on display in the Slype.

An important aspect of mediaeval life is represented by the chantry, a mass recited at an altar for the well-being of the founder while he lived, and of his soul after his death. Chantries stem from the belief in purgatory, when souls who died in a state of grace are cleansed by suffering and so prepared for heaven. In reality, the monastic church as a whole served a chantry function, in praying for the soul of the founder in perpetuity: at St. Albans, twelve poor men prayed daily for the soul of King Offa II, and were given meals in return for their services. A great impetus was given to the chantry idea after the death of Queen Eleanor in 1290, because of the extremely elaborate rituals set up for the peace of her soul by her husband, King Edward I.

Beautiful chantry chapels in Benedictine churches and in cathedrals were a great attraction to pilgrims who liked to look at them. The most sought after positions were around the Shrine and the High Altar and St. Albans retains four chantry chapels in this

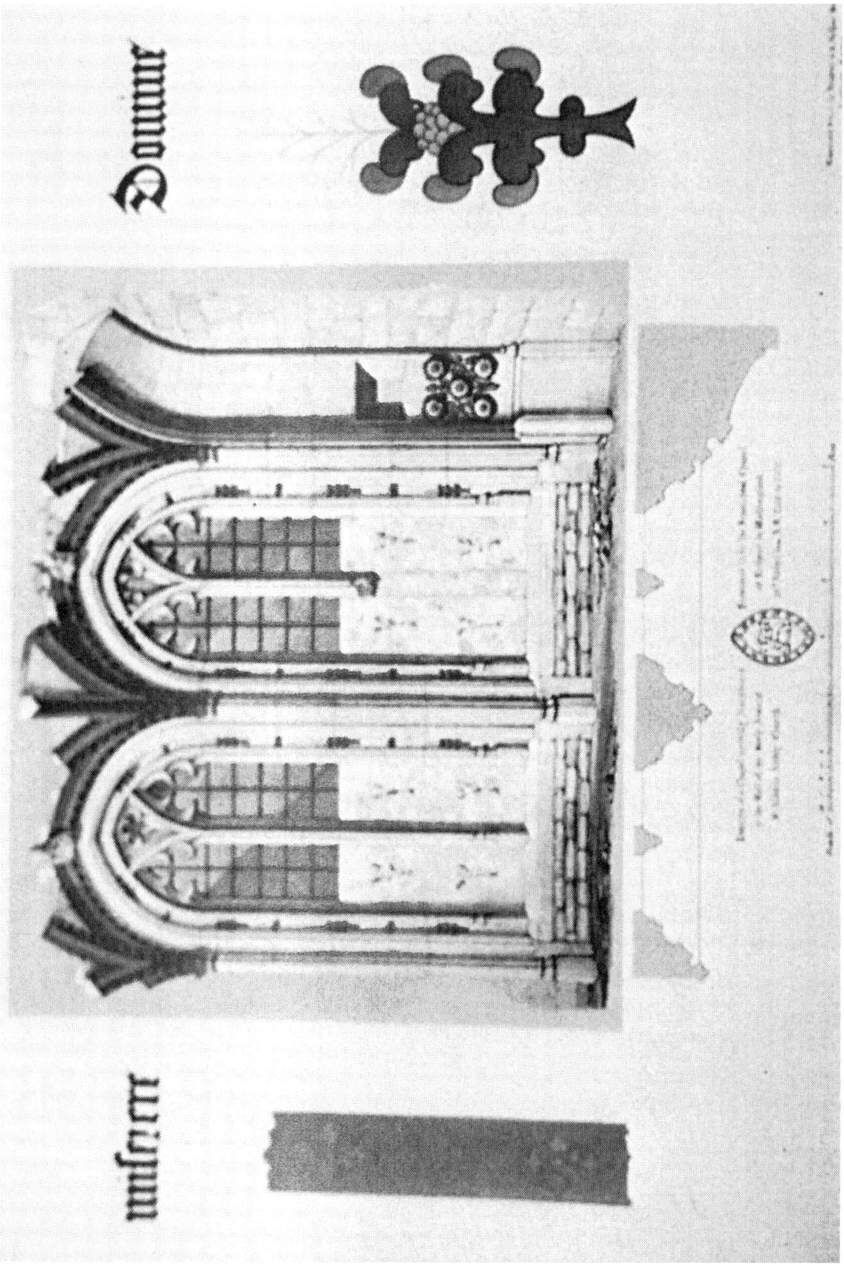

Fig. 66   The Wheathampstead chantry, built 1429. Excavated by Boutell in 1846. Now destroyed.

general area (see rear plan). An economical solution was to place the chapel outside the aisle between two buttresses and Abbot John of Wheathampstead settled for this. His chapel was 'outside the south aisle of the Presbytery in the monks' cemetery'. One had only to knock out part of the wall between the buttresses, build a bit of wall across to join the buttress ends, and vault over the newly-created space to form a mausoleum effect. He constructed his chantry in 1429, during his first term of office. The windows above it had to be partly curtailed. When he resigned, it served for a time as a chantry for his personal friend, Humphrey, Duke of Gloucester. In his second term of office, Wheathampstead hired a marbler to make his tomb for twenty shillings. Most of the chantry chapel was demolished at the Reformation but the antiquary, Charles Boutell, had it excavated in 1846. He found the tomb empty and evidence that the chapel had been vaulted. On the window jambs he found gilding and pigment in red, blue, green and yellow, while an aumbry to the right of the altar had the entwined roses of Lancaster and York painted nearby. It has the inscription 'God have mercy' but no evidence survived either of the shield of arms (he was a Bostock) or of his badges, the eagle and the lamb. Carefully drawn, coloured diagrams of the chapel were published before it was demolished. The site is marked today by the Cedar Tree Door, which was moved from elsewhere in the abbey to fill in the gaping hole.

The Wheathampstead badges were the symbols of his patron saints, the eagle for St. John the Evangelist and the lamb for St. John the Baptist. They stand in circular frames with leafy foliage around (see fig. 45), the same idea as in the Monks' Choir ceiling. He also had the *Christ in Glory* mural at the west end of the Presbytery blotted out (no doubt it was very shabby) and had his badges painted over.

The only royal chantry in the abbey is that of Humphrey, Duke of Gloucester, brother of Henry V. His portrait now hangs in Arras in France; it is believed to be a copy of a contemporary study, made by Jacques de Boucq in the time of King Philip II. Humphrey was a complex character, an ingenious military man, self-indulgent in his private life, ambitious and misguided in his political career. He earned a permanent place in history for his unique contribution to classical learning in the universities of England through the gift to Oxford of volumes from his library; it formed the basis of the Bodleian. He was a close friend of Abbot Wheathampstead but he died in mysterious circumstances on 23rd February 1447. Although murder was suspected, it was never proven.

His chantry chapel occupies the best position next to the shrine, lying open to the interior of the Saint's Chapel, but screened at the south by ironwork (see fig. 77). The triple arches between the piers must have sheltered an east facing altar. Above, in three tiers, are six bays of openwork panelling with canopies. A manuscript in the British Library describes how candles were lit daily in this chapel and the mass read by two priests. Once a year, on the anniversary of his death, thirteen poor men carried torches around his tomb and money was given out to the abbot, the monks and the two local anchoresses at St. Michael's and St. Peter's parish churches. To finance this enterprise, Duke Humphrey had presented the priory of Pembroke as a cell to St. Albans abbey in 1441.

The Gloucester chantry, like certain others, has a vault beneath the floor rather than a tomb at pavement level. Inside it, a mural in black and white painted on the eastern wall depicts a *Crucifix*; Christ is shown as the Mystic Grape, with four chalices collecting the water and blood from his wounds for the two main sacraments of the church, baptism and eucharist. Antiquarian drawings show a skull at the base of the crucifix, illustrating the mediaeval belief that Adam had been buried on the site of the crucifixion, but this skull is no longer visible on the wall.

The best quality chantries had fan vaulting and this one has miniature fan vaults with openwork pendants. Red pigment survives in places. All the carvings on the chantry are of the greatest delicacy. Appearing repeatedly is the Duke's badge, a Garden of Adonis, a bowl of quick growing plants which soon die, a reminder of mortality. This device was popular amongst the Humanists of Italy in the mid-fifteenth century. The shield of arms of Duke Humphrey, carved in low relief, also appear on the chantry; shields figure prominently on chantry chapels as a means of identification.

Abbot William Wallingford, 1476–1492, we are told, 'for the building of his chapel and tomb on the south near the high altar, with railings and marble slab with a figure on it, with other ornaments of the chapel . . . expended £100.' He had chosen the next best position for his chantry. An arch was cut through the thick Norman wall and iron screenwork placed on either side. The original figured slab and altar have both been lost but have been replaced by a modern altar. Fitting out these chapels was a costly business, as vestments, service books, sacred vessels and a brazier to warm the officiating priest, as well as wine, bread and candles were all needed. The large quantities of candles burning in all the chantries and producing smoke and fumes, caused a real ventilation problem in the churches.

The mouldings used on this chantry suggest that the architect was Robert Stowell, the King's Mason who placed the high vaults on the nave of Westminster Abbey and who designed St. Margaret, Westminster. Stowell was absent from Westminster during the correct period, 1481-2. The top of the chantry has a heavy cornice with cresting, whose decorative motifs are very close indeed to bosses in Westminster Abbey. The corners of the chantry are very broadly chamfered.

Fig. 67   Chantry chapel of Abbot William Wallingford, 1476-1483.

The entrance to the chantry is at the south-west, with a square label over a four-centred arch. Filling the spandrils are leaves with finely scalloped edges which are characteristic of Stowell's work. The shield of arms with nine wheat ears in groups of three is sometimes erroneously attributed to Wheathampstead who was John Bostock. The Bostock arms, however, are *sable a fesse argent* cut off at the ends. The shield with nine wheatears also appears on the reredos or High Altar screen, and this is clearly described in the abbey records as being Wallingford's gift.

Digressing briefly from chantry chapels, we will now consider this screen which was built in 1484. A reredos is an ornamental screen of stone or wood covering the wall at the back of an altar. It might also consist of a piece of tapestry or embroidery, a painted panel or a row of statues in niches. A reredos was usually as wide as the altar itself. The murals in the nave of the abbey are considered to be very early examples of surviving reredoses. In the fourteenth century they became very much enlarged, as for example in the chapel at New College, Oxford which was founded in 1380.

The lofty, free-standing reredos at St. Albans cost one hundred marks to build; an almost identical one at Winchester cathedral was probably the work of the same group of craftsmen. The two side doors allowed the priest to walk completely around the altar asperging it. The screen is designed in three bays, and the lowest part in the middle probably holding the painting from Lombardy (including Milan, Bergamo and Brescia) given by Abbot de la Mare. In the thirteen niches above were the statues of Christ and the apostles, and above that a great silver crucifix attended by the apostle John, the Virgin Mary and angels. The sixteen niches on the two side bays held statues of saints; the canopies of these niches have triple gables which merge with the pedestals of the statues above. At the top of the reredos is a heavy cornice.

Because the screen is set in the midst of open arches, it is returned on north and south by shorter screens. There are doorways in these screens with basket-shaped heads. The wooden doors have transoms and traceried panels. An antiquarian drawing by William Stukeley dated 1720 shows the extreme verticality of the eastern face and the recess in the middle for sedilia (see fig. 42). A niche above apparently held the silver statue of St. Alban given by King Edward I; the side niches held angels. The delicacy of the canopy work exhibits virtuoso carving.

To accommodate the screen, the shrine of St. Alban was moved slightly eastwards, to the position it presently occupies. The shrine was no longer visible from the crossing after this great screen had been erected.

We complete our chantry series with the last and finest one, that of Abbot Ramryge, 1492–1521. It is the cage type of chantry, located north of the High Altar; rectangular on plan, it almost fills the arch above. This chantry chapel is considered to be one of the finest in the country.

A drawing of the chantry appeared in *The Builder* for 1895 showing how the design accommodates the three steps leading up to the High Altar. The lowest stage is conceived along the lines of a chancel screen, solid below, and open above. There are four bays with three lights each plus two bays of two lights. The

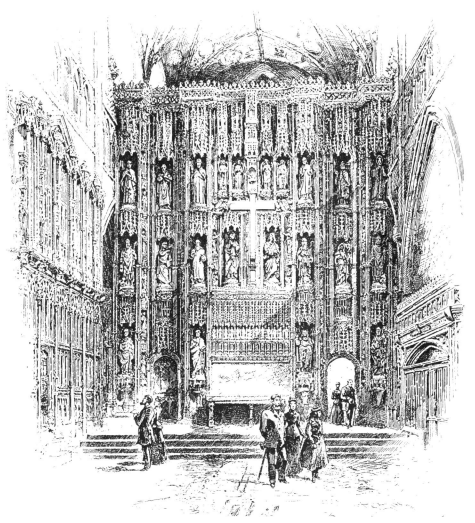

*Fig. 68   High altar screen, gift of Abbot William Wallingford, 1484.
Drawn by F G Kitton.*

door, which is in the south-west corner, has four transoms and the
only mediaeval linenfold panelling in the abbey. The cage in the
upper stage is also solid below with panels, alternating with
niches, above. The all over network of horizontals and verticals is
typical of the late Perpendicular period and ogee domes, a
popular motif in the reign of Henry VIII, are much in evidence.
They appear also at St. George's Chapel, Windsor, which was
completed in 1511.

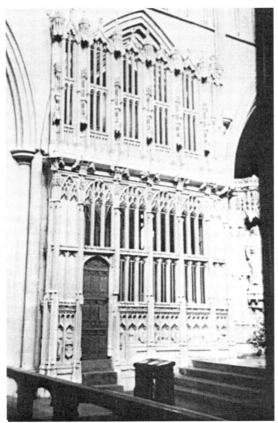

*Fig. 69   Chantry chapel of Abbot Thomas Ramryge,
d. 1521*

The detailing of the chantry is of very high quality, including much use of inscriptions to form decorative bands. The *Martyrdom of St. Alban* is represented in low relief on the spandril of the south door; the figures are in Tudor costume in a foliage setting. Around the cornice are the shields of arms of SS Alban and Amphibalus, of Henry VIII and of the principal cells of the abbey. The shields are of an elaborate, late form and the abbot's shield has two rams as supporters. The rams are from his *rebus*, a symbolical representation of his name, popular among the higher clergy of that day. In this case, the letters RYGE are inscribed on the collar of a ram; alternatively, the letters RYGE appear after a small sculptured ram. The mouldings and buttresses on the chantry are very complex; there is much use of an 'X' form in the tracery and the low relief sculpture is much undercut.

Inside the chapel, there is fan vaulting above, panelling at the sides and three niches for statues at the east end. The slab of the abbot which forms the pavement is engraved with the figure of the abbot and edged by a strip of brass with an inscription. The antiquary Oldfield left a drawing of this.

Ramryge died in 1521, and three abbots followed him, Wolsey, Catton and Boreman. It was under Boreman that the abbey surrendered on 5th December 1539 and to the fate of the building, when it was in the care of the Corporation of St. Albans, we will now turn our attention.

References

BOUTELL (R CHARLES). ('Discovery at St. Albans'). *The Archaeological Journal*. II (1846) 386–7.

BRANDON (J A). An analysis of gothick architecture. 1874.

CAVALIER (H O). 'The symbolism of the brass of Thomas de la Mare.' *Trans SAHAAS* (1929) 274–278.

COOK (G H). Mediaeval chantries and chantry chapels. London. 1963.

DUGDALE (SIR WILLIAM). Monasticon anglicanum. II, pt. 1. J Caley, ed. London. 1819. 178ff.

EAMES (PENELOPE). Medieval furniture: furniture in England, France and the Netherlands from the twelfth to the fifteenth century. The Furniture History Society. London. 1977.

FINUCANE (R C). 'The use and abuse of medieval miracles.; *History*. LX, no. 198. February 1975. 1–10.

HARVEY (JOHN). Henry Yevele, 1320 to 1400: the life of an English architect. London. 1946.

KNIGHT (MAUDE C). 'Humphrey, Duke of Gloucester.; *Trans SAHAAS*. (1903–4). 51–86.

PERRYCOSTE (W B C). 'The Ramryge chantry.' *The Abbey Magazine*. XI, no. 3 (March, 1971) 13 and 15: 'A prayer in stone'. *ibid*. XI, no. 4 (April, 1971) 7–9.

ROBERTS (EILEEN). 'Thomas Wolvey, mason'. *The Archaeological Journal*.CXXIX (1972) 119–144.

. . . 'Robert Stowell'. *Journal of the British Archaeological Association*, Series 3. XXXV (1972) 24–38.

. . . 'Wheathampstead or Wallingford?' *The Alban Link*. I (1974) 4.

ROGERS (JOHN CHARLES). 'The watching loft in St. Albans abbey church'. *Country Life*. 17 January 1931. 74–76.

'The Ramryge chantry'. *Builders Journal and Architectural Record* (27 Jan. 1897).

SPENCER (BRIAN). 'London – St. Albans return'. *The London Archaeologist*. (Spring, 1969) 34–35.

WALKER (LEONARD). To dine with Duke Humphrey. Romford. 1987.

WOOLLEY (ERNEST). 'The brass of Thomas de la Mare, St. Albans Abbey church, description'. *Trans SAHAAS*. (1928) 172–175.

. . . 'The wooden watching loft in St. Albans abbey church'. *ibid*. (1929) 246–254.

. . . 'The Ramryge chantry in Saint Albans abbey church'. *ibid*. (1930) 31–36.

Part IV

THE HIDDEN CENTURIES

Chapter 13

THE DISSOLUTION TO THE CIVIL WAR

Our theme up to now has been architectural development; for three centuries after 1530, deterioration would be a better word. For this period our approach must be almost social history, showing how attitudes to the mediaeval church evolved; how, from being despised and rejected in 1530, concern and care during three hundred years gradually re-emerge.

Abbot Ramryge died in 1521 and Wolsey, who succeeded him, drew the income but did no work. The abbey fell deeply into debt. The last two abbots were Catton and Boreman and under them no fault could be found either in scholarship or in morals. The account books for the last days are pathetically mundane: charcoal was bought for the dormitories, the organ was mended, moles had to be caught and nettles cut down.

The abbey surrendered on 5th December 1539 and the ancient monastic seal of ivory relinquished. The income at the Dissolution was over £2,100 p.a. The abbot was given a pension and the thirty-eight monks annuities. Then, twelve days later, the spoil was seized, a hundred ounces of pure gold, a thousand ounces of parcel gilt and silver, three thousand ounces of gilt plate. St. Albans' relics, some believe, eventually found their way to Cologne. Abbey lands were distributed amongst the nobility, including Anne of Cleves. For a brief period the abbey remained free of episcopal surveillance, but in 1542 it became an archdeaconry of the diocese of Lincoln. It remained there for only eight years, when it was transferred to the diocese of London.

From this time forth, the abbey plan was drastically altered, for a public right of way was cut through the antechapel and the triple arches on the east of the Saint's Chapel were blocked with a rubble wall (see figs. 42, 73, 90). The shrine base had been broken up to provide materials for this. In 1551 the abbot, turned school-master, purchased the Lady Chapel for use as a school, with provisions for this being written into the Town Charter of 1553. The magistrates took over the Great Gatehouse as a gaol and in the same year, the mayor and burgesses purchased from King Edward VI the abbey church to serve their parish, assigning to it the parish of St. Andrew. This chapel was allowed to tumble into disrepair. Four hundred pounds was the price paid for the abbey. Although a thousand people took communion, their annual donations scarcely supported a single priest, either 'from coldness of devotion or poverty'. This was an ill omen for the future.

A sixteenth century mayor of St. Albans, Robert Shrimpton, d. 1605, was a boy at the time and 'remember'd most things relating to ye Buildings of the Abbey . . . of all which he would often discourse in his Lifetime'. He saw the actual destruction itself, defacing the monuments of the dead, breaking up graves and burning bones, removal of brasses and anything hanging on the tombs, like achievements or canopies, which were worth taking away. Shrimpton saw the treasures which were seized, the images of gold and silver, precious jewels and rich stones, costly shrines, altars and tabernacles and rood lofts; pyxes, patens and basins; ewers, candlesticks and crewets; chalices, censers and vessels of gold and silver; rich ornaments and fine linens, costly hangings, altar cloths; jet, marble and precious wood; brass, iron and lead bells.

The next three hundred years are the most neglected in all the abbey's history. The Dissolution seemed a definitive end, and a building in decline is less interesting than a building's growth. The alterations were of a minor character and rather second rate. Our sources are but scattered allusions in *The Corporation Records*, the *St. Albans School Accounts*, the *Marian Survey* and church Briefs. Much was lost in the Old Rectory fire of 1743 although some accounts survive amongst the Gape family papers. The evidence of map makers, print makers and topographical writers must all be gleaned. The furnishings for this period have themselves been dismantled as effectively as the mediaeval ones. We will attempt a chronological narrative, drawing on the dated illustrations and writings which have survived.

Now the villain comes on the scene, Richard Lee, architect and engineer. He had been in the King's service from his youth, becoming an expert in fortification; his work at Berwick-on-Tweed was the first time Renaissance fortification methods were used in England. As early as 1540, the year after the abbey was dissolved, the king granted him Sopwell, both the manor and the priory and there he built himself a mansion, Lee Hall, using the priory church as his Great Hall and overbuilding his other apartments on the lines of the priory foundations. In 1544, he brought back to the delighted king a plan of Edinburgh and its port, and for this service he was knighted, the first English architect ever to receive this honour.

From Holyrood in Scotland he also brought back a bronze lectern which served St. Stephen's church until it was stolen in 1985. He brought back too a brass font in which the kings of Scotland had been baptised; this he inscribed in a boastful way and presented to the abbey church. Lee now wished to purchase the abbey precincts and in 1549 'the defaced house of St. Albans' was assessed for the value of its stone, lead, wood and other materials. Leave to purchase was granted in 1550.

Lee acquired the monastic site except for the church and the Lady Chapel. He could not have the buildings at the west of the church, those surrounding the Great Court, including the stables, the Watergate, the Great Gateway itself, etc., as they were in the use of the Crown. He was given Kitchener's Mead, Pond Mead, the Abbey Orchard and Pond Wicks. Shrimpton tells us that .'the stones and chiefest stuff' taken from the abbey were used in Lee Hall. In fact, Lee had already commenced a piecemeal reconstruction of the mansion on a more up to date H-plan, the work lasting from 1547 to 1557 but he never carried this to completion. Having demolished the buildings and removed the materials, he reconveyed the land back to the last abbot in 1551.

Looking at the ruins of his grand house today, one is reminded of that strange old superstition that the family fortunes of those who profited from the dissolution of the monasteries all ended in blight and barreness. When Mary succeeded to the throne in 1553, she contemplated refounding the abbey, carrying out the so-called *Marian Survey* in 1556 to assess the rents from the various monastic properties. This survey casts some light on the state of the monastic buildings at that time.

When her sister Elizabeth became queen, she was disturbed by the dirty and neglected condition of parish church interiors. She wrote to her Commissioners in 1560/1 ordering that the Ten Commandments be inscribed 'to give some comely ornament and demonstration that the same was a place of religion and prayers'. This was done and the Creed and Lord's Prayer were inscribed near one another. The usual position for these black-letter inscriptions in the English language was on the eastern wall of the chancel or occasionally on either side of the chancel arch. In St. Albans abbey they were placed in the choir, on either side of the western tower arch, in the hollows scooped out in the early fourteenth century to receive new choir stalls (see figs. 21 and 74 right). What pulpit was used at this time we do not know. Very few Elizabethan pulpits survive, because preaching had sunk to a low ebb in the sixteenth century; only four sermons were required to be preached in a year.

When the Corporation purchased the church in 1553, they had acquired both a right and an obligation. They had the right of advowson and could present to the Bishop a candidate of their choice as Rector. They also became responsible for the upkeep of the fabric and to meet this obligation took various steps. From 1556, the son of a burgess could become a Freeman on the payment of four shillings and sixpence towards the upkeep of the fabric.

An interesting sidelight on this period appears in *The Corporation Records*. In 1558, because the glass windows of the school were constantly being broken by boys getting into the schoolyard, it was decided to keep 'the door into Holywell Street' locked and only open at service time. Obviously Sumpter Yard was still a walled enclosure (see fig. 90).

The threat of invasion by the Spanish Armada offered an opportunity which the Corporation quickly seized. Over three thousand pounds of lead were stripped from the abbey roof (what replaced it we are not told) and sold for the making of bullets. The proceeds were used to build a Market House, the rents from which could be used for the upkeep of the fabric. These money raising efforts were soon to prove far from adequate. Because the abbey building was loaned for use in two emergencies, one local, the other national, another source of finance was opened to them.

In 1589 the Assizes were held in St. Albans abbey, apparently during an outbreak of plague in Hertford. In 1594, when plague raged in London, the law courts moved from Westminster Great Hall to the abbey for the Michaelmas term, that is, during October and November. To raise money to fit up the abbey as a law court, a levy was held upon the citizens of the town upon the pain of a fine of twenty shillings or a gaol sentence. It may have been through the influence of Sir Francis Bacon of Gorhambury, 1561–1626, that the law courts were held here. An inscription painted on the wall at the north-west end of the abbey, which is preserved by the antiquary Henry George Oldfield, commemorated this event.

Because the abbey had served the nation in this way, Queen Elizabeth I gave permission to the Archdeacon in 1596 for money to be collected by Brief in five counties (i.e. the Diocese of London) 'once only' for the repair and upkeep of the church. These Briefs nevertheless proved an important source of revenue for abbey upkeep through the years. They were Letters Patent issued by the Sovereign as head of the church, licensing collection in churches throughout England for a specified object; otherwise, it was illegal at that time to collect money outside one's own parish. The Brief was printed on a sheet of paper, and a copy sent to each church. It set forth the royal license, why the money was needed and had a blank space at the bottom to fill in the sum collected. Briefs were read out during the church service after the recitation of the Nicene Creed. A chest, now in the north transept of the abbey church, dates from the period under discussion. It was made by a joiner in the Early Renaissance style, with no Gothic ornament whatsoever. It is made of oak and its legs lift it well off the ground. The decoration derives from the architectural copy books from Germany and Holland which were in circulation at this time. The carved decoration is reminiscent of the slashed costume details of the Elizabethan period.

About the year 1600, a certain Thomas Preston bought an 'Olde Pigeon House and pulled the same down and erected it on (a parcell of ground in or near St. Albans) and afterwards put up a chimney and made thereof a tenement which is now called the Rounde House'. A pigeon house had been erected by Abbot John de la Moote ca. 1400, apparently the very building re-erected upon the foundations of St. German's Gate to make the present public house, the Fighting Cocks, which was restored in 1971.

John Chapple records that the date 1605 was found on the back of wainscot panelling which lined the walls of the Presbytery. A piece of old woodwork which has now been reconstructed into a cupboard standing in the south Presbytery aisle, has carved decoration of that period. Perhaps the 1605 panelling was similar.

The monastic buildings at the west of the church had been retained by the Crown at the Dissolution. These included the Almonry, the Great Gateway (used as a gaol), the Prior of Tynemouth's lodging (apparently part of the Great Gateway), the Deacon's Lodging (not yet located) and the Watergate or Hamme's Tower (south of the Great Gateway, see fig. 71). In 1607 a survey was made of these buildings with a view to putting the King's Stables into repair. They lay to the west of the Great Court. The Great Horse Stable was one hundred and fourteen feet long and it was to be newly planked and and joisted. The Hobby Stable, eighty feet long, for smaller horses and the Sadler's Office, the house of the Master of the Horse and the Forge, were also mentioned as needing repair.

In 1610 the cartographer, John Speed, decorated his map of Hertfordshire with a view of St. Albans on which the walls of Verulamium are outlined and the martyrdom of St. Alban is re-enacted in the foreground. The cluster of buildings meant to represent St. Albans is dominated by two outsize churches, the one in the foreground apparently the abbey. It is cruciform in shape with a crossing tower and high pitched roofs, and is a very schematic rendering.

James I personally visited the abbey on 20th July 1612 on his way from Theobalds to the north. After his inspection, he agreed to issue another Brief for collection in England and Wales 'out of his princely zeal and pious inclination to preserve so ancient a monument and memorable witness of the first conversion of this Kingdom from Paganism to Christianity'. This very Brief was found by a member of the St. Albans Archaeological Society entered in the Churchwardens Accounts at Brington, Northants., for the year 1613. Three readings of the Brief in this church brought in sixteen shillings and eight pence, a higher return than usual as Briefs collected on average only half a crown The Brief *in toto* brought in about £2,000 'which sum was most truly and justly expended' it seems, mainly on the roof over the Saint's Chapel. The archdeaconry official who collected the money was James Rolfe of St. Stephen's parish and his funerary tablet in that church makes reference to the Brief. A verse inscribed under a south window in the body of the abbey church read, in part:

... Offa raised this heap of stones;
Which, after by devouring time abusd,
Into the dying parts had life infusd
By James the First, of England, to become
The glory of Alban's Proto-martyrdom.

The antiquary, John Weever, visited the abbey in 1625 recording the inscriptions on the brasses and tombs then remaining. The brass font from Holyrood, given by Sir Richard Lee, was still in the abbey at the time of Weever's visit.

From the reign of James I survive the famous livery cupboards from which a charity of bread for twenty poor women was dispensed. These are interesting examples of the joinery of the period and are roughly contemporary with the famous staircase at Hatfield House. Motifs, such as the moulded cornice, the brackets and dentils, have been taken from architecture and adapted to furniture making. The decorative hinges and the open balusters on the doors, products of the ancient art of lathe turning, all are worth examining.

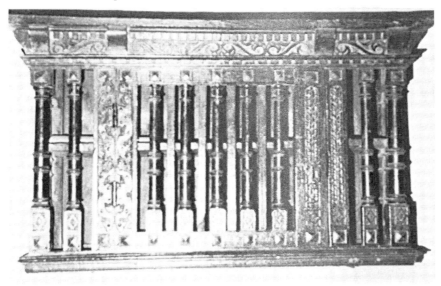

Fig. 70   Livery (or dole) cupboard of the Jacobean period.

The other aumbry has strap work on the end and borders of formalised vines with Tudor roses, oak leaves and acorns, and twisted guilloches. There is no colour applied to the inlay, so the effect stems entirely from the beauty of carved and polished oak.

A remarkable cluster of evidence comes down to us from the early 1630s, in the form of a map, a book and a picture. What had been the stimulus behind this abundance of source material? These were the years when Inigo Jones' career was at its height, when St. Paul's, Covent Garden was being built, when Old St. Paul's was being given a classical skin and when the Queen's House, Greenwich, was being completed.

The book, which we will consider first, is a series of recollections by the antiquary, John Shrimpton, dating ca. 1631. His father Robert, mayor of St. Albans on three occasions, and whom we have already mentioned, was honoured by burial in the tomb of Abbot Ramryge in 1605. John Shrimpton records the macabre details of the opening of the tomb. The proportions of the abbot, whose body had not been covered in earth, were plainly visible. On his chest was a very much decayed silver chalice and in

159

Fig. 71' Ink and wash drawing of St. Albans abbey and monastic precincts in the seventeenth century. Attributed to 'John Lievons'. By permission of the British Library, K. Top. XV–49a.

his hand a crozier broken in two pieces and very rotten. On his feet were boots made of little squares of leather sewn together and these were in good condition. All these relics were appropriated by Thomas Howard, 18th Earl of Arundel and it is not known whether they still survive.

The map, by Benami Hare, dating from 1634, although schematic is a most informative document. (Actually, what survives today in the City Library is only a copy of the lost original.) The land cleared by Lee is called Abbey ruins but the buildings to the west retained by the Crown are clearly shown: the Watergate, the Great Court, the King's Barns and the Guest House range. The abbey church is shown with low-pitched roofs, some with parapets, others with battlements. A tower with a cross suggests the Hertfordshire spike. The Early English clerestory seems to be obliterated, and the Lady Chapel windows are diminutive. The Vintry is full of trees and the gardens north of the nave stretch down to the church. St. Andrew's chapel has disappeared.

The third piece of evidence is a pen and ink drawing attributed to 'John Lievons', supposedly Jan Lievens who shared a studio with Rembrandt van Rijn in the 1620s and was in England under the patronage of King Charles I between 1631 and 1635. The Dutch artists were intrepid travellers and specialised in small drawings representing actual places with great accuracy either as plans for future projects or in hope of finding patrons. This early drawing of the abbey shows clearly some of the monastic buildings still intact, from left to right, the Great Gateway, the King's Stables, the wall between the gateway and the abbey church, the Water Gate, the Great Court and an unidentified building off centre to the right. In the church itself, the clerestory windows are still intact, a Hertfordshire spike is clearly seen on the tower and the shape of the lantern windows has not yet been altered. The line left by the high-pitched roof is still clearly visible on the tower walls. A former mayor, Baskerfield, presented this drawing to the British Museum; it is now in the King's Topography section. The drawing has been engraved at least three times and a watercolour copy appears in C H Ashdown's book, *St. Albans historical and picturesque* opposite page ten.

Turning through the pages of Gibbs' *Corporation Records*, one is struck by the important role church attendance and ceremonial played in the civic consciousness. A 1634 entry tells us, for example, that Aldermen had to conform to the rites of the Church of England. The Mayor was expected to attend church on Sundays and Festival days, accompanied by the Aldermen and four Assistants appointed especially for this purpose. If the Mayor attended divine service without wearing his robes of office, he was fined twenty shillings.

A drawing by Rembrandt in the Teylers Museum, Netherlands dated 1640 was possibly based on sketches taken back by other artists. It misinterprets the Slype roof as a flight of steps rising up to the south transept window which is expressed as a door. There is no record of Rembrandt ever coming to England, and this misinterpretation is understandable when one had never seen the actual building. There is no historical precedent for the south transept being used as a principal entrance.

References

ADDLESHAW (C W O), and ETCHELLS (FREDERICK). The architectural setting of Anglican worship. London. 1948.

ASHDOWN (CHARLES H). St. Albans historical and picturesque. London 1893.

. . . 'The accounts of St. Albans Grammar School'. *The Home Counties Magazine.* (1904) 52–59 and 186–196; (1905) 66–68 and 266–275.

BAKER (ERIC P). 'The cult of St. Alban at Cologne'. *Archaeological Journal.* XCIV. (1937) 207–256.

CAMDEN (WILLIAM). Britannia. Trans. Philemon Holland. London. 1610.

CAVALIER (H O). 'King James I and St. Albans Abbey'. *Trans SAHAAS.* (1930) 25–30.

CHAPPLE (JOHN). A short history of the abbey church of St. Albans. St. Albans. 1882.

CHAUNCY (SIR HENRY). The historical antiquities of Hertfordshire. II. 240–296. London. 1700.

GAPE (ERNEST). 'St. Albans Abbey in the seventeenth and eighteenth centuries'. *The Home Counties Magazine.* V (1903) 123–7.

GIBBS (A E). The corporation records of St. Albans. St. Albans. 1890.

. . . 'Two Briefs for repairing the abbey church of St. Albans'. *Middlesex and Herts. Notes and Queries*. (1895) 97–99 and 142–145.

HOWARD (W WESTON) and PERRYCOSTE (W BERNARD C). 'Some notes on abbey charities'. *The Abbey Magazine*. XI, No. 7. (July, 1971) 6–8; 'Abbey charities II'. *ibid*. XI, No. 8. (August, 1971) 6–8.

JOHNSON (EDWARD A) and WEAVER (O JOHN). 'Excavations at Sopwell, St. Albans. Interim report for 1962–3'. SAHAAS.

KILVINGTON (FRANK I). A short history of St. Albans School. St. Albans. 1970.

KNOWLES (DOM DAVID). The religious orders in England. III. The Tudor age. Cambridge. 1959.

McENERY (JOHN). Trans. 'The Marian survey of St. Albans'. (April, 1974).

OLDFIELD (HENRY GEORGE). 'Hertfordshire Antiquities' with notes by John Meyrick, F.S.A. 9 vols. Hertford County Record Office.

PAGE (WILLIAM). 'The Marian Survey of St. Albans'. *Trans SAHAAS*. (1893–4). 8–24.

SCARISBRICK (J J). The dissolution of the monasteries – the case of St. Albans. Hertford. n.d.

SHAW (S G). History of Verulam and St. Albans. St. Albans. 1815.

SHRIMPTON (JOHN). The antiquities of Verulam and St. Albans. Ed. Carson I.A. Ritchie. SAHAAS. 1966.

WALCOTT (MACKENZIE EC). 'Survey of the site of St. Albans abbey, 2 Edward VI'. *The Gentleman's Magazine*. (1865) pt. ii. 491–494.

WEEVER (JOHN). Funerall monuments. London. 1631.

WILLCOX (REV. FRANK). 'The accounts of St. Albans Grammar School'. *Middlesex and Herts. Notes and Queries*. I (Jan. 1895) 11–15; (April 1895) 39–42; (Oct. 1895) 138–142; II (Jan. 1896) 40–43.

WILTON HALL (H R). 'Notes and memoranda on some Hertfordshire churches at the beginning of this century'. *Trans. SAHAAS*. New series. 1 (189–6) 29–52.

. . . 'Report on the muniments of the Gape family'. *Idem*. XVII (1905) 3–34.

WOOD (JAMES). 'The Fighting Cocks, St. Albans'. *Hertfordshire Countryside*. XXVII, no. 158 (June, 1972) 46–47.

Chapter 14

THE LATER SEVENTEENTH CENTURY

The Civil War, 1642 to 1646, was a menacing interlude. There were sins of omission: the townspeople were hard pressed financially in paying ship money and in supporting, on the rates, royalist prisoners in gaol. Inevitably, the abbey fabric suffered from neglect.

The sins of commission fall into three groups. First was the sheer vandalism inevitable when troops were passing incessantly through the town and actually stationed there for months on end. This is a complicated story in itself. Prisoners were brought from Colchester and from the north and incarcerated in the abbey church and in St. Peter's. An oft-quoted inscription on the south side of the north door of the east face of the reredos read:

'Hugh Lewis, Souldier in his Majesty's army, taken
prisoner at Ravensfield, Northamptonshire. Ser. y --
Day of June, 1645.'

This inscription is very difficult to find today; there is a rubbing of it in the Hine collection of graffiti in the Society of Antiquaries, but even that is so blurred as to be almost illegible. As to funerary monuments, S G Shaw writes of 'the great devastations that have been wantonly committed amongst them, (chiefly by the soldiery of Cromwell)'.

Metal objects are especially vulnerable in time of war and not surprisingly the brass font from Holyrood disappeared. Fuller writes in his *Worthies* that it 'was taken away, in the late cruel war, as it seems, by those hands which suffered nothing how sacred soever to stand, which could be converted to money. There is a wooden one to supply its place, which is said to be made of the same shape with the old font.' The iron grilles on the chantry chapels of Gloucester and Wallingford somehow survived. The brasses, including the incomparable de la Mare brass, were saved by being turned downwards in the Presbytery during the period of hostilities.

Finally, Puritan zeal destroyed many precious things, for parliamentary authority was actually given to destroy surviving images. It must have been at this time that the south facing murals in the abbey nave were defaced, those of *SS Alban and Amphibalus*, *St. Zita of Lucca*, *St. Thomas of Canterbury* and *St. Christopher*. The west facing murals escaped this fate, being already covered by whitewash. William Dowsing of Norfolk was the most notorious of the wreckers going 'about the Country like a Bedlam breaking glasse windows, having battered and beaten downe all our painted glasse . . . and having . . . defaced and digged up the floore of our Chappels' as a contemporary put it. A parliamentary survey of 1649 went carefully over the Crown possessions to the west of the church with a view to assessing damage and William Page prints its contents on page twenty of his *Marian Survey* article, a useful document in the study of the convent buildings.

All was not damage, however; an engraving of the abbey by Daniel King appeared in 1655 during the Commonwealth (see fig. 72). It is one of two illustrating Dugdale's famous *Monasticon Anglicanum*, one of the earliest antiquarian books. In the sixteenth century men like Hall, Holinshead, Leland and Camden, had written down what they had observed. Now Sir William Dugdale, a hundred years later, set out to study and illustrate mediaeval architecture. A group of sympathetic friends gathered round him at the Bodleian Library, forming the nucleus of the Society of Antiquaries. This was refounded in 1717/8 and thereafter a stream of county histories rolled off the press. Although Daniel King produced a charming drawing, how accurate a record is it? St. Andrew's chapel is no more but the arches it shared with the abbey church have been filled in with masonry and supported by buttresses. This wall gave much trouble in the nineteenth century. The roof is neatly leaded and the set of turrets is complete including the bell tower of the Lady Chapel which held the Sanctus bell, now remounted at the west door. There are two porches in the eastern arm, one for the public passage, one to serve as the main entrance to the parish church. The triforium windows are not exposed and the Lady Chapel is given four bays although it in fact has three. The proportions of the north window of the north transept leave much to be desired. One concludes therefore that the King drawing is a general impression rather than an accurate record.

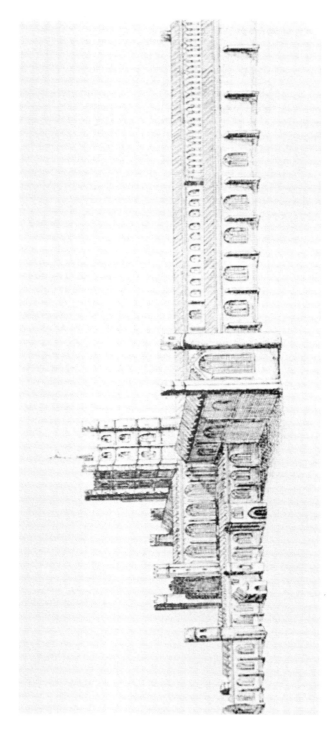

Fig. 72   North elevation of St. Albans abbey engraved by Daniel King, 1655.

The *St. Albans School Account Book* for the year 1658 and thereafter is interesting: candles and candlesticks were purchased to light the school and an hourglass was used to mark the time. Steel andirons, a shovel and tongs fitted out the fireplace inserted in the south wall of the chapel; a view of the south elevation of the Lady Chapel in 1783 shows the flue clearly.

In 1662 the Act of Settlement authorised the use of the Prayer Book once more but there followed a difficult period for the church which was in the hands of the squirearchy for the next two centuries. Then in 1666 the Fire of London occurred with considerable effect upon English church architecture. Eighty-seven mediaeval churches were destroyed and Christopher Wren was given the task of designing fifty-one replacements. Looking at one or two assists in understanding the ideal church interior of that period.

Take for example St. James, Garlickhythe: like other parish churches it had been designed as a setting for Protestant worship in the classical taste so admired at the time. The interior walls were either white, neutral or brown, with no other colour except for the gilding of the decorative details. Wren loved the effect of clear light falling on contrasting surfaces, so replaced coloured glass by plain glass. Exposition was very important in Protestant churches: one recalls Pepys' interest in sermons. It was important that all should be able to see and hear, so the pulpit was placed in a prominent position with a sounding board over it. In this particular church the high box pews are missing, but one should imagine them reaching to the bases of the pillars.

St. Stephen's Walbrook is a good example of Wren's preference for simple, round headed arches and his frequent use of circular windows. As a great wealth of moulded plaster and carved wood adorned his churches, he attracted round him large numbers of fine craftsmen, of which one of the leaders was Grinling Gibbons. Gibbons' font cover at All Hallows, Barking is typical in featuring *putti* and an abundance of flora and fauna.

Wren was a most inventive architect, who enjoyed experimenting with ground plans to fit into confined city sites. A favourite plan was the cross within a square, for example, at St. Martin, Ludgate; the centralised plan was well-suited to contemporary ideas.

Experiments in roofing followed, and Wren tried many variants, including a shallow, saucer dome at St. Mary, Abchurch. When considering the abbey church in the seventeenth century, one should bear Wren's city churches very much in mind.

Topographers paint a melancholy picture of the condition of the abbey at the end of the seventeenth century. Thomas Baskerville of Abingdon called it 'an ancient old fabric, and now much decayed'. Celia Fiennes who rode side-saddle through every county of England in the reign of William and Mary wrote in her journal for 1697 that it was 'much out of repaire . . . the whole Church is so worn away it mourns for some charitable person to help repair it.' Something was being done. *The London Gazette* for December 1681 recorded that Mr Francis Child, goldsmith of Temple Bar, had been appointed by the Bishop of London to receive money collected in England and Wales 'for the repair of the Great and Antient church of St. Albans'. The persons entrusted with the said repairs do humbly request the most Reverend the Archbishops, and the Right Reverend Bishops, and the respective Archdeacons, to further the speedy collection and payment thereof. The Letters Patent of Charles II were dated 26th February 1681.

Apparently this money went on repairs to the timber vault of the Presbytery (see fig. 45). Among the Gape papers is a book recording money received between 1682 and 1684. One of the donors, Sir Harbottle Grimston, gave £100 in instalments; the Bishops of Norwich and Winchester gave money as well as Kings College and Pembroke College in Cambridge. The shields of arms fixed to the springing of the ribs of the vault record the major contributors. When John C Rogers, cathedral architect, was repairing the vault in 1931, he noted the seventeenth century repairs which appeared to him well done. New backbones had been fixed to the lower ends of some of the ribs, badly decayed at the time.

Extra money was needed, however. From Nicholson we learn that the monarchs, William and Mary, made an additional grant in 1689 from some ecclesiastical funds and some old account books amongst the Gape papers show how this money was spent. The outlay was in three main directions: for maintenance, for bringing the fabric in line with current taste and for furniture and fittings. We will look first at maintenance. Expenditure was made on plumbers' work to the steeple, lead for the roof, cleaning the gutters and walls of filth and pulling off weeds, repairing the windows (the roundel in the great east window had been blown down in a gale) making good the great windows at north and south, and mending and glazing the windows in the north and south of the church. The great door needed mending and dust and cobwebs had to be cleaned off the interior walls.

Next, the building was to be modernised. The windows in the lantern were partly filled in to make them round, which can be observed in pictures of the abbey after this date (see fig. 79). The great west doors were encased in deal to effectively cover up the despised Gothic tracery. To make the floor level throughout, huge quantities of earth were brought in to fill the so called 'hollow in the south wing' (in other words, in the south transept) and for 'levelling the ground in the long north aisle'. These floors were then paved in white brick, shown in an eighteenth century engraving. Also shown is the new step at the cloister door which resulted from these changes, as well as the blocked south aisle.

Two windows were newly glazed, one over the north door, the other at the lower end of the south side. These may be the lights provided for the public passageway through the east end of the abbey illustrated in an engraving of ca. 1840. A shilling dated 1696 was found in the masonry of the west porch when it was rebuilt externally, suggesting that the exterior work to the abbey dates from this time.

Finally, money was spent on furnishings and fittings, perhaps the most interesting outlay of all. Evidence for these can be found in contemporary illustrations, as well as in fragments surviving in the abbey today. The new ceiling placed in the crossing tower is shown in an engraving by Storer dated 1820. We have seen how Wren gave interest to the City

Fig. 73   *Public footpath through the antechapel. Engraving ca. 1840.*

churches by varied ceiling treatments: at St. Albans, the crossing below the lantern was filled with a saucer dome of wood supported by ribs (see fig. 74). Light from the lantern was admitted by a circular opening in the middle surrounded by a railing and covered by 'openwork' to prevent accidents. It was adorned by a design of painted scrolls of classic inspiration. Although the false ceiling restricted light, it did prevent draughts. Clear glass filled the pointed clerestory windows of the Presbytery

Fig. 74 View of the crossing looking east in 1820, Storer.

and the walls, including carved stonework, were whitewashed; this neutral interior would be enlivened by the colourful dress of the congregation. Much internal detail is described by Edward Brayley in *Beauties of England and Wales*, 1808.

The old north transept ceiling was already painted with an existing design of shields but, judging from the style, a panel showing the *Martyrdom of St. Alban* must have been added about this time (see fig. 75). It is now preserved in the south Presbytery aisle, and it was clearly painted over a mediaeval panel, similar to the Monks' Choir ceiling, with lettering of the bent ribbon type in a large IHS motif and a mediaeval orle below. The later work has a deep landscape setting with a smooth barked tree and shrubbery to the right and detailed grass and flowers on the hill. An angel plunges down vertically from heaven and Alban, with sunburnt skin and a seraphic expression, holds a long, slender cross. The 'Alban Cross' has been forgotten. Thornhill's frescoes in the dome of St. Paul's, 1716–19, have similar large muscular figures, dramatic poses and simple landscape settings.

We turn now to altar rails. After the mediaeval screen had been torn away, low rails were erected around the altar table. This ensured that it was a fixture; it also kept the dogs away and made certain it was not used by the congregation as a coat rack or a hat stand. Elizabethan communion tables had been protected by rails on three sides, but as the Puritans had ripped out many of these, they had to be replaced after the Restoration. An old drawing shows a straight rail at St. Albans with spiral shafts which could be compared with the turned balusters of the third dole cupboard, installed perhaps for the bread charity of 1716–17 endowed by Richard Hale.

Edward VI had ordered that all stone altars should be replaced by plain wooden tables; on the front of the St. Albans communion table there was a design of Roman arches. These tables would be covered by plum coloured velvet with the IHS monogram embroidered in golden rays. Communion was held only once a quarter as well as at Easter, Whitsun and Christmas and for this the table would be covered by a fair linen cloth on which the church plate would be displayed. At St. Albans, the earliest surviving piece is an Elizabethan chalice of 1560 with another chalice and paten of the seventeenth century.

Sometimes the parish raised money for a special pew for the town officials and churchwardens. In the Gape family papers we read of John Nicholas the Joiner who was paid seventeen pounds three shillings for 'erecting two new pews for the officers of the parish, at the end of the body of the church.' Mr Lord, the Carver, was paid three shillings and elevenpence 'for his work about the same'. This was in 1692–93. This panelling is preserved to the south of the nave altar and its decoration consists of fine foliage scrolls incorporating the arms of St. Albans. It is an important survival as it is both documented and dated. Money was always found to put the corporation pews into good repair even when the church was crumbling over their heads. The Gape papers record money spent in 1693–94 for cushions of serge and worsted with fringe and tow. *The Corporation Records* suggest that more attention was spent on who sat where and on which Alderman's wife was being slighted, than on the essential care of the fabric.

Little evidence has been found on how the church was illuminated. Candles were the only source of light and one would expect silver candlesticks on the table, brass sconces holding single candles attached to the woodwork around the church and a brass candelabrum hanging centrally. At St. Albans, services were held in the morning and afternoon, in daylight hours when less illumination would be necessary, according to the Cumber diaries of 1785. An engraving in Clutterbuck's *History of the County of Hertford* shows a candelabrum hanging before the altar rails.

The Royal Arms, a symbol of royal supremacy, were, according to Brayley, mounted high over the western tower arch. These appeared from the reign of Henry VIII although they did not become compulsory until the reign of Charles II: the St. Albans arms could either be his or those of James II. Some devout Roman Catholics were bitter about substituting what they called a dog and a dragon for the Holy Rood. Some royal arms are moulded in plaster or carved in wood but at St. Albans they are painted on a wooden panel, probably by some sign painter of talent.

The lion and the unicorn are two beautifully carved little figures which adorned the Corporation Pew from the 1820s, when they first appear in engravings (see fig. 74). *The Corporation Records* for 1820 mention 'certain alterations in the old pews'.

On the north of the Presbytery the magnificent Ramryge Chantry still survived and it was appropriated in 1678 by the Faringdons, a local family of Lancashire origins (see fig. 69). They placed their arms (*argent a chevron gules between three leopards' heads sable*) on the chantry chapel and added an inscription. In the Middle Ages, the church's patron had the right to a seat in the chancel so after the Reformation, the Lord of the Manor continued to use his chantry chapel as a particularly grand private pew, where he and his family could sit in splendid seclusion. Their liveried servants sat on a bench behind and there might be curtains, upholstered chairs and even fireplaces for their better comfort.

What the greater did, the lesser emulated. Hence the rise of the box pew, with its doors, lock and keys, and linings of red, green or blue serge fixed with brass studs. The miscellaneous pew sizes in the earliest St. Albans prints suggests piecemeal installation. The sale of these pews emphasised the social hierarchy within the community, with servants sitting on flap seats at the ends and some free benches at the back for the poor. A contemporary engraving shows the restricted circulation which must have resulted. It was common to separate the sexes placing women on the north and men on the south. The panelling is of a simple type, perhaps re-used in a settle now in the St. Albans nave.

From within the box pews, very little could be seen beyond the tall pulpit towering overall, which formed the central focus of the church (see fig. 83). Below it was the reading desk for the clerk who read the responses. The hexagonal pulpit itself was reached by a staircase with twisted baluster rails. The pulpit, which we know from prints, compares well with those in Wren churches not destroyed by bombing, as in St. Stephen Walbrook in London; surviving contracts prove that parts of these pulpits were copied from one another. Panels from the St. Albans pulpit are incorporated in the screen north of the nave altar, placed there by Grimthorpe who finally dismantled it. Each side had a rectangular panel of parquetry with carved mouldings; above are cupids in necklaces between swags of leaves and flowers tied with ribbons. Some parts survive as a chest in the south choir aisle and other parts are found in a cupboard in the south Presbytery aisle.

Obviously, this work is a provincial example of the school of Grinling Gibbons, whose surpassing work can be seen in the choir stalls of St. Paul's cathedral in London. It is interesting to remember that Edward Strong, master mason and quarry owner, 1652–1724, held important contracts under both Wren and Vanbrugh at St. Paul's and elsewhere. When he had made his fortune, he settled in St. Albans, building himself a house here and after his death was buried in St. Peter's church. One wonders if he advised in any way on the interior fittings of the abbey.

Above the pulpit was a fine sounding board or 'type' as it is called in the accounts of the period. A type was often suspended by a chain from the roof and sometimes there is an inscription with the name and date of the craftsman who fashioned it. St. Albans' type had an ogee dome, surmounted by a crown and with

Fig. 75   View into north transept after 1835 by Sargent and Evans.

urns at the corners. These survive at the south-west of the north transept, above panelling which itself may remain from an earlier day: the walls of the Presbytery were panelled with wainscotting to a considerable height.

The galleries in the abbey were the gift of William Hales of King's Walden, Member of Parliament; they dated from 1715. Originally one gallery was sited just west of the tower arch, requiring a new set of Ten Commandments to be placed above the communion table. The Cumber diary for 1785 records how a visiting choir brought a box of tin whistles for their own accompaniment. Orchestral instruments played by 'Pantamies' performed in other church services, according to G C Straker and in 1814 a half-yearly salary of four guineas was paid to John Higdon for playing the 'clarionet' at the church on Sundays.

In the north transept, the gallery held the boys from the St. Albans School and from the Bluecoat School which had been founded in 1713. All were kept in order by the Beadle with his long stave. The parapet of the gallery was panelled and shaped and it was supported by fluted shafts with Corinthian capitals. It is ironic that galleries were installed purely for additional accommodation at a time when the vast abbey building was only fractionally used. Galleries did enable the church interior to take on the cruciform shape so popular at this time.

The font used in the abbey up until the Civil War was presumably the brass font from Holyrood which stood in the Monks' Choir, then known as the Baptistery. Puritans preferred to use a basin but the Act of Uniformity after the Restoration required a proper font, although the Puritan basin was often retained within it. After the brass font disappeared during the Civil War it was replaced, as we learned from Fuller, by a copy in wood.

By the time of the antiquary Oldfield (fl. 1794–1803), the St. Albans font was a white marble basin ornamented with flutes and cabling resting on a carved and moulded base (see fig. 76). It stood on a triangular podium under a baldacchino supported on three columns, its ogee dome surmounted by a dove, symbol of the Holy Spirit. The cover consisted of three openwork trusses suggestive of a crown, like the Jacobean example in Wells cathedral, and was lifted by a screw device. Mingling the exotic and the practical in a curious way, this font was removed to the Slype in 1853 before being transferred to the Workhouse chapel (see fig. 29).

The need to provide for the poor motivated the acquisition of a

Fig. 76   The eighteenth century font.

Poor Chest which still survives in the south Presbytery aisle. It has long strap hinges, triple locks and a painted inscription 'Remember the poor. *Deo Das'*. Above it is the small, homely, carved wooden figure of a pensioner asking for alms. Judging from the costume, it can be dated to ca. 1670–90. The hair is long and the cravat of muslin has two pendant ends. The close fitting coat is waisted and hangs to the knees. The figure wears breeches with short stockings and he carries a tricorn hat with a wide brim and a low crown. This simplified dress succeeded the extravagant styles which flowered briefly after the Restoration. The original figure, removed to the treasury for safe-keeping, has now been replaced by a replica.

The total expenditure on repairs, after the Brief of 1681 and a further grant in 1698 by William and Mary from an Ecclesiastical Fund, amounted to just under £3,000.

References

BRAYLEY (E W). Beauties of England and Wales, VII. Hertfordshire. London. 1808.

CAIGER-SMITH (A). English medieval mural paintings. Oxford. 1963.

CAMDEN (WILLIAM). Britannia. London. 1586.

CLUTTERBUCK (ROBERT). The history and antiquities of the county of Hertford. 3 vols. London, 1815–1827.

DAHL (REV. M E). 'Late Elizabethan church inventories for Hertfordshire'. *Hertfordshire Past and Present*. III (1962–3) 25–31.

FIENNES (CELIA). The journeys of Celia Fiennes. Ed. Christopher Morris. 1947.

FULLER (THOMAS). The worthies of England. 1662.

JONES (CHARLES E). 'The restoration of the cathedral and abbey church of St. Alban'. *Trans. SAHAAS*. (1937) 115–130.

PAGE (WILLIAM). 'The Marian survey of St. Albans'. *Trans. SAHAAS* (1893–94) 8–24.

SHAW (S G). History of Verulam and St. Albans. St. Albans. 1815.

STRAKER (G C). A history of the organs at the cathedral of St. Albans. Gateway Press. 1929.

THREADGILL (ALAN). 'Thomas Cumber – a St. Albans diarist'. *Hertfordshire Past and Present*. XV (1975–76) 10–25.

TOMS (DR ELSIE). The story of St. Albans. St. Albans. 1962.

WILTON HALL (H R). 'Report on the muniments of the Gape family'. *Trans. SAHAAS* (1905) 3–34.

Chapter 15

EIGHTEENTH AND EARLY
NINETEENTH CENTURIES

A drawing from John Oliver's map of 1700 made to illustrate Sir Henry Chauncy's *Historical Antiquities of Hertfordshire* shows the abbey with compressed aisles and transepts and a rather starved Lady Chapel. The surveyor of the abbey church in 1701, we learn from *The Corporation Records*, was called Nicholas Sparling.

In 1703 considerable excitement was aroused by the accidental discovery, while digging a grave for the Gape family, of the tomb of Humphrey, Duke of Gloucester in a vault under the chantry. Thenceforth, until well into the nineteenth century, visitors found this an item of intense interest and described in lurid detail the lead and wooden coffin, the pickle solution, the condition of the skeleton and the sacramental mural at the east end of the vault. Nor did they scruple to purchase fragments of bone from the sexton until in time very little remained of the skeleton. In this is reflected the current Romantic taste for the macabre, for owls, ravens, caverns, mouldering ruins and desolate graves which is found in the poetry of the period. However amusing it may appear to us today, it did lay the foundation for a revival of interest in the Gothic style which led eventually to the rescue and repair of the abbey church.

In that same year, 1703, the fabric of the church suffered a major disaster. During the autumn months repairs were in hand to the south transept window and scaffolding had been erected outside it to that purpose (see fig. 64). Between 26th November and 1st December a hurricane known as 'The Great Storm' raged across England and parts of Europe, one of the most terrible ever experienced. It caused immense devastation. Two million pounds' worth of damage was done in London alone: 8,000 were drowned, twelve Men of War lost within sight of land and 17,000 trees torn

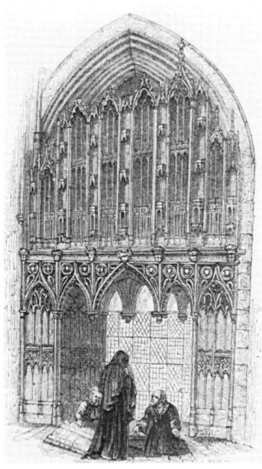

*Fig. 77 Chantry chapel of Humphrey,
Duke of Gloucester, d. 1447.*

up by the roots in Kent alone. The Eddystone lighthouse was destroyed. At St. Albans both the scaffolding and the stone tracery of the south transept window were utterly destroyed but miraculously, the north transept window and the roof escaped damage. John Hawgood, joiner and carpenter who had done work on recent repairs, was commissioned by the Mayor and Corporation to fill in the window with a wooden framework (see fig. 82). His window had five lights and three transoms with interlaced tracery above, a design popular in the Gothic Revival and used also in the Old Rectory (now the home of the Subdean) where it can still be seen. The transept was glazed with diamond panes of clear glass and forty pounds paid for it on 8th September 1704. The window lasted a century and a quarter. Perhaps this meagre insertion prompted an eighteenth century historian to comment 'This noble Fabrick, since it became a parish church, wanted its Abbot's zeal and Purse too for repairs.'

A funerary monument erected to John Thrale who died in 1704 has two portrait busts and some weeping *putti* at the base.

In the early eighteenth century Archdeacon Stubbs had the nave repaved with flags and common bricks, using the money from a legacy. An engraving by John Carter, dated 5th May 1819 and showing still fresh looking tiles, may illustrate this improvement.

Fig. 78   *View in the nave looking north-west
by John Carter, 1819.*

The account books of St. Albans School make melancholy reading in this period. The windows seemed to be the main cause of the trouble, judging from the outlays to plumber, carpenter, bricklayer and glazier in 1711 and the years immediately following.

The Society of Antiquaries was re-founded in 1717 and through the years their members took a close interest in the building and its restoration. Their secretary, William Stukeley, for example, visited the abbey church during his famous itineraries between 1710 and 1725 and published the first drawings of the interior which have come down to us, including two views of the High Altar screen. It was he who noted the careless attitude at that time towards antiquities: the Eleanor Cross was being demolished, the Clock Tower narrowly escaped a similar fate and the ruins of Verulamium were being robbed for road mending.

The Great Storm may have effected more profound damage than the blowing out of a window. Soon after 1721, the architect Nicholas Hawksmoor of Shenley was approached to examine the church. He was occupied at this time on constructing the west towers of Westminster Abbey and was also engaged on Blenheim Palace for the Duke and Duchess of Marlborough; the favourite home of the latter remained the modest Holywell House in St. Albans within view of the abbey. To help raise funds, Hawksmoor prepared for sale a view of the abbey seen from the top of the Clock Tower; one set is inscribed 'Support this venerable pile from being martyr'd by ye neglect of a Slouthfull generation.' The

Fig. 79   North elevation of St. Albans abbey drawn by Nicholas Hawksmoor, ca. 1721.

Corporation paid the Archdeacon three guineas to have them printed. This is the first drawing by an abbey architect to have survived. Hawksmoor shows himself not too particular about details of window tracery, nor even of numbers of windows but he draws the lantern lights partially filled in to make them circular. There is a spire at the south-east corner of the Lady Chapel and a small porch shelters the north Presbytery door. This is the finest early perspective of the abbey we possess, drawn by a skilful architect and it forms an important record.

In 1723–24 during the reign of George I, a new Brief was issued appealing for the sum of £5,775. The Brief described the condition of this 'beautiful, large and ancient fabrick': a great crack had appeared right through to the bottom of the south wall, the north wall was also cracked and was eighteen inches out of the vertical. The roof timbers were decayed and the whole building in a dangerous condition. Sixteen eminent men were chosen as trustees including the first Viscount Grimston and Sir Robert Raymond, Lord Chief Justice, who lived at Abbot's Langley and whose funerary portrait, signed by Sir Henry Cheere, stands in the parish church there.

According to Grimthorpe, money was spent at this time in 'replacing the old oak-ribbed and pannelled and painted ceiling of the working nave, or the ten western bays, by flat deal boards nailed under the old ribs slit in two, with sham pannels of coarse lime-washed patterns'. Sometime in the eighteenth century, the south wall of the Slype was refaced with brick in a diaper pattern.

In 1731 *The Gentleman's Magazine* was founded and it continued publishing until 1914. It included from the start antiquarian articles on historic buildings usually by residents of the locality in question and constitutes a useful source of information on the state of the abbey through the years.

Between 1720 and 1742, Nathaniel Buck was preparing engraved plates for his great work, *Antiquities and Venerable Remains*, which, in the eyes of some scholars, marks the true beginning of the Gothic Revival. Buck drew St. Albans abbey in 1737. Although the proportions are excessively tall and thin, it seems on the whole to have been carefully observed. The projecting water pipes which caused such havoc later on are not suppressed and the cloister arches are still visible along the south transept and the Slype. The bull's-eye windows persist in the lantern but the cedar tree is not yet visible. A few years after this was published, the Old Rectory was consumed by fire in 1743; all the parish and vestry books were destroyed, leaving many gaps in

Fig. 80   South elevation of St. Albans abbey by Nathaniel Buck. 1737.

the post-Reformation history of the abbey.

Buck's engraving was copied many times with his faults exaggerated in different ways by each copyist including one example by Robinson dated 1789. The antiquary F G Kitton wrote an interesting article on abbey engravings in volume thirty-one of *The Antiquary.*.

After another forty years, in the reign of George III, yet another Brief was issued, dated 18th January 1764, stating that the east end was in a bad state of repair due to the decay of the roof, the south wall of the transept leaned outward by twelve inches and the great timber window of sixty years earlier was very rotten and threatening to fall in. The north wall was shattered and cracked in several places. The repairs required over £2,500 but the Brief attracted only a quarter of that sum. Once expenses had been deducted, a mere £600 was left. Clearly the Brief as a method of fund raising had begun to outlive its usefulness.

A drawing of the abbey appeared on the Wren and Andrews map of 1766. The architect for this repair was Robert Mylne and his survey report is the earliest one recorded. He wrote, 'the stamina is totally sound, and I have rarely seen a building so extensive in better order, considering the little care that has been taken of it. There are only two places where there have been unequal settlements, and where the consequences are apparent. The arch of the great south window has pushed the adjoining towers out. The other is more serious and admits of no remedy: the west front of the south (clerestory) wall has inclined twelve inches to the south. All that can be done is to examine the iron tyes.' He recommended 'shutting up every alternate window on the south side, and to put in casements of wood with common glass in the others.' He was paid ten guineas for his work, and the accounts show that the wooden window frame on the south transept was repaired and that carpenters and plumbers were paid for work as well. No money was spent on stone or brick and the ruinous south turrets were left untouched.

Relating to some work on the spire at this time, we learn that the scaffolding used was not the usual network of horizontal and vertical poles but a casing of wickerwork totally enclosing the spire. It was erected by Thomas Birch, basket-maker, of 7 High Street, St. Albans, who was known as 'Twiggy Birch'. He copied an idea first used at St. Bride's, London in 1786 after its spire had been hit by lightning. So far no illustrations of this strange scaffolding in place at St. Albans have come to light, but an illustration survives of a similar one used by Birch at St. Mary,

Islington in 1787. Of this one a detailed record has come down to us. Birch received twenty pounds for his wicker-work of hazel, willow and other sticks. A spiral staircase was woven within which was easily climbed and much safer than conventional scaffolding. It achieved such notoriety that the public paid sixpence to climb to the top. A small print was sold showing the spire enclosed in a tight fitting sock with little tufts sticking out at intervals.

Wealthier parishioners commissioned some interesting works of art during the eighteenth century. William King, who died in 1766, is commemorated in a memorial in the south choir aisle, a work by that distinguished sculptor of Huguenot extraction, Sir Henry Cheere, whose sculptor's yard was at Hyde Park Corner. During his lifetime he effected a transition from the Baroque style to the more delicate and individual Roccoco, clearly seen in the *putti* on the St. Albans monument.

Fig. 81   Wickerwork scaffolding by Thomas Birch, basket maker of St. Albans in 1788 at St. Mary, Islington.

In 1772 the Watergate of the monastery was destroyed (see fig. 71). In fact, the abbey itself was in danger of demolition. The topographical writer, William Bray, wrote in 1777, 'It had a narrow escape, a few years ago, from falling a sacrifice to avarice and mean-spiritedness. The repairs which had been made at different times were found expensive, and a scheme was formed to pull it down and build a smaller church.' Fortunately for posterity, this negative scheme was firmly quashed.

A landmark in the history of the abbey came in 1775 when the architect John Carter published his first drawings of the building (see figs. 23, 37, 63 and 65). He made his living from publishing drawings of mediaeval antiquities, for *The Builders Magazine*, for

Gough's famous *Sepulchral Monuments* and also for the Society of Antiquaries who commissioned him to record important buildings. His drawings form a valuable record and he thundered against mindless destruction and crude restoration of historic buildings. Inevitably, he made many enemies in so doing but he undoubtedly altered the climate of opinion from indifference to a more caring attitude.

Carter's drawings of a crisp and clear-cut appearance, have great beauty in themselves as works of art. He did have a weakness for restoring on paper the building as he thought it should have been, and his guesses were not always correct. He believed, for example, that the arches in the Presbytery were originally open (see fig. 68) and it was only Scott's investigations of the fabric which confirmed that they had always been solid.

Between 1781 and 1803 an antiquarian artist, Henry George Oldfield of Great Scotland Yard, London, was recording topography in Hertfordshire for his patron, John Meyrick, FSA of Fulham. The collection of 1,500 drawings, interleaved with notes by Meyrick, has been bound into nine volumes and is now in the Hertfordshire Record Office. Volume VIII, devoted to St. Albans, contains a unique record of the abbey interior at the close of the eighteenth century. The Saint's Chapel, used as a vestry, had been fitted out by the Archdeacon for the conduct of Consistory Courts, while the painting of *The Last Supper*, given by Polehampton, hung over the Watching Loft. The High Altar screen is shown tricked out with plaster cherubs (see also figs. 74 and 83). The choir occupied the Presbytery and the pews of the Mayor and Corporation stood near the tower arch. Two pews belonging to Holywell House bore appropriate shields of arms. Pews and galleries filled the crossing while the Monks' Choir, which was known as the Baptistery, held the chalice style font (see fig. 76). A long blocked door linking the north nave aisle with an orchard, had recently been opened up by the Archdeacon. Oldfield is highly regarded for his accuracy, and we owe to him too records of the Slype interior, the crypt under the Gloucester chantry, and the ceiling decoration both of the nave and of the south transept.

Another young draughtsman who worked for the Society of Antiquaries was Jacob Schnebbilie who did three views of the abbey. He exhibited at the Royal Academy in 1789. A new romanticism appears in his style, in the swelling ground, the verdant trees, the massing of clouds and the distortions in the buildings themselves. Inert structures are invested with an inner life. People and animals are introduced into his scenes and he brings the river Ver much closer to the abbey building than it really is. The King's Barns in the background show that these old structures were still in existence. Another Schnebbilie view of the abbey shows a gravedigger in the foreground, very much in the gothick taste. Schnebbilie died in 1792 in his thirty-second year. *The Gentleman's Magazine* tells us that this occurred 'after an illness occasioned by too intensive application to professional engagements, which terminated in a total disability of the body.'

Fig. 82   South-west perspective of St. Albans abbey in 1787 by Jacob Schnebbilie.

An important book was published in 1795, *The History of the Abbey of St. Albans* by Peter Newcome, Rector of Shenley. It is an account from the foundation to the Dissolution giving the lives of the abbots and the principal events in the careers of each. This book, described in the *Dictionary of National Biography* as a 'creditable compilation', was one of the sources used in the preparation of the *Victoria History of the County of Hertford*. It is a most readable book, still much sought after by antiquaries and students of abbey history and it doubtless contributed directly to public interest in the surviving building.

The abbey owes a debt of gratitude to the artist, Thomas Girtin, who left some valuable studies of the building. His patron was the well known physician, Dr. Monroe, of the Adelphi in London and of Bushey in Hertfordshire. Girtin, of an impulsive and genial disposition, often sketched with Turner, his personal friend. He abandoned the old water-colour method of making a monochrome study first and then adding colour, using instead an absorbent, cream coloured paper to which he applied rich colour in broad washes, picking out the details in blobs of paint. Thus he invented the modern technique of water-colour painting and had a profound influence not only upon Turner but also upon Constable. Girtin died at the early age of twenty-seven years and was buried at St. Paul's, Covent Garden.

The quality of Girtin's genius comes out in a painting of the abbey interior now owned by the Diocese (see fig. 83). One sees at once that it is an accurate study: Girtin learned much about topographical painting from Canaletto. It is not only an evocative painting but an effective composition as well, subtly composed in terms of light and shade. He makes skilful use of counterchange in expressing the vaults. This record, dated 1795, is especially important as the interior of the church was radically reordered in twenty-five years' time.

Two years later, we read in *The Gentleman's Magazine*, a severe storm once again damaged the fabric of the church. On 25th September 1797, soon after the torrents of rain had in part subsided, an architect reported finding graves open, monumental slabs and the pavement falling into the ground in every direction. The drains near the north door had been blocked allowing the rain to flood into the church. The most frightening damage was done to the pier of the arch next to the north pier of the great tower. The projecting foundation of the column had sunk several inches out of the horizontal. 'I am sorry to say', the anonymous architect writes, 'not any attention was paid to this dangerous appearance' although he pointed out that the stability of the whole building could be undermined by this fault.

The earliest detailed description of the abbey church, inside and out, by a competent architectural writer was published in 1808 by Edward Brayley in volume VII of his important series of books, *Beauties of England and Wales*. The high quality illustrations in the book are by G Shepherd. Brayley and his partner, John Britton, were not scholars but popularisers and for the first time made available to ordinary people accurate and detailed descriptive texts and illustrations of historic buildings. These books were enormously influential.

In 1815, S G Shaw, a stationer, bookseller and bookbinder in the Market Place, St. Albans, wrote a critical but informative account of the way in which the abbey church was failing its parishioners. He wrote, 'Out of this stupendous fabric, the only diminutive part

Fig. 83 View north east into Presbytery. Water-colour by Thomas Girtin, 1795.

of the whole fitted up for religious worship, is contained within the circumference of the tower (see figs. 74 and 75), excepting a small gallery for the use of the boys of the Bluecoat school, in the south transept, and two large pews appropriated to the use of the corporation which are so injudiciously planned, as to place the mayor, and the aldermen sitting near him, with their backs to the minister ... pews are ... kept locked by those who seldom or ever occupy them, to the exclusion of others who would willingly attend divine service if they had such accommodation.' As a result, people 'resort to the dissenting chapels', Shaw concluded.

By the year 1800, church building in England had sunk to its lowest ebb despite the increase in population which accompanied the industrial revolution. In 1818, an Act of Parliament was passed which provided one million pounds for the repair and erection of churches in London and elsewhere; St. Pancras, London, is one example of the 214 churches built as a result of the so-called 'Million Act'. Considerable leadership was given by the architects Nash, Soane and Smirke. St. Albans abbey received a grant from this fund and in 1818 the architect, Lewis Wyatt, was brought in to survey the building. Lewis Wyatt was an elder brother of the more famous James Wyatt, architect of Fonthill, whom he assisted as Clerk of Works at Whitehall, at Hampton Court Palace and at Kew.

R Barnet wrote a guide to the abbey in 1824 in which he lists in detail the internal changes of 1820 and early photographs show some of them. The pulpit was moved from the south side to the north. New pews, neat and uniform, were made and a number of open seats for the poor added, so that there were 450 free sittings altogether. The western gallery, which had been just west of the tower arch, was moved closer to the roodscreen; in this way the usable interior of the church was enlarged to take in the former Baptistery.

An organ was installed in 1820, paid for by public subscription, with the Corporation contributing twenty pounds out of the total cost of £450. It was a second-hand organ, originally built by Father Smith and John Byfield in 1670 for the church of St. Dunstan in the East in a fine Gothic case with four spires. For safety, cast iron pillars replaced the wooden ones under the gallery, but by 1835 the organ had been moved to the north transept (see fig. 75).

With these changes, it is now time to turn our attention to the careers of three men, Cottingham, Nicholson and Scott, whose varied efforts made this crumbling building sound again.

References

AN ARCHITECT. (Effect of the great storm of St. Albans abbey church.) *The Gentleman's Magazine*. (1797) 928.

ANDREWS (H C). 'Henry George Oldfield and the Dimsdale collection of Herts. drawings.' *Transactions of the East Hertfordshire Archaeological Society*. XI (1942) 212–224.

BETJEMAN (JOHN) ed. 'The church in Georgian times'. *Collins Guide to English parish churches*. London. 1958. 33–45.

BINYON (ROBERT LAURENCE). Thomas Girtin, his life and works. London. 1900

BRAYLEY (E W). Beauties of England and Wales. VII. London. 1808

BUCK (S and NATHANIEL). Buck's antiquities; or venerable remains of above four hundred castles, monasteries, palaces, etc., in England and Wales. 3 vols. London. 1774.

CARTER (JOHN). Some account of the abbey church of St. Alban. London. 1813.

COLVIN (HOWARD). A biographical dictionary of British architects, 1600–1840. London. 1978.

EVANS (JOAN). A history of the Society of Antiquaries. Oxford. 1956.

GOMME (G L). The Gentleman's Magazine library . . . a classified collection of the chief contents . . . from 1731 to 1868. London. 1894.

KITTON (FREDERICK G). 'Notes on engravings of St. Albans Abbey'. *The Antiquary*. (1895) 43–52.

NELSON (JOHN). The history, topography and antiquities of the parish of St. Mary, Islington. London. 1811.

NEWCOME (PETER). The history of the abbey of St. Albans. London. 1795.

OLDFIELD (HENRY GEORGE). 'Hertfordshire Antiquities.' 9 vols, with notes by John Meyrick, FSA. Hertford County Record Office. 1781–1803.

RICHARDSON (A E). Robert Mylne, architect and engineer. London. 1955.

STRAKER (G C). A history of the organs at the cathedral of St. Alban. Gateway Press, 1929.

TOMKINS (MALCOLM). 'The duke in pickle'. *Hertfordshire Countryside*. XXXIV, no. 248 (December 1979) 23–24.

WILTON HALL (H R). 'Report on the muniments of the Gape family.' *Trans. SAHAAS*. XXVII (1905) 3–34.

. . . 'Notes and memoranda on some Hertfordshire churches at the beginning of this century'. *Idem*. New series I (1895–6) 29–52.

Part VI

RESTORATION AND A NEW ROLE

Chapter 16

COTTINGHAM AND NICHOLSON

On 3rd February 1832, people living round the abbey heard a crashing sound like the loudest thunder, followed five minutes later by a second crash. A section of masonry wall below the clerestory, where the Early English work joined the Decorated on the south, had given way, and fallen through the south aisle roof, taking timber and lead with it. The area which had collapsed measured about fifteen feet high and twenty-five feet long. Fortunately, neither the nave piers nor the adjacent wall seemed to have been affected.

The Churchwardens and Vestry ordered shoring to be erected as a precaution and this disaster proved another milestone in bringing home forcibly to the parishioners that superficial patching was no longer sufficient. Fundamental repairs were urgent if the building was to continue to stand.

The architect, L N Cottingham, was called in to make a survey. He had been consulted as early as 1827 by the rector, Henry Small,

Fig. 84   The effects of the fall of masonry from the clerestory of 3rd February 1832 can be seen in this south elevation.

to confirm the Wyatt survey but, as usual, nothing had come of it. Cottingham was a Suffolk-born architect who had set up practice in London in 1814. He had received an important commission in 1825 when called upon to repair Rochester cathedral and rebuild its central tower. He was a personal friend of the antiquary, John Carter, and had apparently done some work for the Earl of Verulam.

Cottingham's 1832 *Survey* survives in the abbey Muniments Room among the Wilton Hall papers and is the fullest, early account of the abbey fabric in existence. It is a sad record of dilapidations. The walls of the triforium had been built originally of rubble three feet thick and faced inside with ashlar which was poorly bonded in. Hugh de Goldclif (fl. ca. 1195–1214), it will be recalled, had had a reputation as a 'deceitful craftsman'. When first built, high-pitched aisle roofs had protected the walls from the elements but when they were lowered in the fifteenth century, the wall behind was exposed to the wind, frost and rain (see fig. 71). Pointing had been neglected for three hundred years, so the mortar was disintegrating and the whole south wall leaned twelve inches out of the perpendicular. Consequently, the wall plates no longer carried the roof beams; they rested precariously on the inner, ashlar facing of the triforium and the whole weight of the roof was pushing the walls outwards. Some time before 1764, iron tie-rods had been inserted in an attempt to remedy this: some old photographs show the external S-brackets. In addition to this, rising damp was causing the foundations to fail. On the north, where the adjacent land was not in the ownership of the church but was planted as an orchard, the ground level had ascended higher than the internal pavement and rising damp had climbed six to seven feet. Cottingham wished to dig a trench at the base of the walls to collect the water and carry it away.

The nave roof of the abbey had also been reduced from high to low pitch in the fifteenth century. Cottingham lifted the lead and boarding from the roof and was astonished to see the immense scantling of the timbers used below: the oaks chosen had had to span thirty feet. By now, however, their condition was deplorable. Although some principals had been replaced, others were spliced in a dangerous way and held together by iron. Some were twisted, others completely rotten. Because of the unequal stress, some were carrying much more weight than they were designed to bear. Cottingham wished to remove the entire roof. He proposed reducing the scantling of the timbers by a third, labour in the early nineteenth century being much cheaper than materials. Seasoned oak beams, when sound, are hard as iron. He wanted a new, high-pitched roof over the aisles and a mansard roof over nave and transepts. With tiles on the slopes and lead on the flat top, water would drain off more quickly than with the existing arrangement.

Cottingham then looked at the tower. He wished to remove the Hertfordshire spike, reframing the roofs and floors with lighter timbers, on what he thought would be a sounder principle. The brickwork was very dilapidated because of careless, earlier repairs. He wished to make this good and to plaster it in grey to preserve the 'venerable' look. The belfry frames should be rebuilt in stone, not wood. The waver slats should be of slate instead of wood. The crows would have to be excluded from the tower and from the building generally, as they made a great mess of filth and caused parts to deteriorate. The external galleries, paved in brick, had been so neglected that water penetrated through the defective mortar; this paving he proposed replacing with good York stone.

The south transept was also in poor state. He wished to tie in the west wall by iron chain bars built into the mass of the wall. The wooden south window, designed by John Hawgood in 1704 but now sinking and bulging, he wished to replace in stone to match its twin on the north. The buttresses in his view should all be replaced in stone and all the weeds growing out of the top of the building removed.

The south-west wall of the abbey, from which the conventual buildings had been removed, bore the brunt of the prevailing winds and the external drainage system, with projecting spouts to discharge the water, distressed Cottingham greatly. Wind blew the water back against the walls, causing the mortar to crumble and moisture to get in. He wished to use iron downpipes with proper heads and shoes. In the Middle Ages, much iron had been incorporated in the windows, as upright and transverse bars to support the glazing; unless it is maintained with regular painting, such iron rusts and dislodges the masonry. The abbey ironwork had been shamefully neglected for three centuries and most windows were in danger of falling out. Thirty-two main windows needed replacing and Cottingham proposed blocking twenty little ones located in the staircases. The great west window was especially bad (see fig. 63). On the west front, he wished to repair the stonework, strengthen the buttresses, rebuild the staircases and replace the pinnacles. Inside, the entire face of the clerestory had to be rebuilt. Fourteen thousand pounds was Cottingham's estimate of the total sum the repairs required.

The Earl of Verulam, as Lord Lieutenant of the County, called a public meeting in the Town Hall but only about £4,000 was raised by public subscription. After £1,700 of this had gone in expenses, the residue was applied to the repair, less than a quarter of what was required.

It is hard to determine exactly how the money was spent, although a brief account in *The County Press* for 22nd August 1835 mentions some items. The south clerestory wall had been rebuilt and forty blocked windows in the nave opened up and reglazed. The nave roof was not rebuilt but iron shoes were put on the ends of the rotten beams and the whole releaded. The south nave aisle was given a timber ceiling. The Hertfordshire spike was removed and the lantern windows (up to now still partially blocked) were opened up to their original shape. The great south window was rebuilt in stone and glazed with armorial glass. The shallow, saucer dome over the crossing was finally removed and the plaster cupids scraped off the reredos (see fig. 74). Once again it was merely patch and mend and the fundamental problems were left largely unsolved due to lack of funds.

Six months before the abbey re-opened, a happy appointment was made. In 1835, Henry Joseph Boone Nicholson became rector of the abbey church and for the next thirty years gave strong leadership in St. Albans. He was an exceptional young man, serving in his youth as Domestic Chaplain to the future King William IV and in close touch with the main intellectual currents of the day. His brother-in-law was the distinguished professor, T L Donaldson, founder of the Royal Institute of British Architects, who had been educated at the St. Albans School. Nicholson was a Fellow of the Society of Antiquaries and mediaeval monuments were his lifelong passion. Interest in the Gothic was on the upsurge and local societies were springing up to study and preserve mediaeval buildings. Dr Nicholson, at the suggestion of the Archdeacon, helped to found the St. Albans Society, holding the first general meeting at the Old Rectory on 21st October 1845. Of the first committee, seven out of nine were clergymen. For decades the abbey was their absorbing interest, Nicholson reporting to the members the finds he made and Society membership formed a large proportion of the Restoration Committee. H R Wilton Hall wrote the history of the period in the Society *Transactions* and the keynote of those years, thanks to Nicholson, was 'discovery'.

It was he who had the de la Mare brass restored by Waller, under the supervision of the Society and who had it removed for safety into the Wallingford chantry in 1846. He purchased Totternhoe stone from the foundations of an old barn, said to have been made from abbey stones, for use in repairing the stonework inside the abbey building. He had whitewash removed from the nave pillars, revealing the west-facing murals for the first time in centuries (see fig. 39). The Slype was excavated, the Wheathampstead chantry opened up. Piscinae, altar

Fig. 85   Dr Henry Joseph Boone Nicholson, 1795–1866. Rector from 1835.

stones, tiles, stone coffins, all were lovingly collected, examined and studied. From January 1846, Nicholson kept the building locked, with admission by ticket only, to help raise money for the restoration and to impress upon the public that the abbey was something worth seeing.

During his incumbency, the antiquaries Buckler made their investigations of the building, and wrote *The Abbey Church of St. Alban*, that masterpiece of careful research on the Norman building.

Nicholson opened up the triple arches at the east end of the Saint's Chapel (see fig. 42), uncovering the *St. William of York* mural and arranging for it to be protected under a case of glass and wood. A chromolithograph was made for sale at the time.

To guide visitors, he published *Extracts from the History of the Abbey of St. Alban and a Description of its church*. It is a scholar's book, well documented and packed with interest but more demanding than the average tourist requires today. It remains an important source for students of abbey history.

Fig. 86 The incredulity of St. Thomas *mural in the north transept, engraved by R C Boutell, 1846.*

In 1846 another important mural was uncovered, on a buttress in the north transept. This was *The incredulity of St. Thomas* and almost at once the local Society had an engraving made which records many details since lost. R C Boutell published the picture and a descriptive note in *The Archaeological Journal* that very year.

In the south-east of the nave, the Alchorne window of ca. 1852 exemplifies the searchng spirit of these times. It is believed on stylistic grounds to be the work of William Wailes, the glazier from Newcastle-upon-Tyne who showed his glass at the Great Exhibition in 1851. In a stiff, self-conscious way, it follows mediaeval models in the archaeologically correct manner which A W Pugin and Thomas Willement had pioneered. Its clear, bright colours reflect the early successes at recapturing the secret of pot-metal glass making lost since the Middle Ages.

In 1853 Nicholson had the chalice shaped, white marble font replaced by one more in the current taste (see fig. 29).

With Nicholson, hope and excitement were reborn. In the words of John Chapple, 'he had raised a spirit of enquiry', 'had been successful in causing attention to be directed to the forlorn state of the building' and 'creating in the public mind a desire to see the grand old Church . . . restored somewhat to its pristine beauty'.

References

BOUTELL (R Charles). 'The incredulity of St. Thomas'. *Archaeological Journal*. II (1846) 386–7.

BUCKLER (J C) and BUCKLER (C A). The abbey church of St. Alban. London. 1847.

CHAPPLE (JOHN). A short history of the abbey church of St. Alban. St. Albans. 1882.

COTTINGHAM (L N). 'Report of survey and estimate for the repairs of St. Albans Abbey'. Wilton Hall Papers no. 4 (1832) St. Albans Abbey Muniments.

NICHOLSON (HENRY JOSEPH BOONE). The abbey of Saint Alban – some extracts from its early history and a description of its conventual church. edn. 8. London. 1887.

ROBERTS (EILEEN). 'He sowed and others reaped: H J B Nicholson, 1795–1866'. *The Abbey Magazine*. IX, no. 4 (April 1969) 5–8.

. . . The St. William of York mural and the altar of the relics in St. Albans Abbey. Chichester. 1979.

WILTON HALL (H R). 'Tis sixty years since: a history of the Society from 1845 to 1905'. *Trans. SAHAAS*. (1906–6) 123–146.

. . . 'A list of papers read before the society from its foundation'. *ibid*. (1903–4) 104–114.

Chapter 17

SIR GEORGE GILBERT SCOTT

Thanks to Nicholson, the climate of opinion was changing. On 5th April 1856 a second public meeting was held in the Town Hall, chaired by the Earl of Verulam, with the double intention of raising the abbey to cathedral status and of restoring the fabric. Over four thousand pounds were subscribed and from this period the serious efforts to repair the abbey can be said to have begun.

Mr Gilbert Scott was appointed architect. He had had a romantic interest in St. Albans abbey from his childhood days in Gawcott parsonage, Buckinghamshire and while still in his teens and apprenticed to a London architect, had made his first visit to the abbey, which he later remembered 'with intense delight'. He became abbey architect at the age of forty-five at the height of his success and fame.

During these very years, 1854–58, Scott was engaged in building St. George, Doncaster, in Yorkshire's West Riding; Pevsner describes it as 'the

Fig. 87 Sir George Gilbert Scott, 1811–1878. Abbey architect from 1856 until his death.

proudest and most cathedral-like of this fabulously busy architect's parish churches.' But there is one discordant note in this lovely church: the great east window with its harsh and insistent tracery. This was designed by an active and interfering member of the Building Committee who donated £500 towards the building, a young Q.C. called Edmund Beckett Denison (see fig. 91). Fate brought the two together again at St. Albans. Whereas Denison never ceased (unjustly) to vilify Scott's work, Scott in his *Recollections* still referred to Beckett as his friend. This illustrates the generosity of the man.

Several sources record Scott's work upon the abbey: his own report made to the Earl of Verulam in 1871, the receipts of the works from 1860 to 1878 amongst the Gorhambury papers in the Hertfordshire Record Office, the written account by the Clerk of Works, John Chapple, published in 1874 and the references to St. Albans in Scott's own *Personal and Professional Recollections* of 1879. Sir Edmund Beckett (as Denison was later known) in his book of 1885, refers extensively to Scott's work but with a strong bias against it, and he cites several dates which appear to be inaccurate.

On 20th November 1860, Scott sent Samuel Cundy, Foreman of Outside Work, to survey the quarries at Totternhoe then belonging to the Earl of Brownlow (see fig. 3), indicating his intention of matching the mediaeval stone used in the building with that employed in repairs. Scott had tons of earth removed from inside the aisles of the church to restore the mediaeval floor levels; when he began, the south transept had been filled up to two feet over its entire area. Between 10th December 1860 and February 1861, payments were made to Jackson and Shaw, Builders, for work on the south aisle and north transept. The new roof over the north aisle, which Beckett grudgingly praised as 'good of its kind' and left in place, dates from 1861. During exploratory work at this time, the site of an extra-mural chapel on the north of the church was uncovered.

Rector Nicholson, greatly encouraged, commissioned in 1862 a handsome stained glass window from the newly founded firm of Heaton, Butler and Baines. *Crossing the Red Sea* (Exodus 14) in the top medallion must have symbolised for Nicholson the miracle of restoration work which now engulfed the building. Set in the south choir aisle, it looked through the then open arcade toward the font, hence the appropriate *Baptism of Christ* theme of the lower medallion. This gift proclaimed the rector's faith in the work Scott was doing and set a standard for artistic adornment in the future.

Essential work on drains and foundations began after March 1863, when the purchase was completed by the Ecclesiastical Commissioners of the land to the north of the church. Earth had risen ten feet high to windowsill level and 1,980 tons of earth had to be removed before the walls could be underpinned and drains leading waste water to the river Ver could be constructed.

Meanwhile, in the south transept, the western windows which had been partially blocked for years were re-opened by Scott (see fig. 40). As early as 1863 he found fragments of tabernacle work broken up and blocking the two original Norman sanctuary doors, (see figs. 21 and 43). These he removed, reinstating the doors to smaller dimensions and reconstructing the southern tabernacles. He made a copy to place on the northern side, as it was clear from the marks on the masonry that originally there had been a matching set in that position. In the south Presbytery aisle, some early Norman arches, long hidden under later masonry, were uncovered. He also repaired the masonry pattern where it was defective (see fig. 26).

H J B Nicholson died in 1866, not living to see the Lady Chapel reunited with the body of the church. First steps were taken the following year. A new Gaol having been completed in 1866 near the railway station, the Grammar School Trustees purchased the now empty Gatehouse (see fig. 71), the former Gaol, for their school in 1867 and it was open for inspection of the improvements made at Easter, 1871.

1870 was the year in which the young architectural student, James Neale, saw the abbey for the first time. He looked at the building 'with amazement'. As a project for passing the examination to become a student at the Royal Academy, he began to make measured drawings of the abbey, beginning with an Early English bay in the north of the nave. Soon the task so absorbed him that he was working from six in the morning until midnight. Every drawing was prepared to scale on the spot, to make it as accurate and complete as possible (see figs. 21, 52 and 64). The architect Street for whom he worked, Gilbert Scott and Rector Walter Lawrance of the abbey, all gave him encouragement. Finally he completed his great task, gaining in 1875 the Pugin Travelling Studentship. Neale's unsurpassed masterpiece was printed for subscribers two years later. How different the restoration might have been if Neale instead of Beckett had succeeded Scott as architect.

Not long after this, a crisis occurred. On 1st August 1870, while John Chapple was at worship in the crossing, he heard an ominous crack. He well knew how to interpret this warning sound but restrained his first impulse to flee lest he cause panic in the congregation. He reported to Scott as soon as possible after the service. Examination revealed that the each of the four tower piers had a stratum of inferior mortar, apparently damaged by frost or rain during construction in the eleventh century (see. fig. 74, left). The south wall of the nave, by now twenty inches out of the perpendicular, was not helping the situation. The south-east tower pier was found to be undermined; a cave large enough for a man to stand inside had been excavated and was supported only by timber struts. Furthermore, the four tower piers had been greatly weakened by cutting back their outer casing to a height of thirty feet. The Norman wall had been constructed in the usual way, with a firm casing on the outside, in this instance of Roman bricks, and an inner core of rubble. Once the outer casing was cut away, there was nothing to stop the rubble core from pouring out after the mortar had deteriorated.

To make matters worse, the Presbytery walls next to the tower piers had been pierced with very large openings and all bond with the piers destroyed. Clearly, the whole tower was settling, with cracks appearing in all directions. The north-east pier had actually burst and both the Ramryge chantry and the vault in the north aisle had split and were being crushed (see fig. 69).

Scott ordered the arches to be bricked up and supporting timbers inserted. Although the baulks put in were very heavy, they bent like reeds under the violent compression: the men toiled night and day but the pier continued to crumble. The tower definitely was on the move. Eventually the east and north arches were propped up and with this achieved, the vast project of repairing the tower could commence. Receipts of payments to Miskins, the local building firm, from 14th July to 7th May amount to over £2,000. The feat of saving the tower earns for Scott the title of saviour of the Abbey.

During all this time services had to be conducted in the nave for the first time in four hundred years (see fig. 78). A temporary screen was inserted from the top of the roodscreen to the ceiling to keep out the dirt and noise. Old photographs from this period show a series of scriptural texts which were applied to the architecture and changed from time to time. Solid fuel Gurney stoves, installed by November 1870, heated the nave to a temperature of fifty degrees Fahrenheit (as in fig. 49 right). Perhaps it was at this time that the woodwork from the crossing, particularly from the old Churchwardens' Pew, was adapted to enhance the nave altar; it can be seen in the etching forming the frontispiece to J M Comyn Carr's book of 1877. One can also see the north aisle roof and the two steps leading into the sanctuary at that time.

It would now be appropriate to make some comment on the

flowering of Victorian stained glass design. As mediaeval churches all over the country were being rehabilitated, the need for stained glass became apparent. Mediaeval examples were studied and experiments carried out to recover the lost arts of pot-metal and flashing. These processes were carried out to a state of perfection by John R Clayton (1827–1913) with the encouragement of Scott, and Clayton, with his partner Alfred Bell (1832–95) provided many windows for Scott's buildings. There are two examples of their later work in the abbey, in the west wall of the south transept, dating from 1874 and 1876. Clayton and Bell were noted for their balanced colour, excellent draftmanship and intelligent use of leading. The firm of Burlison and Grylls, operating from 1868 to 1953, whose founders John Burlison and Thomas Grylls trained under Clayton and Bell, are represented in the abbey in numerous windows, three from the lifetime of Scott: the H H Toulmin window on the north of the nave and the E Lawrance window on the south, both of 1871, and the J E Gape window of 1872 in the Chapel of the Four Tapers. Their style is more subdued, with much use of silver staining, intricate nichework and intertwining banners with Gothic lettering. The glazier C E Kempe (1834–1907) who also trained under Clayton and Bell, provided windows for the Lady Chapel in the generation after Scott's death. Scott's role in encouraging the revival of stained glass should not be overlooked.

Having restored the floors of the abbey to their mediaeval levels, Scott proceeded to pave them afresh with tiles. According to Chapple, the old designs were copied and new tiles manufactured by Minton and Co. of Stoke-on-Trent. This was a porcelain firm which worked closely with Pugin and which led in the reproduction of mediaeval tiles. There was much antiquarian interest at this time in newly discovered mediaeval tile kilns and in the uncovering of the superb tile floor of the Chapter House of Westminster Abbey. In the choir and crossing of St. Albans abbey, one can see how closely the old designs were followed by comparing them with original examples of quadrant tiles; the interest of these tile pavements is greatly undervalued. Wherever nineteenth century tile paving is to be found in the abbey, it is Gilbert Scott's work, as Beckett had strong views against the use of tiles for floor covering.

During the repaving work in 1872, the heart burial of Abbot Roger de Norton, d. 1290, was discovered in the Chapel of the Four Tapers in an oriental box set within a hollowed-out stone.

By 1875, the Presbytery was structurally sound and for the

Fig. 88 Minton tiles laid by Scott under the crossing tower, based upon mediaeval examples.

pavement here, Scott chose to copy relief tiles from the abbey Chapter House. These had been discovered 'on the spot' deep under the gas pipes laid in 1877, two square designs in green, and one decorative band in terra cotta. In the repaving, all the grave slabs of the abbots were carefully relaid in their correct positions in the Presbytery.

The Ramryge chantry was repaired (see fig. 69), and the smashed up grave slab of the abbot reinstated in its proper place.

While removing earth from the internal aisles and while opening up blocked arches in the eastern arm of the building, many fragments of carved stone had been found, some with colour and gilding, clearly, the shattered remains of the shrine of St. Alban. Chapple, assisted by the Foreman, Micklethwaite, set about in March 1872 reassembling the fragments. A rectangular Purbeck marble kerb on the pavement of the Saint's Chapel, all that was left after 1539, showed precisely where the shrine had stood; to secure the foundations, they took up this kerb, dug out a trench, filled it with rubble and replaced the kerb. On this a timber base was laid supporting a core of brick which was secured with cement and iron straps. Around this internal mould the marble fragments were arranged and fixed, each in its proper place, with plaster of Paris, shellac and Roman cement. A few pieces, in the frieze especially, were not correctly placed, but the handsome shrine, restored to wholeness once more with vision and enthusiasm, symbolises Scott's fine work for the abbey (see fig. 47).

Much publicity was attracted in *The Times*, as well as in *The Architect* and *The Builder*. The shrine of St. Amphibalus, beautifully carved in Totternhoe stone, was also found and reconstructed. This, too, Scott replaced correctly on its late mediaeval cult site, in the midst of the antechapel (see fig. 49). The Restoration Committee was annoyed that money had been spent on this recovery work without their consent, but John Ruskin generously promised to cover the cost himself, should it prove necessary.

When the Bishopric of St. Albans Act was passed in 1875, restoration work was still in progress. Large murals of the apostles in the clerestory of the choir were uncovered in this year, and the modern paint, which obscured the design of the Monks' Choir ceiling was removed. The Restoration Committee reported that £20,000 had been spent in the preceding five years and that £30,000 was still required.

On 30th April 1877, The See of St. Albans was created by Order-in-Council and on 12th June, Bishop Thomas Claughton was enthroned. A throne designed by Cottingham had been found in store in the crypt of Rochester cathedral and it was brought to St. Albans for the occasion. By this time, the seventeenth century pulpit had had its tester removed. The handsome bronze eagle lectern with angels at its base, still in use in the nave, is Scott's design, indicating once again how much in the spirit of the building his contributions were.

The most frightening defect still to be rectified was the south wall of the nave, which was now fully twenty-eight inches out of the perpendicular. To rectify this, Scott devised an hydraulic pressure system which lifted the weight of the roof off the walls. First, he stiffened the north wall with timbers to help it take the strain. Iron rods like railway couplings were fixed from the north wall to the south and screw jacks applied from the outside. Then the entire mass was dragged back in one piece and in a single motion. The actual straightening took two and a half hours to complete. It was then held in place until it could be adequately underpinned and buttressed. By now the Restoration Committee had been recast and only now a proper legal Faculty granted to carry out the work. The contracting firm which executed the straightening of the nave wall under Scott was Longmire and Burge.

Outside, Scott supported the wall be means of five exceedingly heavy buttresses. He refused to pierce the western section of the

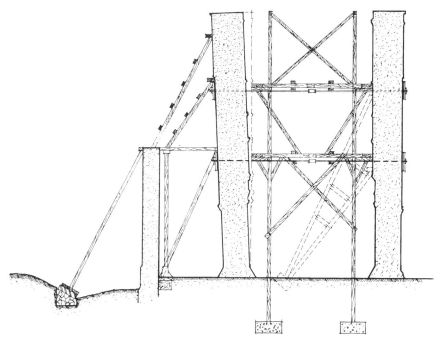

Fig. 89   Detail of part of scaffolding used by Sir G G Scott to straighten nave walls, 1877.

wall with windows, on the grounds that there had been none in that location originally, the abbot's lodging occupying this position (see fig. 84). The big buttresses took the thrust from the flying buttresses under the high-pitched aisle roof which stretched for a hundred feet. For some of the external repairs, Scott used Chilmark stone which unfortunately weathered severely during the next hundred years. He intended to reinstate the former high-pitched roof over the nave, as he had done at Rochester, but he did not live to carry out this plan.

He revaulted five bays of the south nave aisle following the evidence which survived from Trumpington's vaulting. The ceiling of the nave is also apparently Scott's work; it is different in style of construction from the transept ceilings which was Grimthorpe's project.

How to finish the west end bay where John de Cella's south-western tower had been begun but never completed was a problem for which Scott had to improvise a solution (see fig. 36). The unbalanced effect of the arches as he left them has been criticised. Suddenly, on 27th March 1878, before these works were carried to a conclusion, Scott died. The parts left unfinished at his death were carried out according to his plans by his son, J Oldrid Scott. In all, Scott restored twenty-nine cathedrals, ten minsters and over four hundred parish churches. Sir John Betjeman writes, 'many of our churches are still standing today because of the practical steps Gilbert Scott took to ensure their stability.' Scott should receive much more credit than he normally does for his achievements at St. Albans. He worked here for twenty-two years but his labours are under-estimated, partly because of

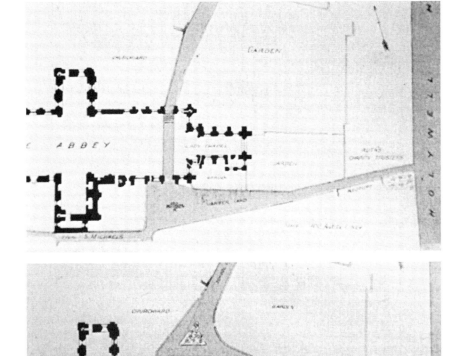

Fig. 90   Scott's plans of 1878 to divert the public footpath which ran through the abbey.

Grimthorpe's campaign of abuse, partly because he did essential repairs instead of imposing his personal style upon the building.

Seven years before his death, in 1871, Scott had protested in his personal report to the Earl of Verulam about the public passageway through the abbey, describing it as a 'conspicuous and barbarous injury' and a 'monstrous piece of vandalism' (see fig. 73). In the spring of 1874, this passage was boarded up at each end to allow restoration work to proceed. Forty-five inhabitants of St. Albans petitioned the Council against stopping the highway, otherwise they would consider themselves at liberty to enforce their right. A counter petition from another group about a week later favoured the closing for a year to allow the repair to be made. On the night of May 20th, a group of people forcibly reopened the passage. A compromise solution was reached when the Earl of Verulam proposed diverting the footpath around the east end of the abbey church; land to the east was purchased, certain walls demolished and the new route agreed in 1878. After so many years of dismemberment, the church was a single entity once more.

References

BECKETT (SIR EDMUND). St. Alban's cathedral and its restoration. St. Albans. 1885.

CHAPPLE (JOHN). The restoration of St. Albans Abbey. St. Albans. 1874.

COLE (DAVID). The work of Sir Gilbert Scott. London. 1980.

COMYNS CARR (J W). The abbey church of St. Albans. London. 1877.

KILVINGTON (FRANK I). A short history of St. Albans School. St. Albans. 1970.

LLOYD (ROBERT RIDGWAY). An architectural and historical account of the shrines of St. Alban and Saint Amphibalus in Saint Albans Abbey. St. Albans. 1873.

NEALE (JAMES). The abbey church of St. Alban, Herts. London. 1877.

POPE-HENNESSY (John) ed. Victorian church art. London. 1971.

SCOTT (G GILBERT). Personal and professional recollections. Ed. G G Scott Jr. 1879.

STAMP (GAVIN). 'Sir Gilbert Scott's Recollections'. *Architectural History*. XIX (1976) 54–73.

Chapter 18

SIR EDMUND BECKETT,
1st BARON GRIMTHORPE

With the death of Scott, a new character moves firmly into the centre of the stage, Sir Edmund Beckett, 1st Baron Grimthorpe, whom Sir Nikolaus Pevsner describes as a 'venomous, pompous, righteous bully'. He was born Edmund Beckett Denison near Newark in 1816, the son of a wealthy baronet who was 'King' of the Great Northern Railway. Raised at Doncaster, Denison was educated at Eton and Trinity College, Cambridge, from which he graduated as Wrangler in 1838. His interest in mediaeval architecture began in his undergraduate years, although one notes that the Camden Society for promoting the study and practice of ecclesiastical architecture was not founded until the year after he graduated, in 1839. Denison married Fanny Lonsdale, the daughter of the Bishop of Lichfield in 1845 and from then on the Church of England interested him deeply; he himself was a rigid evangelical. His career at the Parliamentary Bar was distinguished and he was the leading solicitor of the Great Northern Railway. He began to study architecture

Fig. 91 Edmund Beckett Denison,
born 1816. From 1874,
known as Sir Edmund Beckett,
from 1886, Lord Grimthorpe.
Died 1905.

seriously in 1853 after the parish church of St. George, Doncaster, burned to the ground. It was at this time that he became acquainted with Gilbert Scott. From the experience he gained on the Building Committee, he wrote *Lectures on Church Building* which was published in 1856.

In 1858 the shareholders of the Great Northern Railway built a parish church for the railway workers, Doncaster St. James, designed by Denison and executed by Gilbert Scott. Already, Denison's style is fully developed. 'A church should be well built' he claimed and after one hundred and thirty years this one is still crisp and solid (compare fig. 44). It imitates the Decorated period, in Denison's view the climax of the Gothic style. He preferred natural materials such as well cut stone and considered brick and concrete to be shams. He admired massive tracery, strong and varied. Supports should be strenuous and look capable of doing their job, casting strong shadows. He especially liked 'eyebrows'.

In 1856, an old Archdeacon took Denison, then aged forty, to the fund-raising meeting at St. Albans Town Hall, 'quite by chance' he said. Denison's name does not appear amongst the contributors but it was he who asked Gilbert Scott to act as architect in the abbey restoration. Denison succeeded to the baronetcy in 1874 and, dropping the surname Denison, was henceforth known as Sir Edmund Beckett. He bought himself the Batch Wood estate, building himself a house in his version of the Queen Anne style; this house has been considerably altered in modern times. From this experience he wrote his second volume, *A Book on House Building*, sometimes described as 'How to do without an architect'. He was now approaching sixty years of age.

When did Beckett join the Abbey Restoration Committee? It is hard to say. For one so meticulous, he is remarkably vague on dates. Certainly he was working on repairs to the Presbytery vault by 1872 (see fig. 45); John Rogers, the later abbey architect, records how the boarding was so badly decayed that it was admitting light, so Beckett applied stiffly glued canvas onto the top surface to hold it together, but apparently ignored the infestation of death watch beetle. Then, in 1877, a workman woke him up in the middle of the night to tell him the Early English clerestory was about to collapse again (see fig. 84); in Scott's absence, Beckett had it shored up at his own expense. He claimed that he took over after Scott's death at the request of the Town Committee, who considered him superior to all other candidates.

In the pages that follow, it is hoped to present Sir Edmund objectively, without discussing his mastery of invective, nor (except in passing) his many controversies. He will be discussed as a later Victorian amateur designer. We must ask ourselves to what extent he achieved, or failed to achieve, his own aims and ideals. Incidentally, he was made in 1877 an honorary member of the RIBA but resigned in disgust after eleven years as he despised both architects and antiquarians.

Roofing the nave presented the first problem to be solved. Scott had favoured a high-pitched roof and the Committee of 1878 had concurred because the line of the original roof could still be seen, outlined on the tower (see fig. 71). The problem was the mediaeval parapet, an integral part of the existing, low-pitched roof but incongruous with a high-pitched roof (see fig. 79). Should it be destroyed or retained? The battle raged, in the pages of *The Athenaeum* as well as in *The Builder* and *The Times*. The correspondence makes sordid reading but at least the issues were sufficiently aired for the public to see both sides. The contract for the new roof, high-pitched *with* parapets, was signed in August 1878; Longmire and Burge were to be the builders with work commencing in the summer of 1879.

A view inside the roof shows the timbers after more than a century to be in remarkably good condition. The construction of the trusses is unexpected indeed: the king post has a double prop beneath it and on another plane. Diagonal braces meet the purlins at mid points between the trusses, while posts with angle brackets can be seen at the sides. Along the length of the roof is a raised platform which forms a passage for maintenance. The ceiling underneath the roof is apparently not by Beckett, as it is not tongued and grooved in the manner he used in the transepts. The cost of the roof totalled £4,000.

Looking at the nave roof westwards from the tower, one sees the remarkably steep pitch combined with the contradictory parapets. The structure has lasted well, the very straight ridge making it look new after more than a century. In deference to Scott's wishes, the roof was leaded, although Beckett himself preferred tiles. He had the sheets cast in smallish sizes, only six feet by twelve feet to reduce contraction and expansion. The leadwork was completed by the summer of 1879. Beckett was very proud of the ventilation of the roof space. Trap doors were provided for access and frequent rainwater outlets were provided.

Although the tower looked more comfortable with the visual support of a high-pitched roof (see fig. 20), James Neale claimed that the old pitch had been incorrectly reproduced. At least it

*Fig. 92   High-pitched roof with parapets constructed
by Sir Edmund Beckett, from 1879.
Re-leaded by J O Scott, 1909–1914.*

harmonised with Scott's one hundred foot length of high-pitched aisle roofing.

Beckett had been critical of the old corbel table, asserting that it was made of modern bricks and plaster. The restorer, William White, however, stated that it was the original corbel table of Roman bricks with a fifteenth century string course and parapet above. Beckett's new corbel table was hand carved in Ancaster stone, but time has revealed a funda- mental flaw in the design: the angle was insufficient to throw the rainwater clear of the building.

How to treat the west gable end which now rose awkwardly over the west façade of the building posed a new problem (see fig. 63). Closely related to this was the condition of the old west front generally. Evaluations differed widely. Scott had claimed he could repair it for £200 but Chapple stated that the west buttresses had split clean away from the façade and believed that the old design had been 'churchwardened' past all recognition. The antiquary, Boutell, said it was 'in a truly frightful state of ruinous decay'.

After Beckett had completed the roof, he applied for the Faculty to rebuild the west front, pointing to the spandril which was cracked completely through and to the triforium shafts which were leaning westwards. He feared that the nave arcades would follow. By December, the Committee had given him their backing and early in 1880, a new edition of *The Book of Building* appeared with a chapter added on restoration. By May 1880, the west front

Faculty had been granted to him.

Beckett produced a sketch of what he proposed and passed it to J Oldrid Scott, son of Sir Gilbert, 'in case he liked to work it out as a design for the new faculty'. The inadequacies of the proposal are legion: the big middle porch jabs into the west window, the blind arcading in the three bays are on different levels, the turrets are out of sympathy with the buttress heads and the lancets in the gable are too small. Beckett was annoyed when Scott produced his own design; it was published in *The Building News* on 3rd December 1880. Eventually three submissions went to the Bishop: Beckett's, one from Canon Davys of nearby Wheathampstead parish, and J Oldrid Scott's. Beckett unscrupulously substituted for Scott's professional drawing a rough tracing in writing ink on linen, so that his own work would not suffer by comparison. The Bishop chose Beckett's.

Fig. 93 West front as designed by Sir Edmund Beckett, 1880.

Beckett's scheme owes a certain debt to Lichfield cathedral, the church of his father-in-law. Both have three doors in an *aba* rhythm, and semi-octagonal buttresses at the extremities ending in turrets. The central window has three circles in the head, with two tiers of niches on either side. There is a wide band of cusped members. The large, foiled circles in the west window at Lichfield, Beckett copied inside the antechapel.

A superb drawing in *The Building News* for 17th July 1885, shows the west front as built. It had been altered somewhat in construction, for Chapple, still Clerk of Works, had to make it buildable; some go so far as to claim that he was the architect. The pinnacles have acquired high conical roofs, the window has grown larger, the parapet deeper. The single decorative motifs above the porches have become triplets and the stepped lancets in the gable have grown in size. A pair of arches appear between the porches. Once wonders how carefully Beckett had measured the building before he made his drawing.

The contract was signed on 2nd October 1880 with Longmire as builder and Chapple as Clerk of Works. J Oldrid Scott refused to work under Beckett without control over the design.

All this time the battle to save Wheathampstead's window raged in the press but there was little hope of prevailing, given Beckett's tactics (see. fig. 63). Once the scaffolding was up, he proclaimed the old façade 'thoroughly good for nothing'. As Mosette Broderick of New York pointed out in a recent paper, Beckett preferred to work on a ruinous building so he could rebuild completely without the 'tedium of laborious reconstruction stone by stone'. He despised the Perpendicular period which he described as vile, with the walls all eaten up by windows. Whenever he saw a part he did not like, he claimed it was too rotten to be saved and thus justified his rebuilding. Finding some old Early English mouldings rebuilt into the fifteenth century work, he himself incorporated some Perpendicular mouldings as rubble in his new nineteenth century front.

The middle bay of the new west front retained the same window outline as in the fifteenth century but with new tracery in the head. 'This almost made itself by the necessities of geometrical and mechanical treatment' Beckett said. In his view, a wheel with smaller circles around it was the essential motif. Actually, a wheel is a Norman motif, not a Decorated one, but Beckett never bothered himself with historical accuracy. His practicality comes out in the gently arched sill which removes the weight from the porch below and also in the chamfering of the central gable to reduce light loss. He liked floods of daylight and so used clear glass in his glazing. He had a meticulous eye for detail, each small circle containing more than seventy pieces of glass, no one piece more than five inches wide. The very deep buttresses, he said, were inspired by Lincoln cathedral. The parapet on top gave access to the roof.

To consolidate the three west porches, he had the foundations dug out in places to a depth of twenty feet. He restored the porch floors to their mediaeval levels and in so doing, revealed the step within (see fig. 34). He made the buttresses a foot wider and four feet deeper than before, and immensely increased the strength of construction in order to resist the thrust exerted by the nave arcade. In his search for strength, however, he built too well, cementing the stones so rigidly together than no allowance was made for expansion or contraction. The cross at the apex of the middle porch cast an inner shadow which pleased him very much.

Prominent turrets mark the corners of the façade and low arches near the ground give the deep shadows which he felt so desirable. His arcading, Mosette Broderick points out, is deliberately left empty, although mediaeval practice would have given every arch a piece of sculpture. Despite the expensive craftsmanship commissioned by Beckett, the work still looks machine made and mass produced.

The pinnacles lack harmony with the Norman crossing tower. Octagonal on plan, they have Early English shafted lancets on each face, squared fleurons of the fifteenth century on the frieze and a classical looking finial. Beckett mixed periods flagrantly and so we feel uneasy looking at the building.

Inside the porch are one hundred free standing shafts. Beckett insisted they should be worked by hand and not machine turned to prevent them looking like gas pipes; the rough chiselled surface which he specified has aged and weathered attractively. He added a second tier of shafts where there had been only one tier before.

Mr Plows did all the exterior carving, including the notorious portrait of Beckett as an angel, symbolising St. Matthew. It typifies instead his egocentricity: the tumbled locks and the idealised face give it an almost Byronic cast. The lion, symbol of St. Mark, is rather shapeless, apparently based on a mental picture rather than an actual lion. The ox for St. Luke looks rather like Tenniel's Mock Turtle, with its tiny ears and protruberant muzzle; the scale of the animal's head and that of the limbs have been distorted for artistic effect. Mr Plows seemed more at home with eagles and the symbol for St. John the Evangelist might be based upon an actual bird.

Inside the nave, when the earth had been removed, five steps were revealed, a feature unique in England. It was dictated by the sloping character of the site and gives an impression upon entering the nave of greater height, despite the fact that the ceiling overhead is flat. Three unusual windows opening between nave and porch were uncovered too. Beckett made the new western wall a double one with wall passage within, different on each side of the façade.

In April 1883, the apex stone was placed in position. The west front had cost £20,000 to rebuild.

If one looks by contrast at the west front of Rheims cathedral, one sees the source for Beckett's triple porch design. Such a scheme was never popular in England although it is used on the north transept of Westminster Abbey. His impoverishment as a designer becomes evident: Beckett combined the wide, screen like English front with the French style, which featured three horizontal and three vertical divisions. This muddled thinking increases our unease.

When St. Andrew's Chapel had been demolished in the sixteenth century, the arcade which joined it to the abbey was replaced by a shoddily built wall (see fig. 72 right). Scott died before this could be properly dealt with so, not surprisingly, the clerestory above it still leaned over; Beckett's workmen very easily pushed over this wall for seventy feet of its length. Beckett rebuilt the three western bays entirely, giving them deep buttresses, each with two set-offs, to support the flying buttresses beneath the high-pitched aisle roof. For the sake of unity, he copied Scott's south aisle design on the north but regretted doing so later, due to the excessive scale; as we have seen, he had had no qualms about using massive buttresses on the west façade.

The flintwork of the aisle was meant to remain exposed and unplastered. The windows are entirely of Beckett's design, two cinquefoiled lights with a foiled circle above.

Inside the north aisle, the windows have been given nook shafts and hood moulds. Beckett wondered about vaulting this aisle; only four bays would have been involved, but the transition to the Norman work would have been difficult. Eventually, he left it in such a way that it could be vaulted in future; the flying buttresses which he left exposed, could in that case be hidden within the cones of the vaults. The Early English tower arch in the north-west corner was too far gone to save (compare fig. 36). The three lancet windows in the west wall of the north aisle are his invention, placed there to illuminate the passage in the wall behind. A holy water stoup was moved in here from the porch outside in fragmentary condition but it does not function as it has no drain.

With Scott no longer in his way, Beckett was free to insert four new windows in the blank wall of the south aisle with, he tells us, 'a few variations in patterns'. Actually, he mixed the Decorated and Perpendicular styles. All the windows in the south aisle were rebuilt, he says; only the internal shafts and mouldings were left intact (see fig. 99 left). Whereas in the mediaeval period all the tracery in these windows had been alike, his new patterns, as usual, mix the style periods.

For the clerestory windows, Beckett used small scale glass quarries, set in cast iron frames and supported by iron saddle bars. These were to prove a problem with the passage of time, as the iron corroded causing damage to the stone.

All five of the Decorated piers he found to be covered in cracks which were steadily getting worse due to the deterioration of the rubble filling within the ashlar casing (see fig. 52). These piers he rebuilt and, he claimed, were the only new internal stonework (overlooking his work in the windows). Up to seven tons of cement were poured in from the top and a total of £300 spent repairing them. He was proud that no one could guess they were new: if only this sentiment had restrained his hand elsewhere.

The nave pavement was in a bad state, as the small flags and common bricks laid down by Archdeacon Stubbs were mostly broken and the floor uneven from the vaults sunk below (see fig. 78). The very foundations of the building had been robbed to hollow out these vaults. He filled them up, lowering the floor level to make the rise more gradual and paving the whole with large flags laid diagonally and punctuated by small, black marble squares. The old tombstones were relaid and the spaces between filled with granolithic, a mixture of powdered granite and cement.

He designed very long pews using oaks of magnificent girth. They are so comfortable that they must rate amongst his best designs and are much appreciated by those who sit in them Sunday by Sunday. The backs meet the seats at exactly the right angle.

In lowering the nave floor, he made three altar steps instead of two (see fig. 59). The sanctuary was paved in marble hexagons of three different colours. Noting how the floor level has changed, one must guard against drawing archaeological conclusions from the present appearance of the Norman pier bases.

He wanted a pulpit high enough to be as widely seen as possible, making one cylindrical in shape, carved in stone. He greatly enjoyed designing the overall pattern in low relief, in its combination of pentagons with two shapes of lozenge. A long footnote in his book on restoration describes the proportions used in these. Convolvulous flowers fill the figures. The Bishop, usually so meek, refused to preach from it, calling it a 'rotunda'. This pulpit was dismantled in 1972 but is still kept in store.

The abbey was illuminated by gaslight at this time. A glazed screen was placed across the south choir aisle, allowing a full view of the entire south aisle. It gives easy access but the detailing is dreary and coarse, the middle and side bays discordant and impoverished. It compares badly with some of the mediaeval screens of Hertfordshire, such as those from St. Mary, Hitchin, which are of great delicacy and beauty.

He extended the roodscreen northwards but provided access into the new vestry which served both the nave and High Altars. A door was cut harshly into the mediaeval style panels. This man, so practical and ingenious, was utterly devoid of taste. The nave was reopened for services on 21st October 1885. Its restoration had cost him £50,000.

The south choir aisle once had Norman vaulting as Scott reported in 1871 and as Sophia Lonsdale, Beckett's niece by marriage, confirmed in her memoirs. Possibly it was ruinous; we do not know. It was replaced in any case by a very odd design: the pointed vaults have wide transverse arches with a sunk panel decoration and coarse mouldings of the Norman period. It is another hotchpotch of mixed motifs, bothersome in effect.

The next problem was the cloisters whose blind arcading still survived outside the south wall (see figs. 55 and 80). Beckett found the foundations in this position to be shallow; the wall leaned outwards and the windows were badly decayed. He toyed with the idea of using flying buttresses which would spring over the tracery and preserve it but, deciding the tracery would shortly be weathered entirely away, decided to write it off. He refaced the wall above, supporting it with a system of heavy buttresses which aligned with the nave arcade within. These had foundations sunk into the ground to a depth of five feet. He recessed the windows more deeply to give the play of light and shade he loved so much.

Then he turned to the south transept. As Beckett's personal account of the restoration ends with the year 1885, we have only the reports of others and the visual remains to guide us. The south transept wall was so rotten, he claimed, that it crumbled when the workmen touched it. He therefore rebuilt the lower west wall, destroying the blind arcading of the east cloister walk as well as the book lockers which survived (see fig. 80).

The entire south face of the transept is new and Beckett manufactured 'Roman' bricks when none were to be had. He replaced Cottingham's stone window by his especial pride, his giant lancet composition (see fig. 99). The central lancet in the

Fig. 94   Reredos, The resurrection of Christ, by Alfred Gilbert, from 1890.

group is the highest in England, and each mullion weighs thirty-two tons. The upper parts of the lancets illuminate an attic room under the newly raised roof. One pleasing aspect is the texture of the glazing: in technical matters like this Beckett did excel. Note how he retained Cottingham's heraldic glass. The south transept turrets feature the polychromy much favoured by followers of Ruskin. However, these turrets represent Beckett's style at its worst; there is no effect of diminished weight as the eye ascends, with a top-heavy result. The details are gross in scale, for example, nail-head ornament as big as cannon balls. The roof is brutal in its seating and incongruous in its enormous weight. Apparently no attention is paid to carrying off the rain, yet somehow the Ancaster stone he used appears very often crisp and new. Inside, the new south transept ceiling was beautifully tongued and grooved throughout, completely airtight in its construction. The roof was tiled. In 1886, Beckett was elevated to the peerage, becoming Lord Grimthorpe at the age of seventy years.

The Slype was partly rebuilt (see fig. 29). The south wall, the only surviving portion of the twelfth century domestic range, was fortunately retained, but its external facing, in diapered brickwork of the eighteenth century, he replaced by plain new brick to harmonise with the old brick wall surrounding Sumpter Yard. The two end walls he cut away and rebuilt in brick, opening a new doorway on the eastern side and placing lights at the west.

The carved Norman doorway which joined the Slype to the cloister he retained, to reset in the middle of the south wall of the south transept where no door had existed before. An inner order was added to it, of squares filled with formalised flowers and nutmeg pattern. No one could confuse this with Norman work, despite his hope of tricking the antiquaries. The south transept was deemed complete in 1887.

The pulpit at the crossing was presented by the Freemasons of England at a cost of £700. It is signed by Goldsmuir and dated 1885.

The Wallingford screen was being restored by Faculty between the years 1884 and 1889 by Henry Hucks Gibbs, 1st baron Aldenham of Aldenham House near Elstree. Gibbs was both banker and scholar, serving the Bank of England as Director, then Governor, and contributing to *The New English Dictionary* as a philologist. He had hoped to restore the Lady Chapel, but lost to Beckett in an acrimonious lawsuit. For the work on the Wallingford screen, Gibbs chose Arthur Blomfield as architect.

The sculpture on the screen, which Sir Nikolaus Pevsner describes as 'repulsively ungenuine' was by Harry Hems, 1842–1916, the prolific sculptor of Exeter. His work is to be found in most parts of England; his collection of newspaper cuttings of himself is said to have numbered 26,000 items. A long battle raged about the figure on the cross (see fig. 68); Beckett, as an evangelical, opposed it, but this time Gibbs had his way, and the mediaeval scheme of Christ on the cross was eventually reinstated.

For the reredos, Blomfield brought forward Alfred Gilbert, 1854–1934, famous as the sculptor of Eros in Piccadilly Circus. The reredos, carved in marble, shows *The Resurrection of Christ*: a nude figure of Christ rises from the tomb, still swathed in graveclothes and flanked by two angels whose iridescent wings are a mosaic of seashells. The inscription reads, 'Come unto me all ye that labour'. Although commissioned in 1890, the reredos was never actually completed but Richard Dorment, Gilbert's biographer, considers it 'one of his most original and . . . compelling creations' (see fig. 94).

Gibbs also financed the dividing and rebuilding of the great organ to given an unbroken view through the whole length of the building.

Some of the abbey's finest glass, in the east window of the Saint's Chapel, commemorates H H Gibbs, Lord Aldenham. An angel figure occupies each of the six lights, with the central four playing musical instruments. Although from the studios of Burlison and Grylls, there is nevertheless marked William Morris influence, in the glowing colours, long rhythmic lines and strong sense of design. Arched wings, counterchanging red and blue, adorn the upper spaces while golden beams of light fan out below. Kenneth Gibbs, Archdeacon of St. Albans and a son of Lord Aldenham, commissioned this fine window (see fig. 44).

Meanwhile, Lord Grimthorpe was reworking the north transept between 1888–9; it is just as assertive as the south but veiled behind a softening screen of trees. There is no doubt which parts are his as the textures demonstrate which surfaces were meant to be plastered and which parts exposed. The twin shafted lancets on the lower stage of the ground floor are his contribution. The steep gable is crowned by a Celtic cross but the brash turrets argue with the Norman tower. In the gable end is a Norman style twin window, marred by the unhistoric addition of an oculus (a large, circular window) above. This is another lapse of taste and judgement.

Here in the north transept, he destroyed the still surviving great Perpendicular window inserted by Abbot William Wallingford. The rose window which replaced it consisted of concentric rings of lights, plain circles and cusped ones, with lozenges in the intervals. It has the merit at least of strength. The clear glass (which he favoured at clerestory level) he handled extraordinarily well, each circle containing a different geometrical pattern of great ingenuity. Grimthorpe the mathematician was a genuis and these designs of radial symmetry, ninefold, fourfold, fivefold, formed a masterpiece of the glaziers' art. Nothing comparable existed outside the Islamic world.

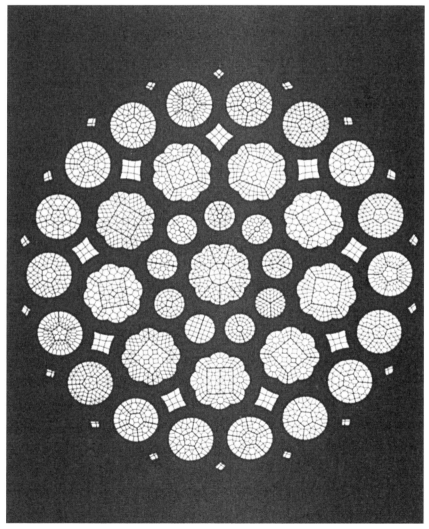

Fig. 95   Rose window, north transept, designed by Lord Grimthorpe, 1888–89. Glazing bars now destroyed. Courtesy Dr Rowland Mainstone.

The bobbin pattern carved around the window has been copied from the Slype arcading (see fig. 29). The Latin inscription claiming he had destroyed all the work of Wheathampstead is inaccurate, as this abbot seems to have done no work at all in the north transept. The flat ceiling, an unadorned copy of the old, carefully tongued and grooved, is also by Grimthorpe.

He turned next to the Presbytery, raising the pitch of the roof and covering it with tiles, paying due attention to light and ventilation within. A central gangway under the roof allowed one to walk the full length of the Presbytery inside. Then his abysmal taste reasserted itself: he could not resist inserting tracery into the chaste Early English lancet windows (see fig. 41). Because of the high-pitched roof, a new gable end was created at the east and this was designed with typical Grimthorpe fantasy (see fig. 48): a foiled, triangular window has Tudor roses at the base and centre combined with Early English mouldings. There is a parapet at the gable adorned with tumbling trefoils and an unusual cross form at the apex. The pinnacles are typical of his style: lancets under cusped arches are expressed in fat and bulbous mouldings. The caps are octagonal and ribbed with stiff-leaf finials and end stops.

The great geometric window at the east of the Presbytery, high over Alban's shrine, Grimthorpe reproduced along the former lines, except for variations in the cusping and his favourite inflated mouldings (see fig. 44). The eastern wall is composed of coursed flintwork with brick and heavy, decorative bands with naïve, outsize patterns.

As Chancellor and Vicar-General of the Diocese of York, Grimthorpe was conscious of the need for Consistory Courts and he adapted the St. Albans antechapel for this use. He erected a wall along the east of the Saint's chapel, adorned on the eastern face with a bold niche treatment. Some units were trefoiled, others pyramidal, all supported on Purbeck shafts. The varied heights gave a restless effect and again he used a favourite motif, the tumbling trefoil. The shrine of St. Amphibalus, Britain's first known Evangelist, was relegated to a gloomy corner at the east of the north aisle. Grimthorpe's ornate wall was not, apparently, popular and lasted only forty years; it was discreetly removed in the 1930s by the architect Blacking (see fig. 42).

Finally Grimthorpe turned to the Lady Chapel (see fig. 49). He replaced the old wooden vault by a copy in stone, but pointed it more sharply thus altering the internal spatial feeling. The vaults were made to spring from long, pendant brackets carved by John Baker. There was no precedent for these at St. Albans, although well known examples exist at Exeter cathedral. There is a carefully observed design of the oak at the south-west corner, and a study of the filbert on the north-west. The glazing of the east window was the gift of the Corporation of the City of London in 1880. Around the lower stage Grimthorpe provided blank arcading based upon fragments surviving at the east and west of the chapel when the school moved out. The capitals were carved by John Baker in fruit and foliage patterns based on the plants which grow in the locality, good quality examples of late Victorian sculpture. In the south-east corner, Grimthorpe improvised a sedilia and a door where these had been lost in earlier centuries. It forms a study in contrasts, 1880 work below, and 1310 canopy work above. Black and white marble paved the chapel floor.

Outside the chapel, a complete refacing took place (see fig. 50). The parapet was quite new with its sunk lozenge pattern. The buttresses before refacing were much enlarged to support the new stone vault. The ancient materials of flint, brick and stone have been used in the distinctive Grimthorpe fashion, while the gables to the buttresses rise above the parapet with a restless and assertive effect. After a hundred years, the Ancaster stone still looks amazingly new. As Chapple said, 'You cannot copy it; better it if you can'.

The Chapel of the Transfiguration received his attention in 1891, gaining a parapet of tumbling trefoils (see fig. 50, lower right). The windows at the ends and sides are different, an ancient tradition of the St. Albans archdeaconry of which Grimthorpe was probably unaware.

In 1893, with the laying of the floor in the Lady Chapel, the Grimthorpe era was drawing to a close. He himself had said, 'the great fault of architects was that they know nothing of practical building'. Yet, in 1897, we find Lord Grimthorpe beginning to repair his own restoration work: the roof tiles had to be stripped and relaid, the parapet coping stone had to be renewed, the south aisle roof needed repairs, the bases of the shafts in the west portal had cracked and so had certain window sills. Had he fallen short of his own high standards, or should we be charitable and call it 'making good'? One hundred years later, much damage was discovered, caused by his use of ironwork with stone which had corroded and allowed damp penetration. We have already mentioned his too rigid cementing of stone together without space to expand. In his youth, he had been a typical product of his age, influenced by Pugin and by Ruskin. In his latter years, the world had passed him by. Men like William Morris, Charles Rennie

Mackintosh and Charles Voysey moved in another sphere. A marble bust of benign demeanour can be seen in the north transept, Grimthorpe, no doubt, as he saw himself.

He died in 1905 and was buried under a modest stone in the north-east corner of the churchyard. Like Wren, if you seek his monument, look about you. Does anyone admire him unreservedly? He had exemplary ideals: know what you are doing, build well, be bold, be strong. But he did not know his limitations and would never listen to critics. His great qualities were marred by arrogance, bad taste and a lack of historic sense. Like us all, he was human but his strengths and weaknesses were on an heroic scale.

References

'Abbey rival returns'. *Herts. Advertiser*. 12th October 1990.

BECKETT (SIR EDMUND, 1st BARON GRIMTHORPE). Lectures on church building. 1856.

... A book on house building. 1876.

... A book on building. London. 1880.

... St. Albans cathedral and its restoration. St. Albans. 1885.

CHAPPLE (JOHN). The restoration of the abbey of S. Alban. St. Albans. 1874.

... The restoration of the abbey church of S. Alban. St. Albans. 1876.

... A short history of the abbey church of S. Albans. St. Albans. 1882.

COX (JOHN). 'Carvings in the Lady Chapel'. *The Alban Link*. II. Spring, 1975. 4–6.

DORMENT (RICHARD). Alfred Gilbert, sculptor and goldsmith. Royal Academy of Arts. London. 1986.

FERRIDAY (PETER). Lord Grimthorpe, 1816–1905. London. 1957.

GIBBS (HENRY HUCKS, 1ST BARON ALDENHAM). Account of the high altar screen in the cathedral church of St. Albans. 1890.

JONES (CHARLES E). 'The restoration of the cathedral and abbey church of St. Alban'. *Trans. SAHAAS*. 1937. 115–130.

KITTON (F G). 'Lord Grimthorpe: a biographical sketch'. *Hertfordshire Illustrated Review*. I. 1894. 149–153.

MARTINEAU (VIOLET). 'Uncle Grim (from recollections of Sophia Lonsdale)'. *The Alban Link*. XX. Autumn 1984. 17–22.

OLDING (SIMON). 'Harry Hems – sculptor'. *The Alban Link*. XVIII. Autumn 1983. 25–31.

The Church Builder. 'St. Albans abbey; the battle of the roofs'. April, 1879.

Part VII

THE TWENTIETH CENTURY

Chapter 19

J OLDRID SCOTT AND JOHN C ROGERS

J Oldrid Scott, 1842–1913, the second son of Sir Gilbert, trained in his father's office and assisted him on many important buildings, like the Foreign Office in Whitehall. He himself restored Beverley Minster and Tewkesbury Abbey. His fine drawings of Gothic revival churches were frequently shown at the Royal Academy.

After the death of his father in 1878, he carried on the work at St. Albans; Scott's proposal for the west front would have saved Wheathampstead's Perpendicular window (see fig. 63). The domineering Beckett shoved him aside from the principal restoration work. The two were engaged inevitably in many public controversies but these do not concern us here.

A personally self-effacing man, J Oldrid's contribution to the abbey was church furnishings of high quality. Believing that the thirteenth and fourteenth century Gothic was the apogee of the national style, he tried to reproduce it faithfully. The tomb of the first bishop, Thomas L Claughton, 1877–1890, was his scheme with the figure carved by the sculptor Forsyth. A new bishop's throne was provided in 1903 to replace the box like Cottingham throne as a memorial to John W Festing, bishop from 1890–1902 (see fig. 96). Scott's drawing shows it arranged in three tiers; the bottom one is rectangular with flying buttresses projecting at the rear. The middle tier is cruciform with a steeply gabled roof and slender, crocketed pinnacles at the four corners. The top tier has an octagonal lantern. Alban, unfortunately, is shown incorrectly as a Roman soldier. The stalls which commemorate Festing as well as Archdeacons Ady and Mildmay and other notables, are by Scott also. They have what Beckett's work lacked, a sense of scale and sufficient plain surface to act as a foil to the rich decoration. The stall end figure of an angel musician is appealing and appropriate to the choir.

Fig. 96   *Bishop's throne, designed by J Oldrid Scott, 1903*

H H Gibbs, we have seen divided up the great organ into halves, one north and one south, so that a view could be obtained throughout the length of the building; Scott's 1907 design for the case is a highly satisfactory one.

Practical tasks were undertaken in these years as well. The fifth and sixth bells were recast by John Warner of Cripplegate in 1901. The lead of the roof, proving inadequate, had to be stripped off in sections and recast between 1909 and 1914 (see fig. 92); the reroofing was paid for out of the Grimthorpe bequest. In the years before the first World War the plan to vault in stone the four western bays of the north nave aisle was again resumed. Funds for this purpose were collected and plans, drawn up by J O Scott, hung for some time at the west end of the nave. The war intervened, however, and the money afterwards applied to providing a war memorial.

J Oldrid Scott, who died in 1913, is chiefly remembered at the abbey for the mellow graciousness of his choir furnishings.

The eminent Sir Herbert Baker, 1862–1946, made a modest contribution to the abbey. The protegé for twenty years in South Africa of Cecil Rhodes, and associated in 1912 with Lutyens in New Delhi, his notable London buildings are South Africa House, 1933 and the Bank of England, 1921. At St. Albans, he prepared a scheme for rebuilding one of the apsidal chapels to the east of the north transept as a missionary chapel (see fig. 19), but again, with the outbreak of war, the money was put to other uses. He reorganised the Saint's Chapel as a memorial to Edgar Jacob, bishop from 1903 to 1919 and his personal friend.

The first memorial to the dead of World War I was a colourful and dramatic canvas, *The passing of Eleanor*, painted by Frank Salisbury, then still in Harpenden. It represented a scene in the 1907 Pageant which had impressed him strongly. Ten years later the mayor, Arthur Faulkner, purchased it for the abbey to celebrate the freeing of Jerusalem by the British army and to honour the fallen of Hertfordshire. This much loved work, for which local people had posed in costume, was stolen from the south transept in October, 1973.

The second major memorial was the glazing of the great west window (see fig. 93). Michael Furse, bishop from 1920 to 1944, warmly backed this project to honour the dead of the diocese; by diverting the vaulting fund and by collecting from the parishes, £4,000 was raised.

The glazier selected was Ninian Comper, 1864–1960, noted for his 'sensitive, expensive and unmistakable workmanship' as Gerard Irvine puts it. Comper had been articled to C E Kempe the glazier and later to the architect Bodley, his especial master. The window was dedicated in 1925 and typifies Comper's work in the predominant blue, white and gold, to which deep burgundy touches give contrast. Heraldic display, of parish and diocese, regiments and allies, occupies the three rose motifs in the head to which a band of angels gives a firm foundation underneath. With considerable panache, Comper triumphs over the limitations of the nine narrow lights below, by which Beckett had hope to foil any glazing schemes, preferring clear glass himself. The crucified Christ, a gleaming, silvery figure, forms the central, vertical motif; he is shown as the youthful, beardless Christ of the Greek tradition which Comper so much admired. Golden trumpets fanning out at his feet give additional focus. The lower band is a dense and vigorous group in darker tones, the patron saints of the allies, with Roman soldiers behind, typical of Comper's eclectic style. Above, in the middle band, against an architectural setting, the banners of the allies dramatically unfurl.

It is instructive to realise that the abbey possesses not only two windows in the south wall of the Lady Chapel by C E Kempe (1834–1907) the glazier to whom Comper was articled; it also has two examples by Comper's pupil, Christopher Webb (1886–1966) in the north-west corner of the nave. Thus several generations of a single glazing tradition can be studied in this one building.

The stalls in the Lady Chapel, 1940, are also Comper's work, 'the greatest church furnisher since Wren' Irvine claims. Nearby, in London Colney, All Saints Convent possesses one of the chapels for which he is particularly renowned. He was knighted in 1950 for his services to glazing and his ashes are buried in Westminster Abbey under windows of his design.

Meanwhile, administrative changes within the Church of England had been taking place. By the Enabling Act of 1919, executive powers had passed from the Dean and Churchwardens to the Parochial Church Council. Having appointed a Fabric Committee to care for the building, a local man, John C Rogers was selected as Architect and Surveyor to the Fabric. This was in 1919. Woodwork was Rogers' particular speciality; indeed his book *English Furniture* published in 1923 contains superb drawings of constructional methods which 'have not been, nor are likely to be, superseded' in the words of Margaret Jourdain.

Appropriately, in the restoration of timber work lay Rogers' great contribution: in 1930–31 he undertook the repair of the painted wooden vault over the Presbytery (see fig. 43). His report, published in a local journal, begins with historical background based on meticulous observation below and above and informed by the knowledge of a craftsman who knew wood and what it could do. His vivid account of the work reads like a detective story.

First he acquainted himself with the method of construction by crawling over the dusty and dangerous vault; he found a severe infestation of still active death watch beetle. Supporting his workmen by ropes slung over the roof trusses above (even so the foot of one man went through the vault) one and a half tons of dust were removed from the top surface of the vault alone. Great cavities, as big as a man's arm, became apparent in the ribs and the huge bases were so eaten away that only a few 'stalactites' remained. About twenty-five cubic feet of solid oak had been consumed by beetle in the six hundred years of the vault's existence; the whole structure was dangerous in the extreme. In one pocket near the tower, charred wood was found, evidence of an earlier fire and its repair.

C Miskin and Sons were taken on as contractors. Rogers' problem was to effect the repair without altering the essential structure, without obtruding on the visible surfaces and without discolouring the painting; all this was to be achieved *in situ*. The challenge was formidable. The whole area below was covered in scaffolding and the wooden shields taken down. From each 'pocket' a few boards were removed so the dust inside could be cleared. Insecticide treatment was given to all members and hollow ribs were filled with plastic wood. A light metal backbone was then applied to the ribs; the iron strips six inches wide by three-eighths of an inch thick were brought in by a turret door near the end of the gutter. The whole vault, in effect, was suspended by supports from the nineteenth century roof trusses above; other members were bolted to the masonry walls by angle irons. The decayed feet of the wall posts were sawn away and replaced by short piers of stock bricks resting on the stone springers below.

All this time, Prof. E W Tristram of the Royal College of Art was working on the painted decoration of the vault (see fig. 83), and two watercolours showing the discoveries he made still hang on the west wall of the Presbytery. A joint report by Rogers and Tristram was published with photographs in *Country Life* in May 1931 informing future generations of this remarkable repair.

Wasting no time, Rogers turned his attention to the timbers in the great crossing tower (see fig. 21). He conducted a survey in May 1931, completed the work and published a full description in a local journal within the year. His account, fluent and lucid, has a plan, sections and an isometric drawing, executed in a neat, thorough and meticulous style. Four tons of solid rubbish produced by birds and vermin were removed by a vacuum process. Steel reinforcements were inserted and oaken wedges placed in loosened joints. Canvas was glued above the flimsy old tower ceiling, sound insulation placed upon it and a floor of stout deal planks laid in the ringing chamber. One hundred gallons of insecticide was applied to the forest of timber to destroy the death watch beetle. The belfry timbers were not examined because of the presence of the bells; Rogers disapproved of the heavy water tank placed on that level by Grimthorpe without regard to the strength of the timbers.

Finally, the Watching Loft was dusted out and treated against beetle infestation in the floorboards (see fig. 61). Its light and airy position had protected it against worse attack and no structural repairs were necessary. Rogers once again published a masterly analysis of the structure, this time in *Country Life*.

Prof. E W Tristram continued his work on the murals during the thirties (see fig. 39). He had shown an early interest in wall painting even as a student; influenced by Lethaby, his life's work became the copying and recording of English mural paintings. Now mainly in the Victoria and Albert museum, these watercolours form, in effect, a national record of murals. His method of restoration, sadly, proved to be unsound: his application of wax dissolved in turpentine and driven in by heat was impenetrable to moisture and deterioration often ensued. Trimstram's waxing has not yet been removed from the north transept, the south choir aisle nor the *Holy Trinity* mural.

The architect J A R Blacking was called in to carry out some special commissions. His marble font of 1933 is of the chalice type with a bowl of fluted white supported on a black moulded pedestal. The font cover is a lofty, openwork spire in three diminishing tiers on the mediaeval pattern, but all details are executed in the classical idiom and gilded. The furnishings of St. Michael's chapel, at the east end of the north aisle, are his design, but follow the lead of Comper in taking the altar seriously and not treating it as a sideboard or mantlepiece. He replaced the ponderous Grimthorpe niches on the west wall of the antechapel by an unadorned wall with central access into the Saint's Chapel (see fig. 42).

To mark the jubilee in 1934 of the change ringers of Hertfordshire and of the cathedral, it was decided to add four new bells to the existing peal, bringing the abbey peal up to twelve, the only example in the diocese. At the same time, the existing eight bells would be overhauled and retuned and the cracked fifth bell recast. It was established with experts that the abbey tower could withstand the additional thrust. Mears and Stainbank, bellfounders of Whitechapel, were to undertake the work at a cost of £500. Two bells were financed by individuals (Dr Madge and E P Debenham), one by the county ringers and the fourth by public subscription. The delicate task of lowering the bells by winch was effected through a panel opening in the tower ceiling. All eight were then transported by cart to the Whitechapel foundry where the recasting and retuning took place. The dedication of the new peal took place on the day of King

George V's Silver Jubilee, 6th Mary 1935.

When Sir Mortimer Wheeler and Mrs Tessa Wheeler were carrying out their excavations in the early thirties in the Roman city of Verulamium, Dean Cuthbert Thicknesse (1936–1955) had the foresight to obtain a considerable supply of Roman bricks to be laid aside for future repairs to the abbey as required. This stock was to prove invaluable in major repair work both to the great crossing tower as well as to the nave.

Meanwhile John C Rogers pursued the mundane tasks of cathedral maintenance. He carried out drainage works on the north side of the building and in 1937 installed a modern heating system. An external boiler house and chimney were required (see fig. 99) and in digging the trenches to receive the heating ducts, the embossed tile floor of the mediaeval chapter house was uncovered. Arranging for this to be cleaned and photographed, Rogers altered his plans to site the new structures well clear of the ancient remains to protect them. Whilst digging in the south choir aisle, fragments of gilded and painted clunch from the shrine base of St. Alban were discovered (see fig. 47). Once again, Rogers published a report in the archaeological society's *Transactions*.

Rogers died in 1939, but his historical approach, his superb architectural drawings and his thorough recording of the work done, set a standard of excellence for those who follow.

References

CARTMEL (G W). 'The bells'. *The Alban Link*. XXI. Summer 1985. 32–39.

COMPER (JOHN NINIAN). 'The English altar and its surroundings'. *Some principles and services of the Prayer Book practically considered*. J Wickham Legg, ed. London 1899. 41–129.

FERRIDAY (PETER). Lord Grimthorpe, 1816–1905. London 1957.

KELL (J R). 'St. Albans abbey bells'. *The Abbey Magazine*. September 1969. 12–15.

. . . 'About the abbey'. *The Alban Link*. VI. Spring 1978. 1–4.

. . . 'Maintenance and improvement, 1900–1977'. *The Alban Link*. VIII. Spring 1979. 3–5.

'Obituary: John Oldrid Scott, FSA.' *Journal of the Royal Institute of British Architects*. 28 June 1913. 614.

Idem. *The Times*. 2 June 1913.

ROGERS (JOHN C). *English Furniture*. edn. 2. Country Life. 1950.

. . . 'The great tower of St. Albans abbey church.' *Trans. SAHAAS*. 1930. 56–64.

. . . 'The watching loft in St. Albans abbey church'. *Country Life*. 17 January 1931. 76.

. . . 'St. Albans abbey church: the painted wooden vault . . . its history, structure and recent repair.' *Trans. SAHAAS*. 1931. 122–136.

. . . 'Some notes on excavations in and about St. Albans cathedral during the summer of 1937.' *Trans. SAHAAS*. 1937. 140–143

ROGERS (JOHN C) and TRISTRAM (E W). 'St. Albans abbey: the restoration of the presbytery roof.' *Country Life*. 28 March 1931. 390–392.

SKEAT (FRANCIS W). Stained glass windows of St. Albans cathedral. Chesham and Luton. 1977.

STRAKER (G C). A history of the organs at the cathedral of St. Alban. London 1929.

TRISTRAM (E W). English medieval wall painting: the thirteenth century. 2 vols. Oxford, 1950.

. . . English wall painting of the fourteenth century. London, 1955.

WALLER (J G). A critical examination of the armorial bearings and decorations on the ceiling of the monks' choir of the abbey church of St. Alban. Westminster, 1889.

Chapter 20

CECIL BROWN AND GEORGE PACE

The distinguished architect and draftsman, Cecil Brown, served as Surveyor to the Fabric for twenty-three years, from 1939 to 1962. His noteworthy achievements elsewhere include restoration work on St. Paul's cathedral (designing and inserting the stainless steel chain which girdles the drum of the dome, for which he received the RIBA Silver Medal) and the sensitive restoration, from a pile of ruins, of St. Lawrence Jewry in the city of London.

Shortly after his appointment to St. Albans, war broke out; he therefore organised the fire protection of the building, including a system of dry risers and the provision of a fire pump in the Slype. Fearing bomb damage, the twelve abbey bells were lowered in 1941; eleven of the bells remained in the south Presbytery aisle for the next five years, with the remaining one placed in the north transept turret. During the tedious hours of fire watching in the cathedral, he commenced an isometric drawing of the tower and transepts to a scale of one inch to six feet. This *tour de force* of the draftsman's art, on display in the Exhibition Gallery, was dedicated to King George VI. As well as presenting the original drawing to the abbey, he produced for sale reduced photographic copies.

Early in the war years, clergy stalls for the Lady Chapel were designed by Sir Ninian Comper and dedicated in 1940. Further work on this chapel was deferred until after the war, when improvements were financed by members of the Kent family: the rehabilitation of the organ in 1952 and a new lectern in 1954. Eighteen new pews, designed by Cecil Brown at a cost of £955, replaced the 'dilapidated chairs' in November 1955. Rectangular panels and consoles feature in the design. On his altar frontal, in dull gold brocade embroidered in blue, green, burgundy and glittering gold thread, a serene and monumental Virgin with two attendant angels cradles the holy child. Hassocks and cushions, designed by Joan Hudson Wakely, were worked between 1960 and 1972.

The restoration of the Norman crossing tower was Brown's great contribution to St. Albans (see fig. 20). The Roman tiles of its fabric, collected more than eight centuries before from Verulamium, had deteriorated badly, not only from gas fumes and from weathering, but also from the destructive cement used by Grimthorpe in pointing. Brown introduced a full time, resident stonemason to the abbey staff. The first appointee, Walter Barrett, with a single casual assistant, removed and turned every Roman brick in the vast crossing tower, resetting each in soft mortar. Necessary replacements came from Dean Thicknesse's stock of Roman bricks. If any abbey workman deserves recognition, it is surely Walter Barrett, for his heroic achievement.

The ceiling of the tower, which dated from the sixteenth century, was in a badly decayed condition, its painted decoration bleached and peeling. With funds from the Yapp Trust (a private bequest) Brown had a replica made, its sixteen panels brightly painted with red and white roses around four central heraldic shields (see fig. 22). One of the original panels has been preserved in the north Presbytery aisle; the others remain covered up in the roof.

Brown's skills embraced stained glass design: two windows, coloured medallions set in clear glass, overlook the antechapel at north and south. *St. George and the Dragon* on the Dymoke-Green window on the north dates from 1954; the arms of Toulmin on the south date from 1955. Both were executed by Francis Skeat. The style reflects that of the glazier, Christopher Webb (1886–1966) whose striking window of 1955 in the south Presbytery aisle depicts *The martyrdom of St. Alban*. It, too, features a coloured figural group framed in a wreath (here roses) set on a field of clear glass; as well as beautifying the building, it also admits the light.

In 1955 the restoration of the mediaeval murals in the nave, which were very grimy and suffering from Tristram's well-meaning but misguided attempts at preservation, was taken in hand. This work, financed mainly by the Pilgrim Trust (which also lent the scaffolding) was directed by Prof. R W Baker of the Royal College of Art and by his wife, Mrs Baker, in consultation with E Clive Rouse and Cecil Brown. New solvents were applied in a gel base to remove the wax coating, revealing the masonry pattern on the four tower arches in all its beauty; here foliage bands were also revealed (see fig. 22). A *trompe l'oeil* frieze was discovered in the choir clerestory, imitating jutting blocks of coloured marble. A fifteenth century restoration of the murals was confirmed, in which the colour of the crosses had been altered from brown to green, indicating the high regard in which these paintings were held in the Middle Ages (see figs. 26, 39). Elsewhere in the building, repair to internal plasterwork was carried out, aided by a grant of £1,000 from the Fraternity of Friends.

While the above dusty work was in progress, the organ had been removed for rebuilding. The design, by Ralph Downes and Peter Hurford, was carried out in 1962. It has three manuals and pedals and seventy-three ranks. Since it required an enlarged instrument, Cecil Brown designed the central Positive case for the choir organ, facing east and surmounted by the royal arms, in recognition of the Queen's personal gift to the rebuilding fund. Brown's designing skill is apparent in the harmonious relationship of the new canopy to the earlier design by J Oldrid Scott, and by the sympathetic way in which the new tripartite case emerges naturally from the lacy parapet of the choir stalls.

We owe to Cecil Brown's foresight the establishment of a Muniments Room, in which all correspondence, documents, drawings, maps, minutes, plans and other archive material, hitherto scattered amongst various cupboards, was gathered into one spot over the south Presbytery aisle for safekeeping. Having been arranged and indexed, it is now available for study as required.

Cecil Brown retired in 1962 and died twenty-one years later, on 6th January 1983 at the age of eighty years. The Bishop of Peterborough remembered him for his 'never failing urbanity, his exact and precise solution of problems, and his total demolition of pretentious and ill-formed criticisms'.

George Gaze Pace succeeded Brown in 1962 and served as Consultant Architect for a dozen years. As an architectural student, he had received a number of important prizes and practised mainly in Yorkshire with ecclesiastical work as his speciality. Amongst his outstanding works can be mentioned the University Library at Durham, the post-war restoration at Llandaff cathedral and the King George VI Memorial Chapel and tomb at Windsor Castle. He wrote prolifically on architectural subjects and his masterly drawings of Gothic detail at the Royal Academy's Summer Exhibitions always evoked admiration.

His work at St. Albans commenced in a modest way with the cleaning of some architectural treasures. The High Altar was meticulously cleansed in 1966 and the nineteenth century sculptures treated so as to better blend their yellowish stone with the mediaeval canopy work behind (see fig. 68). Between December 1970 and January 1971, the Ramryge chantry was cleaned of accumulated grime (see fig. 69). Using sectional, mobile scaffolding, every inch was dealt with, first with a dry, vacuum process and soft brushes, followed by a wet treatment using finely sprayed water, soft brushes and sponges. Immaculate once more, the intricately detailed and delicate carvings can be appreciated to the full.

By 1968, executive powers of the abbey had passed to the Cathedral Council. The re-ordering of the nave now assumed high priority. With the

Fig. 97   George G Pace, 1916–1975.

passage of time and the evolution of liturgical ideas, the Victorian arrangements with their bulky rigidity grew more and more irksome. The heavy choir stalls on their wooden platforms obstructed the view of the altar and raised a barrier between celebrant and people. Grimthorpe's massive pulpit halfway down the nave was another immovable obstacle. A more open, flexible arrangement, with a closer bond between altar and people, expressed in a westward facing celebrant and congregation closer to the altar, seemed desirable. If pulpit and choir stalls were of modest scale and easily moved, the internal spaces could be more freely adapted. Great diocesan events, like the Easter Youth Pilgrimage, the Nine Lessons and Carols at Christmas and the International Organ Festival, could have the setting each required. 'Function determines furnishing' Dean Noel Kennaby declared, opening the debate in February 1969 in *The Abbey Magazine*. George Pace, asked to draw up reordering plans, looked on the project as twofold: enhancing the beauty of the building, and 'leaving the options open'.

While the reordering work was carried out in the summer of 1972, nave services were moved temporarily to the crossing and for the first time in a hundred years, the nave was entirely cleared of furnishings. A thorough house-clean took place first, to lift the dust from the Norman plaster and to cleanse the grime from the stone revealing its creamy beauty. The triforium windows, hitherto blocked, were brought to life by hidden lighting which enhanced the soft, green, mediaeval glass. Examining a cupboard in the north nave wall revealed the blocked Norman door which had once led into St. Andrew's chapel: reinstating this exit gave quicker and safer egress to the vast crowds attending special abbey events.

The massive stone pulpit was taken to pieces, all eight tons of it as well as the one ton staircase; preserved in sections, it may one day find a role in another building. The choir stalls on their built up platforms were dismantled and the timber preserved for other uses. Permanent pews were cleared from the nave and replaced by chairs; one range of aisle pews was removed to facilitate processions.

When the altar space was being widened, an immense vault was discovered underneath, cubical in shape, twelve feet square; it was filled with rubble, no doubt by Grimthorpe. Before the altar space was rebuilt, ducts were laid for loud speaker and microphone cables. The ironwork formerly around the altar was removed and adapted as radiator covers at the west of the nave. The noisy wooden ramps up to the altar were replaced by silent ones in solid stone.

Light oak choir stalls were designed which could be sited in a good relationship with the organ without obstructing the view of the altar. Nave seating was moved forward one whole bay, creating more space around the font which enhanced the dignity of the important rite of baptism. One thousand kneelers were commissioned by the Fraternity of Friends for which George Pace devised four *Light through stained glass* designs. The abbey colours of blue and gold are featured with a careful range of harmonies introduced. The patterns are studies in rectangular form, overlapping, interlacing, intersecting. They show great simplicity and restraint and, worked by the women of the diocese, give colour and unity to the nave today.

A Bach oratorio on 2nd December 1972 marked the reopening of the nave and in countless ways, church life has been deepened by the new flexibility and freedom the reordering has allowed.

Pace's enrichment of the Saint's Chapel demonstrates well his idiosyncratic style (see fig. 42). The Gothic, he believed, when required in the twentieth century, should be given a twentieth century treatment. In this chapel, the gilded ironwork of chandeliers and candlesticks harmonises completely with the thirteenth century chapel, yet expresses with conviction the twentieth century. How has this been achieved? Realising that verticality is the essential quality of the Gothic, Pace kept this emphasis throughout, using as his main motif a rectangular form. Unlike the Gothic, however, his curves turn out, not in, and his forms have blunt ends, not sharpened ones. The shapes reach and soar and truly enhance the mediaeval setting without intruding. His *Alban and Amphibalus* banner is similarly distinguished.

Dean Noel Kennaby, who worked so closely with Pace and directed him, retired in the spring of 1973; his likeness in bronze can be seen in the Hudson Memorial Library in a bust by Margaret Wilding.

Tragically, George Pace died prematurely on 28th August 1975 at the early age of fifty-nine. In the words of his obituary in *The Times*, he 'made an individual and distinctive contribution to his profession without ever becoming known to the general public.' His design for the new nave pulpit at St. Albans was never realised.

References

CARRINGTON (BERYL). 'Echoes of Victoria fade out of abbey'. *Herts. Advertiser.* 21 July 1972. 66.

'Discoveries in St. Albans Abbey: work on restoration of wall paintings'. *The Times.* 2 August 1960. 10, 14.

HAMMOND (PETER) ed. *Towards a church architecture.* London 1962

HURFORD (PETER). The organs of St. Albans Abbey. Minehead. 1962.

KENNABY (NOEL M). 'On furnishing the house of God'. *The Abbey Magazine.* IX, no. 2. February 1969. 1 and 3.

'Mr Cecil Brown, meticulous work in church restoration'. *The Times.* 15 January 1983 and 25 January 1983.

PACE (GEORGE G). 'Modern church architecture'. *The church and the arts.* F J Glendenning. ed. S C M Press. 1960.

... 'Principles and precepts'. *Making the building serve the liturgy: studies in the reordering of churches.* Gilbert Cope. ed. London 1962.

... 'The reordering of the nave'. *The Abbey Magazine* IX, no. 3. March 1969. 1 and 3.

PERRYCOSTE (W B C). 'The Ramryge chantry'. *The Abbey Magazine.* XI, no. 3. March, 1971. 13 and 15; 'A prayer in stone'. *Ibid.* XI, no. 4. April, 1971. 7–9.

ROUSE (E CLIVE). 'Paintings on the walls and timber ceilings of the central tower of St. Albans cathedral'. *Trans. SAHAAS.* (1953) 98–102.

Chapter 21

ANDREW ANDERSON AND THE NAVE RESTORATION

Andrew Anderson of Norwich who, as Consultant Architect and Surveyor of the Fabric, replaced George Pace in 1974, obtained a suitable pulpit from a redundant church in Norfolk. Placed on castors and treated to match the colour of the choir stalls, it was set one bay closer to the altar than the former pulpit had been.

The Wallingford chantry was restored to its original chapel function and set aside as a place for meditation (see fig. 67). A burning bush design by Anderson, worked by Annie Crawley, adorns the aumbry curtain, while the famous de la Mare brass, housed since Nicholson's time in the chantry, was moved to a more accessible place in the north Presbytery aisle.

A scheme to floodlight the abbey was selected by the City and District of St. Albans in 1975 to mark Architectural Heritage Year. On weekends and special occasions, the glowing building, which hovers like a beacon over the darkened hill, is a breathtaking and inspiring sight. A gift shop was opened in the Slype in 1976 (see fig. 29), to be run by volunteers with the proceeds to abbey maintenance.

Pat Russell designed forty-

Fig. 98 Andrew Anderson, as portrayed in the corbel table of the restored nave.

248

four new cushions for the canons' stalls in the choir in 1977. In trammed tent stitch gros-point and petit-point on canvas, heraldic designs with inscribed banners overlay a ground of roses. Jill Watson of the Abbey Embroiderers directs this very considerable undertaking: each cushion will require five hundred hours to complete.

A magnificent frontal for the nave altar was designed by Joan Freeman in 1978. On a deep blue ground, cream coloured polygons overlapping to form white, symbolise the Holy Spirit. Across this ground a golden phoenix, symbol of the Eucharist, hovers, built up of shallow arcs of glittering gold suggestive of feathers, wings and flames. A mood of inspiration, joy and hope infuses this lovely piece.

In numerous ways, the building continued to be beautified, its spiritual potential deepened. Behind the scenes, however, a much more serious plan was underway, a major restoration of the fabric, a fundamental work which will occupy the Surveyor over a period of years. The essential first step was a major structural survey, the first for many years. Many pockets of masonry decay, leaky leadwork on the roof and buckling window glazing were reported in September 1974 to the Dean and Cathedral Council. A programme of restoration in ten annual stages was recommended to maintain the building in a 'stable, wind and watertight condition'. There was no alternative but to accept the report.

Consulting engineer Professor Jacques Heyman plumbed the tower but found little sign of movement in this key component (see fig. 20). Rattee and Kett of Cambridge, specialists in making good old buildings, were appointed building contractors. A building compound was set up on the south of the building and a temporary sleeper road constructed from the west front. Mrs Veronica Gillmor was appointed in May 1978 to represent the Cathedral Council to the contractors, to visit the site daily, to attend the architect's monthly site meetings and observe the architect's liaison committee. Her articles in *The Alban Link* in the spring of 1979 and in *Abbeynews* in September 1979 plus the Surveyor's annual reports to the Fraternity, unfold a picture of the first major restoration since Grimthorpe.

Most urgently needing repairs were the nave roof and clerestory (see fig. 92). Work in four stages would begin on the south, first the half nearest the tower, then the western portion, followed by a repeat operation on the north. Scaffolding from ground level across the aisle roof and along the clerestory face, fitted with lightning conductors and a hoist for materials, required two months to erect.

A quarter of the south wall is of Roman tiles and flint. This needed some repointing and a few tiles inserted from the reserve supply from Verulamium. To tackle the decayed limestone, a detailed drawing was made with every stone measured and numbered so that the Cambridge office could follow the work in progress. Decayed stones were cut out.

All the stone in the building other than the flint is limestone and it is difficult to differentiate now the mediaeval from the later work. York stone, extremely hard, was used nearest the tower. No working drawings either of Sir G G Scott or of Grimthorpe have been found, but Scott apparently used Chilmark stone which weathered severely and Beckett, Ancaster, which was also worn, but not so badly.

The hand carved string-course of the parapet had been badly designed, with an angle insufficient to throw rainwater clear of the corbels, so water had settled and caused decay. A replacement with a corrected angle was cut by machine in Cambridge from Clipsham, a very hard limestone, creamy in colour. Old corbel heads, weathered beyond recognition, were cut out and craftsmen in the Cambridge yard began to carve replacements, using the durable 'Ancaster hard white' stone.

Meanwhile, long ladders had been leaned against the steep roof surface and plumbers began stripping the old lead from the roof, beginning at the tower (see fig. 92). Laid between 1909 and 1914, it was amazingly thin and pitted, almost spongy in texture. Eight to nine bays were cleared at a time, the exposed roof protected by tarpaulins. The old leading was melted down in Watford, impurities removed and the weight made up with fresh lead. Seven tonnes were needed for the first quarter of the roof. New sheets, 210cm by 75cm, were recast each weighing sixty-five kilogrammes. The lead arrived from the foundry in rolls.

With the roof timbers exposed and cleared of accumulated dust by vacuum, they could be examined carefully. The wood was in remarkably good condition, with only one small patch infected by death watch beetle. This was removed and preservative applied to all timbers in a dripping technique.

The rolls of new lead were beaten flat in a workshop high in the scaffolding. To lift each sheet, two men were required. On the roof, each piece was secured at the head by large brass screws and washers. The side edges were bent up at a ninety degree angle, held upright by copper tingles. Using a large, round, wooden mallet and a dowel shaped piece of wood, the seams were beaten

into neat, overlapping rolls. Horizontal laps alternate. At the
eaves, the lead was trimmed even and beaten to an under curl. In
March 1979, the first phase of the roof repair was completed,
costing about £100,000. Work on the western half of the south
nave roof was in progress by the following June.

Parts of the gutters and downpipes were badly corroded and
fractured, allowing the wall face to be soaked with rain. The
downpipes were replaced in lead and fixed with bronze bolts. The
eastern heads were repaired and painted and fitted with an
ingenious sieve, designed by the Master Plumber, to catch debris.
A checklist was worked out for regular inspection and clearance of
both gutters and downpipes.

Meanwhile, work was proceeding on the ashlar work in
parapet and clerestory and window mouldings replaced where
required. The newly cut stones were inserted and the sound areas
of old stone cleaned by sprays of water and thorough brushing.
The finished effect is in shades of cream but in time it will weather
to a perfect match.

Reglazing the clerestory was imperative. The century old
leading had deteriorated and the glass buckled alarmingly. After
experimenting with a window in the south choir aisle, a larger
sized quarry was selected to admit more light. The glazier, Dennis
King of Norwich, used twenty-five per cent cordelé glass and
many of the quarries are engraved with signatures of donors.
Grimthorpe's cast iron framing and saddle bars had corroded and
stained the stone; instead of iron, an alloy was used, delta bronze,
which would not discolour the wall.

During this time, sculptors in Cambridge were completing the
twenty-two new heads for the corbel table. Most of the heads are
the work of John Shuffleton, a St. Albans' woodcarver who had
once worked for Faith Craft, Abbey Mill, until that firm closed
down. Each head weighs about a hundredweight, and was pinned
in position by a mortice and tenon joint, filled with lime slip.
Three heads portray local people, the bespectacled *Bishop Robert
Runcie* (1970–1980) later Archbishop of Canterbury, the *Dean*, and
the late churchwarden *Rob Kell*, who had an unrivalled knowledge
of the fabric. *Robert Mylne*, the eighteenth century surveyor, was
also included as was *Sid Warner*, the mason in charge. Carved with
particular affection and tumbled locks is the present Surveyor,
Andrew Anderson himself (see fig. 98). Besides these portraits are
the traditional grimacing beasts, horned animals with flaring
nostrils and pointed teeth and a bevy of ladies, some old, some
young, in a mediaeval fashion show, one wearing a goffered veil,

another with templars, a third with barbette and fillet. The nineteenth century heads were cleaned to blend in with the new. For how many decades will these patient heads support the heavy parapet?

The west front, even on first inspection, had caused concern (see fig. 93); buttress tops were laminating, and vertical pressure cracks were visible. Grimthorpe had built too well, cementing the stones rigidly together without regard for expansion and contraction: today, a lighter lime mortar is used. A guard rail had to be erected in 1978, but prolonged frost that winter had caused rapid deterioration. Stones began to fall and for protection, scaffolding with safety platforms was erected across the entire front.

Removing decayed stone in the vault of the central porch revealed the root of the trouble, a defective valley gutter between the west window and the porch gable. Great chunks of stone were removed and taken to Cambridge to have the decay cut away so that the sound remainder could be used on the restoration. Bits of Wheathampstead's great west window, used by Grimthorpe as rubble, have been carefully preserved (see fig. 63).

By February 1980, the scaffold tower on the north-east nave was almost complete; on this section, no restoration work had been done in the nineteenth century and decay was severe. The same principles of repair established on the south were followed on the north but at the eastern end, large chutes were inserted to dispose of rainwater from the parapet gutter. A pair of louvred doors in a lead covered dormer were inserted in the roof to make access for maintenance easier and to help ventilate the roof space.

Phase IV of the restoration dealt with the exacting repair of the disintegrating Early English style clerestory; the blind arcading, hood moulds, moulded and shafted window frames as well as ashlar walling, Grimthorpe's work, all had to be completely replaced. Frank Fielden, a mason who died tragically in a fall from the scaffolding on 11th September 1980, was commemorated by a portrait head in the corbel table on the north side. By July 1983, the scaffolding had been moved to the north-west buttress to repair the dangerous stonework on the pinnacles.

The vast nave restoration project was deemed complete by January 1984 at a cost of £1,750,000, the bulk of which had been collected by volunteers in a myriad of ingenious ways. An exhibition of embroidery and vestments and an antique auction could be singled out from scores of money-making projects. No state aid was forthcoming; indeed, fifteen per cent value added tax was required on every pound spent. The restoration, of course, will not be complete until the remaining parts of the building have been similarly repaired and six further phases are envisaged, as funds become available.

Meanwhile, within the church, further improvements were being made. In the north transept, the Chapel of the Persecuted Church was dedicated on 24th March 1981, the first anniversary of the murder of Archbishop Romero in San Salvador. The chapel is simplicity itself, consisting of a platform supporting a free standing altar whose frontal was designed and executed by Patricia Leighton. A coarse sisal tapestry in warm earth colours, a plain Greek cross is woven into a striated ground suggestive of early dawn. A crucifix on the wall, a *Christus Rex*, from the chapel at Verulam House, provides a focus for meditation.

A cathedral treasury had been established by the autumn of 1981 in the north Presbytery aisle to house historic church plate. Designed by F Jasper Jacob, the three glass cabinets appear to float, although actually suspended from beams spanning the aisle. The Goldsmiths' and Silversmiths' Companies as well as the Friends financed this project which allows precious silver vessels from the parish churches of the diocese, as well as silver from the abbey and the city, to be freely viewed and admired by visitors.

Repairs to the bells were carried out in January 1982 by the Whitechapel bell foundry at a cost of £6,000. The old wooden headstocks of the ninth, tenth and tenor bells were replaced, the pulleys and wheels renewed and the clappers and fittings refurbished, which greatly improved the sound of the bells.

Four great hangings showing *The Elements* (earth, air, fire and water) *in Salvation*, had been hung in the south nave aisle by November 1982, designed by Sister Regina of Turvey Abbey in Bedfordshire and worked by the Embroiderers' Guild. Each panel, which measures eleven feet by five feet, has a plain border in a solid colour within which six or more scriptural passages are illustrated in a bold and abstract style. Textural contrast is the keynote, with applied coarse fabrics: wool, felt, leather, silks, velvets; details are embroidered, couched, crocheted even glued. The colours rust, burgundy, dull orange, gold, yellow, moss green, grey blue and turquoise predominate. The vigorous modern design carries well in the far reaching spaces of the nave.

References

ANDERSON (ANDREW). 'The cathedral and Abbey church of St. Alban, Hertfordshire: inspection'. September, 1974.

. . . 'Memorandum: stone repair policy'. September, 1978.

. . . 'Surveyor's annual report'. *FFSAA 30th annual report*. 1978-9. 12-14.

. . . 'Surveyor's annual report'. *ibid*. 1979-80. 12.

GILLMOR (VERONICA). 'Restoration of the nave'. *The Alban Link*. VIII. Spring 1979. 6-8.

. . . 'What's been going on?' *Abbeynews*. LXVII. September 1979. p.1.

. . . 'Restoration of the nave, part II'. *The Alban Link*. X. Autumn/Winter, 1980. 7-8.

. . . 'The story of the restoration of the nave, 1978-1983'.

KRETT (PAT). 'The pennies roll in'. *The St. Albans Review and Express: The Royal visit*. 15 July 1982. 20.

Chapter 22

THE CHAPTER HOUSE AND THE SHRINE

Bishop Robert Runcie, who was enthroned on 14th March 1970, drew attention on his first visitation to the lack of facilities for the ever increasing numbers of visitors to the abbey. The Institute on Romeland, purchased in 1893 as parish rooms and for diocesan purposes, had become inadequate for modern needs. Dean Peter Moore, collated on 3rd November 1973, whose vision for the abbey was to restore it to a place of pilgrimage and prayer, requested the architect, William Whitfield, to make a design study for a new Visitors' Centre.

The site proposed was south of the south transept, where the monastic chapter house had stood in bygone years. Planning permission was applied for in the spring on 1973; while the local planning authority recognised the need for the proposed new facilities, the unique archaeological importance of the intended site precluded the granting of permission to build there. An appeal was lodged by the Cathedral Council, a public enquiry held and on 1st September 1977 planning permission was granted by the Secretary of State, provided the site be thoroughly excavated first. This was carried out in the spring and summer of 1978 under the direction of Professor Martin Biddle and Magister Birthe Kjølbye-Biddle and the foundations of three earlier chapter houses, two apsidal and one square-ended, were revealed, as well as carved stones and other finds. The remains of eleven abbots and three other worthies which were uncovered during the dig, were reinterred with great solemnity in the Presbytery of the abbey alongside other abbots. The ceremony, on 21st November 1979, formed part of the 15th centenary of the birth of St. Benedict and a handsome commemorative stone, with lettering by David Kindersley, was laid over the spot.

Foundation work for the modern building was commenced in February 1979 by the contractors, Messrs. Harry Neal Ltd. The

Fig. 99   South transept, south face, as rebuilt by Sir Edmund Beckett after 1885. On the right, Chapter House, designed by William Whitfield, 1982.

building was officially opened by H M the Queen on 8th June 1982 on a gala day of general rejoicing. The Right Rev. John Taylor, the Lord Bishop of St. Albans, was present. The cost, originally estimated at £600,000 had risen, before completion, to £1,000,000.

The new building was conceived, not as a small scale cathedral, but as a replacement of one of the monastic buildings so long missing from the southern side of the abbey. Half a million hand made, Roman style bricks had been ordered from the Bovingdon Brick Works, and a French stone chosen for the dressings which would weather like the Ancaster stone used by Grimthorpe on the south transept façade.

Approaching the building from the south, the slim, rectangular structure with its apsidal end appears pleasingly proportioned in relation to the south transept. The gabled turret storey, a third the way along the roof, and the arched south-west porch, help to mask the adjacent boiler house. Deeply set windows in the southern wall, in three tiers and segmentally arched, give a sculptural quality to the elevation. The west façade has three boldly arched lights, their sills deeply splayed, linking the new building in scale to the great cathedral beside it. The handmade bricks present a pleasing texture while the silvery stone facings lend quality to the finish.

An external stairway descends on the south and east to the crypt, but a splayed, pyramidal feature on the north-east, which conceals the kitchen and includes the entrance to it, is the least satisfactory part of the exterior.

On entering the foyer, a wide range of shallow steps leads the eye to the higher levels of the Slype and the cathedral. Overhead, a great, suspended horizontal cross, the underside of the gallery above, forms the dominant impression, again directing movement towards the cathedral entrance, where the ancient west doors of the abbey are displayed on either side, their rugged tracery picked out in light from east and west (see fig. 65). The foyer itself is gently illuminated by light filtering through the glass and timber grid of the doors and by the generous windows on two walls of the shop, raised on a mezzanine floor to the west. From the pavement of the foyer rise great rectangular piers of brick, past the giant cross to arches supporting the roof. The east and west walls of the foyer, also arched, are whitewashed to maximise the light.

The refectory, on the ground floor to the east, is the principal room of the building; its ceiling is deeply coffered on the diagonal, while narrow, vertical windows overlook the abbey orchard. Steep, narrow stairs lead from the foyer to the lavatories on the

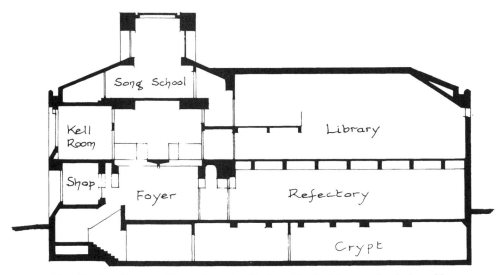

Fig. 100 The Chapter House, longtitudinal section looking north, designed by William Whitfield, 1982.

basement level and along a passageway with storerooms, the crypt is reached, a plain, low, apsidal space of squarish proportions.

A newel staircase of twenty-six steps leads from the ground level to the first floor and the upper side of the huge cross feature, in the form of a carpeted gallery with simple but effective iron railings. A feature is made of the arched, central space above and glimpses from this suspended gallery to the floor below gives a sense of excitement and space, very much of the twentieth century. At the head of the cross, a window opens on the pleasant, southward view; the foot of the cross leads to the Michael Stair descending to the south transept. The Kell Room (a chapter room and clergy vestry) is at the western arm of the cross; here hangs a portrait by Frank Salisbury of John Watkins, virger, churchwarden and lay canon, 1903–1950. A passageway eastwards, past general offices and counselling rooms, leads to the Hudson Memorial Library, an apsidal room with a handsome, open, timber framed roof in dark stained wood. Two tiers of fenestration light the room. The book collection is built up of three libraries, that of Canon C E Hudson, who endowed the library, that of the former Bishops' College, Cheshunt and the Beardsmore collection of antiquarian books of local interest. Displayed on the walls of the library are historic prints and paintings. A gallery, which gives additional space for study, is reached by newel staircase. A portrait of Dean Peter Moore by D MacLean, 1983, hangs in this library, commissioned by the Cathedral Council, 'as a token of respect for all that he has done to initiate and promote the idea of building (this) magnificent building'.

Climbing a further twenty-seven steps, the Song School is reached, a sunny room in the gabled turret with choir vestry facilities and music library. The administration offices are also located here.

The building has been justly praised for the quality of the finishes and for the craftsmanship and beauty of the detailing. Criticism has been voiced on the tight circulation, the numerous steps (a lift having been omitted on grounds of cost), poor acoustics and internal noise penetration. Some of these problems can be traced to the Brief presented to the architect: so many functions requested, so little space allotted. In 1991, major repairs were required on the roof. Most people agree, however, that a new dimension has been added to cathedral life and a warmer, livelier atmosphere is apparent to all, visitors and congregation, who use the building.

The completion of the Chapter House allowed two bays of the north choir aisle, assigned to vestry use since 1877, to be cleared of furnishings, exposing to view once more the *Holy Trinity* mural. An Exhibition Gallery was established here in 1983, where visitors could learn of the abbey's work, past and present, through attractive exhibits arranged by local experts, working voluntarily.

To complete the link between Chapter House and cathedral a staircase of oak, limed and waxed, was hallowed on 1st February 1986. This gives separate clergy access during services. Called the Michael Stair, it commemorates the life and service of Michael Gresford Jones, a much loved bishop, 1950–1969. An opening had been cut through the seven foot thick wall, where interlaced arcading from the Norman slype had been mounted by Grimthorpe (see fig. 29), opening onto a gallery supported on great trusses and leading to the straight flight of the stairs themselves. The newel posts have mitred heads. Oaks were donated from the diocese to make these stairs, which Andrew Anderson designed.

In 1987, an altar frontal was presented by the Mothers' Union for their Chapel of the Four Tapers. Jane Lemon of Salisbury was the designer. A rose motif, symbol of the Virgin Mary and of purity, is laid on a deep blue velvet ground. The petal lines of the design, upward swinging and joyous, are expressed in the appliqué of slubbed silk fabrics in white, lemon, cadmium yellow, greenish yellow and three shades of blue. Gold couched threads give emphasis. The heart of the rose, off centre, is a deep blue globe enclosed in a golden crown of padded stamens. This frontal is a piece of quite exceptional beauty.

Engraved glass by Sally Scott had been placed in three lights above the west doors by October 1988. Standing figures of the *Virgin and Child* with outstretched arms are enclosed in a delicate wreath of lilies, thorns and roses. Flanking creatures fill the outside lights, a unicorn, symbol of purity on the north and a peacock, symbol of immortality on the south.

Soon afterwards, five glass panels with engraved inscriptions by David Peace replaced the oak doors of the former inner porch. The inscriptions on the doors at north and south face outwards, the north reading, 'I will light a candle of understanding in their hearts' (Esdras 14:25), the south 'Seek him that made the seven stars and Orion' (Amos 5:8). Each text is arranged as an oval medallion cut by a diagonal. The three middle panels are fixed, their texts disposed in a flattened quatrefoil, with candle and sword motifs superimposed. The Alban prayer, 'We worship and adore the true and living God who created all things' continues, 'Almighty God, we thank thee for this place built to thine everlasting glory. May we be faithful witnesses following his example in the fellowship of the saints. Amen.' This text faces inwards but David Peace's letters form a pleasing pattern however viewed. These glowing, transparent screens enhance the west end with lightness and beauty and inspire those passing in and out.

The great rose window in the north transept designed by Grimthorpe contained clear glass up to this time. In 1988 the glazier, Alan Younger, was commissioned to design a replacement and fill with stained glass the sixty-four panels of this vast window which measures fully thirty feet across. Amenity Societies expressed concern about the project, pleading for the retention at least of the nineteenth century glazing patterns, but the scheme went ahead and one original leaded roundel can be seen on display in the south transept. Fortunately, Dr Rowland Mainstone's skilfull photo-montage records the ingenious and varied geometric patterns of the earlier scheme (see fig. 95).

On 26th September 1989, HRH the Princess of Wales unveiled the completed window, in which the colour blue predominates, with much red and white and touches of green and gold. The existing concentric circles the artist has interpreted as the universe with the earth at the centre. Triangular areas of colour have been used in a non-objective way to suggest the infusion of spirit into matter. This splendid and munificent enrichment of the abbey interior was the gift of Laporte Industries of Luton, who devoted £75,000 to mark their centenary year in this magnificent way. It is the first example in the abbey of non-objective stained glass design.

Meanwhile, the Purbeck marble shrine of Alban, reassembled in 1872 from many fragments, had grown dilapidated and collapse was imminent (see fig. 47). In 1984, the Fraternity of Friends resolved to restore the shrine; the following year, a symposium of experts was convened to discuss the many problems of repair and conservation. In the ensuing months, a photographic survey of the shrine was made, the Purbeck marble studied to find its place of origin, the red, blue and gold pigments on the inner vaulting analysed and a photogrammetric survey conducted to define and number the myriad fragments comprising the shrine.

A sum of £150,000 was required for the work. After the Friends had made an initial donation of £10,000 and churches in North America dedicated to St. Alban had contributed, a public appeal, led by the late Sir Eric Cheadle, opened in October 1991. The desired total was achieved in just three months.

The sculpture conservators, Harrison Hill of Brigstock, Northamptonshire, were entrusted with the restoration. The dismantling of the shrine, which began in April 1991, proceeded more quickly than expected. Because the fragments had not been thoroughly cleaned in 1872, the adhesives used (Roman cement, plaster of Paris and shellac) were less tenacious than feared.

To ensure a secure and damp-proof foundation for the reassembled shrine, Prof. Martin Biddle excavated the site, revealing Chapple's foundation trench and a vault of 1770 date. No trace was found of Alban's burial place or of earlier monastic remains.

Reconstruction commenced in the spring of 1992 with Andrew Oddie of the British Museum, an expert on shrines, as adviser. The photogrammetric survey ensured that each piece was correctly replaced, including all fragments found since 1872. A light, pressed steel framework supports the monument, which is held together by special adhesives and by stainless steel and other suitable dowels. The twelfth century slab, previously laid on top of the shrine although part of an earlier monument, was not replaced due to its excessive weight. The spiral Purbeck shafts included in the 1872 reconstruction, are also believed to be from elsewhere and were not reinstated. A major piece of Purbeck marble had been found for repairing the northern side of the shrine, where parts were restored if the original form was sufficiently sure. If viewed from six feet the monument should look perfect; if viewed from six inches the restored parts should be clearly seen.

In 793, King Offa II founded a monastery at a famous pilgrimage site, to honour Alban, Britain's first Christian martyr. Twelve centuries later, it is fitting that his shrine, restored to splendour, speaks still to modern pilgrims of his faith and sacrifice.

References

ANON. 'New exhibition area'. *The Alban Link*. XIII. Autumn, 1981. 10–11.

ANON. 'The shrine of St. Albans; further restoration proposed'. *The Alban Link*. XXI. Summer, 1985. 18–25.

BIDDLE (MAGISTER BIRTHE KJØLBE and PROF. MARTIN). 'Excavation below the shrine of St. Alban'. *Abbeynews*. CCXVI. January 1992. 4.

BIDDLE (PROF. MARTIN). *St. Albans abbey chapter house excavations 1978*. FFSAA Occasional Paper no. 1. 1979.

. . . 'Dismantling the shrine'. *The Alban Link*. XXXV. Sept. 1991. 4–7.

CLOVES (JEFF). 'A stairway from heaven'. *St. Albans Review and Express*. 30 January 1987.

CARRINGTON (BERYL). 'Shrine resurrection'. *Herts. Advertisier*. 18 December 1991. 10.

GOODWIN (ROB). 'A challenge to designers'. *The St. Albans Review and Express: The Royal Visit*. 15 July 1982. 16.

HOWARD (H W) and PERRYCOSTE (W B C). 'Abbey houses'. *The Abbey Magazine*. XI, no. 11. November 1971. 12–13, 15; *Ibid*. XII, no. 2. February, 1972. 11–13.

MACMILLAN (ROBERT) and MAINSTONE (ROWLAND). 'Cathedral glass'. *The Times*. 2 July 1988.

MAINSTONE (ROWLAND). 'Conflicting colours'. *Building Design*. 6 January 1989.

SYMONDSON (ANTHONY). 'Chapter and verse: William Whitfield's new multi-purpose chapter house at St. Albans'. *The Architects' Journal*. CLXXVII, no. 25. 22 June 1983. 42–47.

S.S. 'Requiescant in peace' (*sic*) FFSAA 31st annual report 1979–80. 8–9.

List of Officiating Clergy

Abbots

Anglo-Saxon

Willegod	793 –	796
Eadric	796 –	ca.810
Wulsig	ca.810 –	ca.830
Wulnoth	ca.830 –	ca.840
Eadfrith	ca.840 –	ca.860
Wulsin (Ulsinus)	ca.860 –	ca.870
Alfric	ca.870 –	ca.890
Ealdred	ca.890 –	ca.910
Eadmer	ca.910 –	ca.930
No properly constituted abbot	ca.930 –	ca.970
Alfric II	ca.970 –	ca.990
Leofric	ca.990 –	ca.1042
Leofstan	ca.1042 –	ca.1064
Egfrid	ca.1066 –	ca.1070
Fritheric	ca.1070 –	ca.1077

Norman and Mediaeval

Paul de Caen	1077 –	1093
Richard d'Albini	1097 –	1119
Geoffrey de Gorham	1119 –	1146
Ralph de Gobion	1146 –	1151
Robert de Gorham	1151 –	1167
Simon	1167 –	1183
Warin	1183 –	1195
John de Cella	1195 –	1214
William de Trumpington	1214 –	1235
John de Hertford	1235 –	1263

Roger de Norton	1263 –	1290
John de Berkhamsted	1290 –	1302
John de Maryns	1302 –	1309
Hugh de Eversden	1309 –	1327
Richard de Wallingford	1327 –	1336
Michael de Mentmore	1336 –	1349
Thomas de la Mare	1349 –	1396
John de la Moote	1396 –	1401
William Heyworth	1401 –	1420
John (Bostock) of Wheathampstead	1420 –	1440
John Stoke	1441 –	1452
John Bostock (re-elected)	1452 –	1465
William Alban	1465 –	1476
William Wallingford	1476 –	1492
Thomas Ramryge	1492 –	1521
Thomas (Cardinal) Wolsey (non-resident)	1521 –	1530
Robert Catton	1531 –	1538
Richard Boreman or Stevenage	1538	

Rectors and Deans

George Wetherall	instituted	12 May 1553
William East	"	1555
James Dugdale	"	25 February 1556/7
Edward Edgeworth	"	5 March 1578/9
Roger Williams	"	7 March 1582/3
John Browne	"	1627
	deprived	1643

Ministers

George Newton	appointed	1644
John Geree	"	1646
Job Tookey	"	1649
John Oliver	"	1653
Richard Roberts	"	1655
Nathaniel Partridge	"	1657

Rectors and Deans

Edward Carter	instituted	20 February 1662/3
John Cole	"	16 December 1687
" "	"	9 September 1713
Benjamin Preedy	"	13 September 1754
Joseph Spooner	"	23 January 1776
Joseph Nicholson	"	28 November 1796
Henry Small	"	4 July 1817
Henry Nicholson	"	13 February 1835
Sir John Hawkins, Bart.	"	18 October 1866
Walter Lawrance	"	30 October 1868

Dean and Rector

Walter Lawrance	collated	18 July 1900
George Blenkin	"	28 November 1914
Edward Henderson	"	25 April 1925
Cuthbert Thicknesse	"	17 March 1936
Kenneth Matthews	"	12 November 1955
Noel Kennaby	"	25 January 1964
Peter Moore	"	3 November 1973

Bishops of St. Albans

Thomas Claughton	enthroned	12 June 1877
John Festing	"	7 October 1890
Edgar Jacob	"	16 May 1903
Michael Furse	"	22 April 1920
Philip Lloyd	"	6 January 1945
Michael Gresford Jones	"	28 September 1950
Robert Runcie	"	14 March 1970
John Taylor	"	14 June 1980

Glossary

abacus   the flat slab at the top of a capital of a column. Fig. 13.

apse   a vaulted end to a chancel or chapel, either semi-circular or polygonal.

arcade   a series of arches on piers or columns. Fig. 52.

arch   basket arch: a three-centred arch formed by two segments of circles of equal radius, joined at the top by a segment of larger radius.
four-centred arch: a pointed arch with four arcs, two on each side, the upper arcs having lower centres than the lower arcs.
two-centred arch: an arch formed of two equal curves meeting at a point.

ashlar   masonry formed of squared blocks of stone with finished faces laid with fine joints.

aumbry   a cupboard or recess for the storage of vessels used for communion or mass.

ballflower   a decorative motif consisting of a globe-shaped three-petalled flower containing a ball. Fig. 53.

batten   square-cut timber, which can be up to eight inches wide by four inches thick, but more generally much smaller, say two inches by one inch.

baulk   a length of timber of massive width and thickness.

bay   a unit or part of a building, that is repeated to form the whole design, often separated from the next bay by a column or buttress. Fig. 25.

blind arcading   a range of arches on a wall surface, without openings. Fig. 59.

boss   an ornamental knob or projection at the joining of ribs in a vault or ceiling. Fig. 56.

broach-spire	an octagonal spire rising from a square tower without any parapet, each of the four angles of the tower terminating in a broach, an inclined portion of masonry.
canted	tilted or not square.
cantilever	a projection which is self-supporting without supports along its length, as in a cantilevered beam, canopy or balcony.
carrel	a niche for study, used by a monk in a cloister or bay window.
cavetto	a hollow curved moulding.
chamfered	splaying a right-angled corner of stone or wood so that a surface is formed at forty-five degrees to the two faces.
chord of apse	an imaginary line joining the extremities of the curve of the apse walls.
clasping buttresses	buttresses that extend around both sides of the corner.
clerestory	the upper stage of the main walls of a church, containing windows.
cock-loft	a small, upper loft.
colonnette	a very small column. Fig. 32.
corbel-table	a range of corbels (i.e. projecting blocks) just below the eaves.
cornice	a projecting ornamental horizontal moulding at the top of a building or wall.
crenellation	the top of a wall or parapet formed into a regular pattern of alternating raised and lower portions, similar to battlements. Fig. 63.
crockets	carved leaf shapes, at regular intervals, on gables, pinnacles, etc. Fig. 33.
cusp	the point where two curves meet in a Gothic arch or tracery, thus 'cusped' and 'cusping'.
dado	the finishing of the lower part of a wall, from the skirting to waist height.
dagger	a pointed motif used in window tracery, rounded or pointed at its head, rounded at its foot and cusped inside. Fig. 64.

dentils	a series of small square blocks used decoratively in a cornice or string course.
dog-tooth	an ornament consisting of carved, four-cornered stars. Fig. 35.
ecclesia	a church building designed primarily as a setting for the Eucharist and to house a congregation.
echelon	a stepped or staggered arrangement of parts, each part being parallel to the others but aligned differently. Fig. 17.
end stop	the decorative conclusion to a moulding. Fig. 53.
feretory	a shrine behind the high altar to store relics that are intended to be carried in processions.
finial	a pointed ornament at the top of a gable, canopy or pinnacle, often a *fleur de lys*. Fig. 42.
flash	to cover colourless glass with a film of coloured glass.
fleuron bands	a band of carved, floral decoration. Fig. 53.
foil	a leaf-shaped curve in tracery, separated by a cusp from the next foil. Quatrefoil: having four such curves. Trefoil: having three such curves.
grisaille	of windows, composed mainly of white glass, partly painted with foliage and leaded into more or less complicated patterns.
groined cross vault	the junction of two barrel vaults without any ribs.
hood-mould	a projecting moulding on a wall above an arch or doorway to throw off the rain.
impost	a bracket-like moulding on a wall to carry the side of an arch.
jamb	the side of an opening in a wall (for a door, arch or window).
keeled shafts	stone shafts having a continuous, raised vertical line or lines. Fig. 53.
label	see hood mould.
lancet window	a pointed-arched window of narrow proportions. Fig. 99.

lantern

the part of a tower rising above the roof which has windows all around it. Fig. 22.

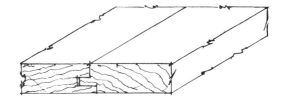

lapped, tongued joint

lights

the openings between window mullions.

mansard roof

a roof with a steep lower slope, and a shorter, shallower slope above this.

martyrium

a church which houses a congregation but is also a memorial shrine built on a hallowed site.

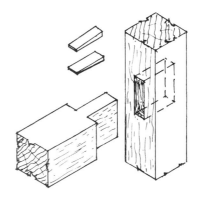

Mortise and tenon joint

mullion

a vertical upright dividing a window into lights.

newel

the central pillar of a winding staircase, or a post at the angles of a square staircase.

nook shaft

a shaft in the angle of a pier or wall, or in a window or door jamb.

ogee arch

a pointed arch in which each side is formed of a compound curve, the upper one of each side having its centre outside the arch. Fig. 55. Nodding ogee: an ogee in which the pointed apex projects from the wall surface.

opus anglicanum	embroidery in silk and gold thread which reached a height of excellence in the thirteenth and fourteenth centuries. Fig. 11.
pilaster	a shallow pier or rectangular column slightly projecting from a wall.
piscina	a built-in stone basin with a drain for washing the vessels after communion or mass, usually in a niche south of the altar.
plinth	the projecting base of a wall or column. Fig. 38.
pointing	the finishing of mortar joints in brickwork.
pot-metal	stained glass coloured in the melting pot so that the colour pervades the whole substance.
putlog holes	holes in masonry or brickwork to support scaffolding.
quarry (glazing)	a small diamond-shaped or square piece of glass in mediaeval leaded glazing.
respond	half a pier, forming part of a wall and carrying one side of an arch.
roundel	a circular, ornamental feature or a circular portion of window tracery.
saddle bar	a small iron bar to stiffen the lead-work in a window.
saucer dome	a shallow dome without a drum.
scantling	generally used to describe the dimensions of the cross-section of squared timber.
sedilia	stone seats for clergy in the south wall of a chancel.
severy	a bay or compartment of a vault. Fig. 45.
shaft ring	a ring carved round the shaft of a column.
silver stain	when white glass is stained yellow by firing on the surface with a derivative of sulphide of silver.
sleeper wall	low walls beneath the ground floor, usually at intervals, to carry a timber floor, or built between piers and/or walls to stabilise them.
soffitt	the underside of any part of a building, except a ceiling. Fig. 26.

spandril	the surface above the curve of an arch and below the apex.
springer	the first stone laid in an arch.
stiff-leaf	a form of sculptured foliage, usually on capitals or bosses. Fig. 35.
stilted	when an arch rises vertically before the start of its curve.
stoup	a shallow stone dish for holy water near the entrance to a church.
strap work	decoration resembling fretwork usually on ceilings, screens and monuments.
string-course	a projecting horizontal band in a wall that is often moulded.
strong mullion	a mullion that is of greater thickness than the other mullions in a window.
tie-beam	a horizontal beam to tie together the feet of the rafters in a roof, to prevent the thrust pushing out the walls.
tierceron	a secondary rib in a vault, leading to the ridge rib. Fig. 45.
tracery	the intersecting ribwork in the upper part of a Gothic window. Plate tracery, the earliest form, has openings but in the solid stone filling a window head. Fig. 37. Bar tracery has mullions continued by intersecting ribwork to form a decorative pattern in the window head. Fig. 44. Reticulated tracery is formed of ogee shapes to produce a net-like appearance. Fig. 50 left.
transom	a horizontal part of the framing of a window, below its head and above its sill.
triforium	an arcaded wall passage facing the nave, above the aisle and below the clerestory. Fig. 53.
truss	a frame, often of timber, usually carrying a roof.
tumba	a shrine shaped like a tomb chest. Figs. 47 and 54.
tympanum	the space or wall above a lintel and below an arch.

vault

barrel vault: a tunnel vault, without ribs. Tierceron vault: a vault with tierceron ribs (secondary ribs leading to the ridge rib). Fan vaulting: a form of ribbed vaulting with the ribs radiating from a shaft or boss.

voussoirs

the wedge-shaped stones in an arch.

wall plate

a timber laid along the top of a wall to carry the ends of the rafters.

waver slats

shutters consisting of thin, movable strips.

General Bibliography

ADDLESHAW (G W O) and ETCHELLS (FREDERICK). The architectural setting of Anglican worship. London, 1948.

ASHDOWN (CHARLES H). St. Albans historical and picturesque. London, 1893.

CARTER (JOHN). Some account of the abbey church of St. Alban, London, 1813.

CHAUNCY (HENRY). Historical antiquities of Hertfordshire. London, 1700.

CLUTTERBUCK (ROBERT). The history and antiquities of the county of Hertford. 3 vols. London, 1815–27.

COOK (G H). Portrait of S. Albans cathedral. London, 1951

CUSSANS (JOHN E). History of Hertfordshire. 3 vols. London, etc. 1870–71.

DUGDALE (SIR WILLIAM). Monasticon anglicanum. 6 vols. Ed. J Caley, etc. London, 1817–30.

GESTA ABBATUM MONASTERII S. ALBANI A THOMA WALSINGHAM (AD 793–1401). Ed. by Henry T Riley. 3 vols. Rolls series. London, 1867–69.

NEALE (JAMES). The abbey church of St. Alban, Herts. London, 1877.

NEWCOME (PETER) The history of the abbey of St. Albans. London, 1793.

REGISTRA JOHANNIS WHETHAMSTEDE, WILLELMI ALBON ET WILLELMI WALINGFORDE, ABBATUM MONASTERII S. ALBANI (1459–88). Ed. by Henry T Riley. *Registra Quorumdam Abbatum*. ii. 1–291. Rolls series. London, 1873.

ROYAL COMMISSION ON THE ANCIENT AND HISTORICAL MONUMENTS AND CONSTRUCTIONS OF ENGLAND. Inventories . . . Hertfordshire. 1911.

. . . St. Albans cathedral. London, 1952.

TRANSACTIONS OF THE ST. ALBANS AND HERTFORDSHIRE ARCHITECTURAL AND ARCHAEOLOGICAL SOCIETY.

WILLIAMS (L F RUSHBROOK). History of the abbey of St. Alban. London, 1917.

Index to Authors Used

Addleshaw, G W O,
  and Etchells, F, 162
Anderson, A, 254
Andrews, H C, 192
Anon, 192, 229, 240, 247, 262
Ashdown, C H, 162

Baker, E P, 162
Beckett, E, 211, 229
Bede, 21
Betjeman, J, 192
Biddle, B K, and Biddle, M, 262
Biddle, M, 262
Binyon, R L, 192
Bond, F, 44
Boutell, R C, 149, 201
Brandon, J A, 149
Brandt, M, 67
Brayley, E W, 178, 192
Buck, S, and Buck, N, 192
Buckler, J C, and Buckler, C A, 44, 201

Caiger-Smith, A, 178
Camden, W, 162, 178
Campbell, E M J, 12
Carrington, B, 247, 262
Carter, J, 55, 192
Cartmel, G W, 240
Cavalier, H O, 149, 162
Chapple, J, 162, 201, 211, 229
Chauncy, H, 162
Clapham, A, 44
Cloves, J, 262
Clutterbuck, R, 178
Cole, D, 211
Colvin, H, 192
Cook, G H, 149
Coldstream, N, 121
Comper, J N, 240
Comyns Carr, J W, 211
Conant, K J, 21
Cottingham, L N, 201
Cox, J, 229
Cussans, J E, 273

Dahl, M E, 178
Dodwell, C R, Pächt, O,
  and Wormald, F, 67
Dorment, R, 229
Dugdale, W, 149

Eames, P, 149
Evans, J, 192

Ferriday, P, 229, 240
Fiennes, C, 178
Finucane, R C, 149
Fox and Sorrell, 15
Fuller, T, 178

Gape, E, 162
Garrod, H W, 131
Gem, R, 29
Gibbs, A E, 162, 163
Gibbs, H H, 229
Gildas, 21
Gillmor, V, 254
Gomme, G L, 192
Goodwin, R, 262
Grabar, André, 44
Gunther, R T, 131

Hammond, P, 247
Harvey, J, 44, 86, 131, 149
Hastings, M, 121
Henwood, G A, 131
Hewett, C, 107
Horlbeck, F R, 67
Howard, H W,
  and Perrycoste W B C, 163, 262
Howgrave-Graham, R P, 131
Hurford, P, 247

Johnson E A, and
  Weaver, O J, 163
Jones, C E, 178, 229

Kahn, D, 67
Kell, J R, 240
Kennaby, N M, 247

General Index

A

Abbey:
  endowment of: 3
  inventories: 24
  precincts: 155, 157

Abbots:
  Eadmer: 23
  Ealdred: 23
  Geoffrey de Gorham: 41, 60, 62
  Hugh de Eversden: 118, 123
  John de Cella: 10, 91, 209
  John de Marins: 111
  John de la Moote: 133, 157
  John de Hertford: 97
  John of Wheathampstead: **Fig 66**.
    75, 138, 143, 145, 226, 252
  Michael de Mentmore: 11
  Paul de Caen: 28, 35, 41, 49–51,
    55, 60, 62, 74, 115
  Richard Boreman or Stevenage:
    148, 152
  Richard d'Albini: 60
  Richard de Wallingford: 128, 130
  Robert Catton: 148, 153
  Robert de Norton: 98, 106, 206
  Simon: 74
  Thomas de la Mare: 129, 146, 165
  Thomas Ramryge: **Fig 69**. 146–8,
    153, 207, 244
    tomb opening: 159–161
  Thomas Wolsey: 148, 153
  Warin: 74
  William de Trumpington: 74, 103,
    113, 209
  William of Wallingford: **Fig 67**.
    140, 144, 145, 224, 248
  Wulnoth: 20

Abbots:
  lodging: 209
  remains: 255

Act:
  Bishopric of St. Albans (1875): 208
  Enabling (1919): 236

Settlement (1662): 167
Million (1818): 191

Adrian IV, Pope: 64

aisles: 37–39, 80, 101–2, 125

Alban:
  arms: 133, 148
  badge: 138
  bones: 3, 15, 18
  burial place: 3, 15, 37, 261
  chapel: 98
  cross: 90, 171
  cult: 113
    see also saints, cult of
  early references to: 13–15
  general: 18
  Germanus visits shrine: 17
  Life of St. Alban: 74
  martyrdom: **Figs 6, 28, 62**. 13–14,
    17, 60, 90, 114, 136, 148, 171, 242
  miracles at shrine: 15, 17
  not as Roman soldier: 114
  on bishop's throne: 233
  prayer: 260
  representations of: 60, 90, 94, 114,
    115, 136, 138, 146, 148, 233, 242
  reliquary: 114–5
  sarcophagus: 97–8
  scourging: 114
  shrine: *see shrine*
  silver statue: 146
  tapestries depicting: 60
  tomb: 15, 111–2
  Walter of Colchester's carvings: 94

Aldenham, Lord: *see Gibbs*

alignment of Abbey: 36–37

almonry: 35, 157

altar beam: 94, 95

altars, 24, 37–8, 42, 44, 74, 89, 90,
  92, 116, 117, 134, 144, 199, 253
  rails: 171

ambulatory: 98

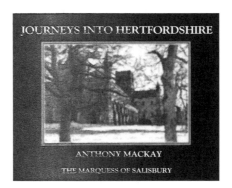

JOURNEYS INTO HERTFORDSHIRE

Anthony Mackay

This exceptional book of ink drawings reveals an intriguing historic heritage and captures the spirit of England's rural heartland, ranging widely over cottages and stately homes, over bridges, churches and mills, over sandy woods, chalk downs and watery river valleys.

Every corner of Hertfordshire has been explored in the search for material, and, although the choice of subjects is essentially a personal one, the resulting collection represents a unique record of the environment today.

The notes and maps, which accompany the drawings, lend depth to the books, and will assist others on their own journeys around the counties.

Anthony Mackay's pen-and-ink drawings are of outstanding quality. An architectural graduate, he is equally at home depicting landscapes and buildings. The medium he uses is better able to show both depth and detail than any photograph.

The Book Castle

FORGOTTEN FAMILIES
of Hertfordshire and Bedfordshire

Evelyn Wright

This book tells the story of families once famous but whose fame is now mainly forgotten. They all lived in Hertfordshire and Bedfordshire in the 16th and 17th centuries, and include the Bechers of Renhold (of Becher's Brook fame), the Mordaunts of Turvey Abbey, Lady Cathcart of Tewin, the Bull family of Hertford, the Nodes family of Stevenage, the Docuras of Lilley and the Wicked Lady of Markyate Cell. All the families were related to each other, forming an intricate network over two counties: Hertfordshire and Bedfordshire. The author is one of their 20th century descendants. The book includes pedigrees showing the relationship between various families, and illustrations of many of the manor houses and mansions in which they lived.

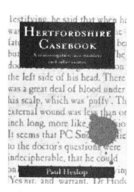

HERTFORDSHIRE CASEBOOK

Paul Heslop

This is a book about crime and punishment in Hertfordshire. It spans from the time when perpetrators were hanged for murder almost up to the present day.

Cases range from the 19th century killing of Constable Benjamin Snow, to the murder of retired Colonel Robert Workman at Furneux Pelham in 2004. There's the case of Mary Ansell, hanged in 1899 for poisoning her sister, a chapter on the infamous Coronation Riot at Watford in 1902, and two 'domestic' murders, at Rickmansworth and Waltham Cross, when Charles Coleman and George Anderson were hanged, Hertfordshire's last executions. The case of Duffy and Mulcahy, the so-called Railway killers, is included, along with two others of national notoriety: the kidnap and murder of Muriel McKay, and the rape and murder of Janie Shepherd, whose body was discovered on Nomansland Common, near Wheathampstead. There's the case of 20-year old Nicola Brazier, abducted, raped and shot dead near Wormley, and Graham Young, who poisoned his workmates. More recent cases include the killing of PC Frank Mason at Hemel Hempstead, and 81-year old Joan Macan, murdered in her garden at Ashridge. In many of the latter cases information has been obtained first-hand from detectives who were involved in the investigation.

The
Book
Castle

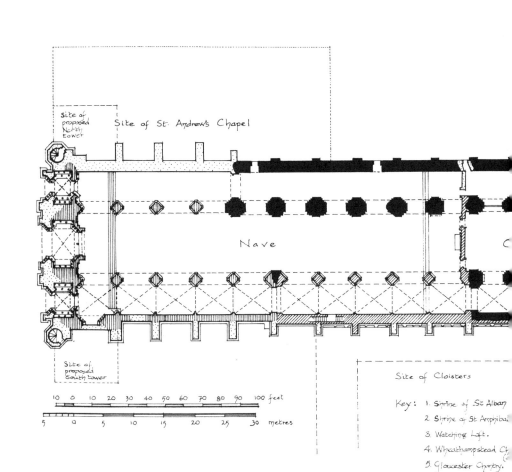

Site of
proposed
North
tower

Site of St. Andrew's Chapel

Nave

Site of
proposed
South tower

10 0   10 20 30 40 50 60 70 80 90 100 feet

5   0   5   10   15   20   25   30 metres

Site of Cloisters

Key: 1. Shrine of St Alban
     2. Shrine of St Amphibal
     3. Watching Loft.
     4. Wheathampstead Ch
     5. Gloucester Chantry.
     6. Wallingford Chantry
     7. Ramryge Chantry.

PLAN OF THE ABBEY TODAY

BMR based upon Chapple

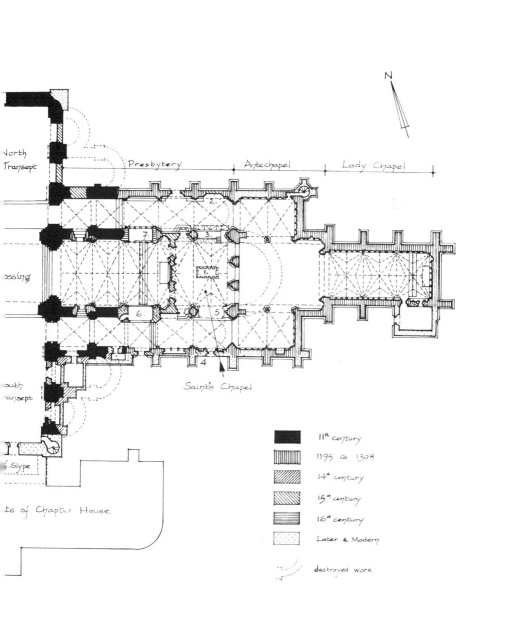

North
Transept

Presbytery | Antechapel | Lady Chapel

crossing

South
Transept

Slype

Site of Chapter House

Saint's Chapel

N

11th century
1195 to 1308
14th century
15th century
16th century
Later & Modern

destroyed work